ALSO BY PAUL G. STOLTZ

Adversity Quotient

Adversity Quotient at Work

ALSO BY ERIK WEIHENMAYER

Touch the Top of the World

THE

ADVERSITY
ADVANTAGE

TURNING EVERYDAY STRUGGLES INTO
EVERYDAY GREATNESS

PAUL G. STOLTZ, Ph.D. AND ERIK WEIHENMAYER

A FIRESIDE BOOK
PUBLISHED BY SIMON & SCHUSTER

NEW YORK   LONDON   TORONTO   SYDNEY

FIRESIDE
Rockefeller Center
1230 Avenue of the Americas
New York, NY 10020

First Fireside trade paperback edition January 2008

FIRESIDE and colophon are registered trademarks of Simon & Schuster, Inc.

For information regarding special discounts for bulk purchases,
please contact Simon & Schuster Special Sales at 1-800-456-6798
or business@simonandschuster.com

Designed by Ruth Lee Mui

Manufactured in the United States of America

4   6   8   10   9   7   5   3

Library of Congress Cataloging-in-Publication Data is available.

ISBN-13: 978-0-7432-9022-7
ISBN-10:   0-7432-9022-4
ISBN-13: 978-0-7432-9023-4 (pbk)
ISBN-10:   0-7432-9023-2 (pbk)

We dedicate this book to Mark Weihenmayer (1959–2006)
and to those who face adversity every day,
yearning to emerge stronger and better.
May adversity become the pathway through which you flourish.
Your greatness is needed.

CONTENTS

FOREWORD

STEPHEN R. COVEY

Many years ago, while on a sabbatical from my university, I was wandering around the stacks of a library in Hawaii and pulled down a book that caught my interest. What I read was so inspiring, so compelling, and so profound that it changed my life from that moment on. These were the three sentences I memorized:

Between stimulus and response, there is a space.
In that space lies our freedom and power to choose our response.
In those choices lie our growth and our happiness.

Just think about it—between whatever has happened to you or is now happening to you and your response to it, there is a space in which you have the power and freedom to choose your response. Those chosen responses will govern your growth and your happiness. In fact, they will govern your achievements and your contributions.

In other words, we are not animals. Animals possess no self-awareness, no space between stimulus and response. As human beings, we are not merely products of our genetics, our conditioning, or our present circumstances. *The Adversity Advantage* in-depth, magnificent example of these three sente had such a profound impact upon me. I'll repeat them again. Between stimulus and response, there is a space. In that space lies our freedom and power to choose our response. In those choices lie our growth and our happiness.

This is not a theoretical book, even though there is extensive theorizing. This is not a book full of abstract idealism, even though it shows how the ideal can become real. Instead, this book is a synergistic product of two marvelous individuals who teamed up to share what they have learned from their respective experiences, Erik from climbing the seven highest peaks on the seven continents of the world, Paul from his life's work decoding and strengthening the human relationship with adversity. Their work together on this book was just like a climb, a grueling ascent through innumerable obstacles, culminating in this powerful message from the top of the world. Just think about it for a moment. Erik brought his insights from the mountains; Paul added his newest thoughts and helped Erik shape those insights into a lesson plan for readers all over the world hoping to achieve everyday greatness. Between adversity and the response is a space. In that space are the power and the freedom to choose to crumble, or to elevate ourselves and others, as these two authors do by sharing their work with us.

Primary greatness lies in character and in contribution. *Secondary* greatness is found in prestige, wealth, position, and the kinds of achievements that make no solid, lasting contribution to others. All of us want our children and grandchildren to develop primary greatness. They may also attain secondary greatness. But few people ever achieve both. A few celebrities do, but most celebrities achieve only secondary greatness. Many everyday people achieve primary greatness, particularly parents who raise children of character and contribution.

There is one common thread that runs through all greatness: the effective use of the space between stimulus and response; in short, how do people deal with adversity, setbacks, suffering,

heartache, disappointment, and injustice? Do they become vi͟
consumed by the metastasizing cancers of cynicism, criticizing,
complaining, comparing, competing, and contending; or do they
learn to "harness" the power, energy, and wisdom embodied in
the difficult moment, the difficult space between stimulus and response?

How ironic it is that what enables us to grow and to experience
true joy in life is the very thing most people spend their lives trying
to avoid. A life of convenience and comfort is the course of least resistance and contributes nothing. Couch potatoes contribute nothing. I take as a mantra for life: grow or die. Keep learning and
contributing . . . or die. I believe this is true not just symbolically
but literally. When we stop growing and learning, we die mentally,
we die emotionally, and we die early physically. Hans Selye, arguably the most quoted expert on stress, taught that what keeps our
immune system strong and the regenerative forces of the body ac-
tive is meaningful work and contribution—the essence of which is
adversity. Let's live our lives in crescendo!

Want to learn a new language? Pay the price—practice, suffer,
and deny yourself. Want to strengthen a muscle? Exercise it until
the fiber breaks, and within twenty-four hours you will become
stronger. (I'll never forget how a strength trainer taught me this
principle many years ago. He said, "Stephen, keep lifting the weight
until you feel you can't go any farther. Then go one more. No pain,
no gain." I asked him why this was so. He said, "When you go a little farther, the muscle fiber ruptures; nature repairs it within a
forty-eight-hour period; and it becomes stronger.")

Dr. Viktor Frankl wrote the foreword to one of Hans Selye's
books. Frankl was the Austrian psychiatrist who wrote the marvelous international bestseller *Man's Search for Meaning*, wherein he
described his experiences with adversity while imprisoned in
the death camps of Nazi Germany. He described how, when his
captors put him under white lights, stripped him naked, and began

performing ignoble sterilization experiments on his body, he truly became aware of the space between stimulus and response and used it to find a meaning in his suffering. He then worked with others to help them find meaning in their suffering. One time the Nazi guards burned his manuscript, and the meaning he found in that setback was to write it again, better. One time a prisoner wanted to commit suicide. Dr. Frankl asked him why he didn't. He said, "Because of what it would do to my suffering wife." Dr. Frankl helped him to understand how this realization gave his life meaning. Someone who has a "why" can live with any "what" and with any "how." Dr. Frankl eventually would become the "father" of logotherapy, one of the most powerful psychotherapeutic approaches ever developed, and particularly influential throughout Europe.

When Frankl wrote the foreword to Hans Selye's book, he brought out the importance of harnessing the energy, power, and wisdom of adversity—even though he didn't use the word *harnessing*, as this book does. Dr. Selye believed that this is the reason why women live longer than men (six to eight years longer, on average). The key difference: a woman's work is never done. Women multitask and deal with many different adversities coming from different directions. They typically have meaningful goals and causes to which they are committed and contributing. Many men die shortly after retirement—particularly those who've become too career-focused during their working lives and then want to shift to a more pleasurable, stress-free lifestyle. They lose their sense of meaning.

Dr. Selye talked about the importance of *eustress*, the good kind of stress which comes from having meaningful work, goals, and projects that contribute to society. *Distress* is the negative kind of stress that comes from trying to avoid the stresses and adversities of ⸱⸱. One key lesson is this: no challenge and adversity, no deeper ⸱⸱ of meaning and purpose.

The remarkable thing about *The Adversity Advantage* is how applicable it is to every facet of life—physical, mental, social, emotional, economic, spiritual. Want to make a new contribution? Make a new preparation. Pay the price. Swim upstream against the cultural currents. Turn the TV way down. Want to live a healthy, long life? Stress your body, but don't overstress it. Participate in aerobics, strength training, and flexibility exercises. Push yourself wisely. Eat wisely. Subordinate taste to nutrition until you reeducate your taste buds. Want to improve your relationships? See love as a verb, rather than as a feeling.

One time a man came to me asking for advice about the difficulty he was having in his marriage. Love, he said, was gone; and he was concerned about the effect on his children. I said, "Then love her." "How do you love when you don't love?" he asked. I continued, "Love is a verb, not a feeling. Love the feeling is the fruit of love the verb. Why do you think mothers are so bonded to their children? Because of the suffering they went through to bring children into the world and all the sacrifices they made raising them. Love the feeling is the product of love the verb. Love is the service you give to another—caring for someone more than you care for yourself. Listen to your wife; you have two ears and one mouth—do the math." He answered, "I don't know if I can do all that." I responded, "Just try it for thirty days. You've gone for thirty years—what's another thirty days? Just give of yourself in loving ways. Stop criticizing, finding fault, and blaming. Serve her. Listen to her. Anticipate her needs. Just practice these habits for thirty days. You'll find that love *is* a verb, and that love the *feeling* will return." It did. Love those difficult to love—the adversity advantage.

Businesspeople, do you want more customers? Give second-mile service. Go beyond what others do. Look on your customers' difficulties and problems as the adversity advantage—a situation where you can provide this kind of caring and creative service, where you go way beyond what is normally expected. You'll get these customers for life.

Want to build a strong, high-trust, high-productive culture in your organization so that everyone is focused on second-mile service? Use the adversity advantage. Pay the price with your people. Get to know them, listen to them, and understand them—their pains, their hopes, their desires, their problems, and their self-doubts. Be true to them behind their backs when the easier way would be to join others in criticizing them. If you are critical, then go and give them feedback. This will take courage, particularly if you do it in a humble—not an arrogant—way.

Want to grow spiritually? Let service be your mantra for life. Never retire from meaningful work or meaningful projects. Where much is given, much is required. There is too much pain in the world to ever retire from meaningful work, even though you might retire from your occupation. This kind of service will mean seeking out adversity on a daily basis, but you'll learn to take on these challenges, summon your strengths, engage your core, and explore alternatives. You'll learn to pioneer possibilities, pack light and right, suffer well, and then deliver this kind of great service on a consistent, regular basis.

The magnificent principles in this book represent the tallest mountains on the seven continents of the world. They are presented inductively so that you can *earn* the insights, not just *learn* them. Inductive thinking means moving from the specific to the general. Deductive thinking means starting with theory (the general) and then applying it to specific situations. In *The Adversity Advantage* you start with the specifics, Erik's mountain experiences, and then are led to the general by a very wise author. Dr. Paul Stoltz is best known for his *adversity quotient*, which has become the most widely accepted method in the world for assessing and strengthening our ability to deal with adversity. Over half a million people have measured their AQs and begun the journey of strengthening how they deal with adversity. He has written two internationally acclaimed books, works with top leaders worldwide, and has done groundbreaking research in at least twenty-one countries to gain an understanding of those rare people who don't just deal well with adversity but convert it into fuel to achieve greatness.

This book is filled with tools, principles, inventories, and challenges that are practical and compelling. I found that the very process of studying this book led me to look carefully at myself with an awareness of how the challenges of my life can be the fuel that will enable me to swim against the stream, against cultural currents, against all forms of adversity inherent in my most important goals.

Setbacks are inevitable, but misery is a choice.

This book can help equip us to harness and utilize the hard moments to achieve the greatest heights of growth and contribution. That's where true happiness is—true joy. This book has inspired me to develop a greater appreciation for adversity and to see the mother lode of wisdom and possibilities to be found in adversity. It has inspired me to be an alchemist, to turn lead into gold.

I also had to pay the price myself with this book. It's not something you just quickly skim to get the main points. You have to earn those points by working with the material and trying to internalize it. One of the best ways to learn this material is to teach the essence of the seven steps to your loved ones and others who might be interested.

I can hardly believe what these two authors have done—teamed up, roped together, because they want to bless and elevate other people—you can feel the integrity and sincerity of their souls breathing through these pages.

I often ask audiences, "How many of you have achieved your present level of success, whatever it may be, partly or largely because someone believed in you when you didn't believe in yourself?" Usually, about two-thirds of the audience members will raise their hands, and when you listen to some of them, you see tears shed by both speakers and listeners. Erik began to lose his sight during the summer between his eighth-grade and ninth-grade years. He basically felt that life was over for him. He didn't have a personal relationship with a man named Terry Fox, who lost a leg to cancer and made the decision to run across Canada from east to west. But Erik says that, with the little sight he had left, he pressed his nose against the TV screen one day, tears pouring down his face, and watched Terry Fox run. He says, "I watched as the miles took a tremendous toll on his amputated leg and its primitive prosthetic. He hobbled along, mile after mile, fighting the pain of blisters and raw skin, at times using a pair of crutches to propel his body forward." Then he adds something very significant: "What struck me most was the look on his face. It was the look of extreme contradiction—complete exhaustion combined with ultimate exultation. I will never forget that look. I see it in my mind every day. In his thin face was the trace flicker of an intense internal light that burned power into his struggling frame. The image filled my sagging spirit and gave me a feeling of utter courage."

Later he explains, "I believe that inside each of us is something I can only describe as a light, which has the capacity to feed on adversity, to consume it like fuel. When we tap into that light, every frustration, every setback, every obstacle becomes a source to power our lives forward. The greater the challenge, the brighter the light burns. Through it, we become more focused, more creative, and more driven, and can even learn to transcend our own perceived limitations to bring our lives more meaning."

Dear readers, pay the price with this book. The dividends will be abundant and will last forever.

INTRODUCTION

What if, as a result of completing this book, you could use any, and I mean *any,* adversity to your advantage? What if you could convert your everyday struggles, big and small, into the kind of fuel that powers you past everyday normality to everyday greatness?

Isn't there something incredibly riveting about the human struggle with adversity? Not only is it the central strand of our story, shared across eras and cultures, but we also read about it in all the great books, are spellbound by it in popular movies, and wrestle with it in our own lives every day. Why adversity?

Maybe it's because within that struggle lies the essential wisdom we all need to become the kind of person we hope to be, or to nurture the kind of team or organization we envision. In fact, after spending the past few years working on this book, I'm convinced that adversity holds the key to achieving everyday greatness in life, business, and society.

Note: The pickax signals Erik's voice throughout.

We don't have to go looking for adversity. It tends to find us. During the summer between eighth and ninth grades, I began losing the last traces of my sight. I could no longer see enough to walk around by myself, so my brothers and parents had to lead me. I'd reach out for their shirtsleeves with the terror of a small child being left behind in a department store. I hated what was happening because it represented utter helplessness. Everything I knew was ending. The loss was like a storm descending on me with such force, such viciousness, that I thought I'd be crushed by it.

Late that fall, I was watching a TV show called *That's Incredible.* I could still see a little out of one eye, though I had to crane forward to just a few inches away from the set. Being featured that night was an athlete named Terry Fox. Terry had lost a leg to cancer, and when not yet discharged from the hospital, made a decision to run across Canada from east to west. With my nose pressed up against the screen and with tears pouring down my face, I watched Terry run. The miles took a tremendous toll on his amputated leg and its primitive prosthetic. He hobbled along mile after mile, fighting the pain of blisters and raw skin, often using a pair of crutches to propel his body forward.

What struck me most was the look on his face. It was a look of extreme contradiction: full of exhaustion yet radiant with exaltation. In his thin face was the trace flicker of an intense internal light that burned power into his struggling frame. The image filled my sagging spirit and gave me a feeling of utter courage. Many would have retreated from such hardship, but—surprisingly—Terry faced it head-on and literally ran into its midst. It was while staring into Terry's face that I first wondered how we could harness that great storm of adversity swirling around us and use its power to make ourselves stronger and better.

Although I was inspired by Terry, I learned early on that inspiration is not enough. If a person embarks on a mountain expedition unprepared and unequipped, the fierce wind, the frigid cold, the steep and technical terrain will do him in every time. Likewise, in order to consistently convert everyday adversity, big and small, into genuine advantage in our lives and enterprises we need some powerful and proven tools. And no one is better qualified to teach us about those tools than the guy I teamed up with to write this book, Dr. Paul Stoltz.

Paul is perhaps best-known for his *Adversity Quotient,* or AQ, theory, which has become the most widely adopted method in the world for measuring and strengthening our capacity to deal with adversity. Decoding the human relationship with adversity has been and continues to be Paul's lifework.

It was through Paul's groundbreaking research that we met. His focus on people who harness life's tough stuff led him to launch the Global Resilience Project, an effort now involving studies in twenty-one countries. His quest was to gain a better understanding of those rare people, like Terry, who don't just deal well with adversity but learn to convert it into fuel, to achieve everyday greatness.

You might remember, from your history textbooks, those medieval alchemists who toiled mysteriously to turn lead into gold. I call the people like Terry, the people Paul has highlighted in his research, modern-day alchemists. I believe that inside each of us is something I can only describe as a light, which has the capacity to feed on adversity, to consume it like fuel. When we tap into that light, every frustration, every setback, every obstacle becomes a source to power our lives forward. The greater the challenge, the brighter the light burns. Through it, we become more focused, more creative, and more driven, and can even learn to transcend our own perceived limitations to bring our lives more meaning.

All of us can be alchemists, taking the lead that life piles on top of us and finding ways to transform it into gold. I strive to be an alchemist every day. I climbed the Seven Summits—the tallest peaks on each of the seven continents—not only because I love to climb but also to shatter people's perceptions of what's possible. And somewhere along the way, I learned more about the advantages of adversity than I ever imagined I would.

There is something inherently compelling about an ascent. I believe that deep inside us, we all strive to move forward and up, to scale new heights. Paul and I have, therefore, organized this book into Seven Summits, based on seven guiding principles that will help you use adversities to your advan-

tage, as a way to infuse some practical greatness into your daily life. I begin
each Summit—each chapter—with a story from one of the seven actual summits that I climbed. In between, Paul draws from my lessons and his worldwide research to teach you how you can generate power from your everyday
struggles, elevating you and everyone you touch.

By "everyone," Erik and I hope you include the people you interact
with through your work, your community, your family, and more.
This is because the ripple effect—both positive and negative—of
how you relate to adversity extends out to all whom you influence,
including many who are unaware of your impact. That's the potential power of *The Adversity Advantage*, and it's why Erik and I love
the word *elevate*. To elevate means to "raise to a higher level or position," or to "raise one's mind or spirit to a more enlightened or ex-
alted level." And when you really come down to it, isn't that what
you want to do with your life, what every parent hopes to do for a
child, what every leader ultimately wants to do for his or her organization?

You might be thinking that any sensible person seeks less adversity, not more. Right? Here's the problem. While you can certainly
have an enjoyable life, you cannot reach be-
yond pleasure to even the most basic level of
greatness without a healthy dose of the very
thing most people seek to diminish. Why?
Because adversity alone has the unique
power to inspire exceptional clarity, purge any vestiges of lethargy,
refocus your priorities, hone your character, and unleash your most
potent forces. Even minor setbacks provide fertile soil for elevating
behavior. If you eliminate adversity, you miss out on life's deepest
riches, highest gifts, and most potent lessons. The more adversity
you escape, the less you become.

> You cannot elevate anyone or anything to its highest potential without adversity.

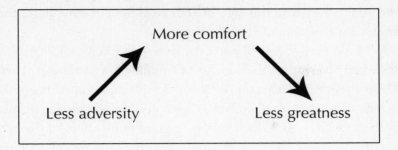

In my first books introducing the Adversity Quotient (AQ), I talk in depth about *Quitters, Campers,* and *Climbers*—the three categories of response to the daunting challenge of leading an ever-elevating life. Quitters simply give up on the ascent—the pursuit of an enriching life—and as a result are often embittered. Campers generally work hard, apply themselves, pay their dues, and do what it takes to reach a certain level. Then they plant their tent stakes and settle for their current elevation. Climbers are the rare breed who continue to learn, grow, strive, and improve until their final breath, who look back on life and say these precious words: "I gave it my all." It's no coincidence that Climbers are the people we most admire, are drawn to, and seek to become. One of the major discoveries of my research is that at the heart of the difference between Climbers and Campers or Quitters lies what they do with adversity.

Relentlessly pursuing a life or building an organization rich in purpose can be tough. The weather on the mountain is rough—and intensifying. That's why Quitters abandon the ascent and Campers hunker down. Only Climbers take on the immensely gratifying challenge of learning, striving, improving, and contributing until their final breath.

According to our poll of more than 150,000 leaders across all industries worldwide, many people quit (5 to 20 percent), most camp (65 to 90 percent), and a rare few climb. In fact, when leaders are asked, "What percentage of your workforce is camping?" the most common response is "80 percent."

This is a *tragic* loss of potential, at a time when camping is increasingly costly, and the benefits of climbing are particularly rich. But my previous books stopped short of explaining something powerfully distinct about Climbers. I have discovered that the people with the highest AQs don't simply respond more effectively to adversity. Whether they are driving a new business model, forging an exceptional team, or simply finding ways to accelerate their own development, they *use* adversity. And in this process, they unleash tremendous energy and innovation, and gain momentum. This book will teach you how to use your adversities to unleash your personal best.

We learn from those who shatter our notions of what's possible. The extremes of the space program created countless practical products for everyday use back on earth; and in just the same way, through extreme examples of what people can do with adversity we learn practical ways to dramatically improve what we do with our own.

My research led me to Erik Weihenmayer because he is a Climber in the truest sense of the word. He attacks life as he attacks a rock face—with a relentless determination to elevate himself and everyone around him, whether through his stirring narratives as a keynote speaker, his groundbreaking and highly visible adventures, or his outreach to marginalized people throughout the world. Climbers strive to improve themselves and their worlds. With regard to anything that matters, phrases like *almost, at least we tried,* or *there's no way* are outside Erik's vocabulary. The words that are true to his character are *more, better, smarter, faster, richer,* and *higher.* Such words define him, pouring out like warm breath on an icy morning.

In short, Erik is the living embodiment of every lesson offered in this book. And, while we will provide many everyday examples,

Erik is the true exemplar of *The Adversity Advantage*. In this book, I will help decode Erik's emotional DNA so that you can infuse his inner tenacity and greatness into your own life. Erik will provide you with his best terrain-tested wisdom and insights, using spellbinding stories to help you fundamentally rethink and retool your relationship with adversity.

The good news is that after teaching people about the power of adversity in business and in life for the past twenty-two years, I know that everyone can learn the practical tools for harnessing adversity as a vital life force. The new principles and practices offered in this book are crafted not for superheroes or impossible extremes. They are devised for us normal folks, for you and for me, so that we can begin to achieve everyday greatness in our own day-to-day lives.

In Summit One—Take It On!—we will define in a simple, practical way the adversities you face. You will learn how you, those around you, and even your organization can *take it on*—get past the frustration, helplessness, anger, and even acceptance of adversity and reach the point where you can embrace and benefit from its force. You'll learn why you are better equipped for the big adversities than you are for the everyday onslaught of energy-draining annoyances, hassles, difficulties, and challenges. You will begin to get a sense of how adversity can be both the ultimate competitive weapon for a business and the ultimate fuel for a life. You will learn where you currently reside on the Adversity Continuum—the ultimate gauge of your relationship with life's tough stuff—so you can begin your journey to higher, more elevating levels. You will complete your own Adversity Inventory, and emerge with a clearly defined Summit Challenge.

Summit Two—Summon Your Strengths—challenges the conventional wisdom that natural strengths are the driving force of success. This chapter will help you decide what you want to do, why you want to do it, and what strengths you need to tap, grow, and gain from others to achieve your Summit Challenge. You will develop your Adversity Strengths through the powerful combination of courage, discipline, tenacity, and desire. You will break through your notions of what you and others can or should attempt to do. You will rethink how you team up with others in business and in life.

In Summit Three—Engage Your CORE—you'll learn how to handle every adversity better and faster. You will gain vital insight into your lens on life, as well as the foundations of AQ and the four CORE dimensions that determine how people respond to adversity. You will learn how the greatest organizations and leaders in the world engage their CORE. And you will devise your own personal CORE Strategy for moving forward along the Adversity Continuum to begin turning specific adversities into real advantage.

In Summit Four—Pioneer Possibilities—you will learn how to devise signature systems for making the impossible possible. You will create strategies that others simply fail to see. Learn how you and your organization can gain tremendous traction and momentum through the force of adversity. You will rethink how you approach limitations, as well as expand your perception of what's possible. You will learn to apply "possibility pioneering" tools to shift from "what now?" to "what if?"

As you climb higher to Summit Five—Pack Light, Pack Right—you will learn from Erik's vivid world of climbing how packing poorly will cripple you but how carefully choosing the right things, people, obligations, and pursuits will strengthen you. The more weighed down you are, or your organization is, the less agile and effective you are when attacking adversity. Kill agility, and you suffocate alchemy. In this chapter you will gain the clarity to spring-clean your life so you can rise up, rather than crumble under the weight of each new adversity.

No matter how fortunate you may be, you will eventually be

given the opportunity to suffer. So the question is whether you will suffer poorly or well. This is the subject of Summit Six—Suffer Well. Adversity alchemists have the amazing capacity to suffer well—to elevate those around them through their own losses and hardships. They turn pain into beauty. Suffering can be tragic, debilitating, and stultifying, or it can be high-octane fuel for accelerated alchemy. Potent reactions usually involve heat. That's why character is forged in the flames of adversity. Done right, suffering can fuel greatness.

Summit Seven—Deliver Greatness, Every Day—is the culmination of the preceding six summits. It brings together the most important ideas from the entire book, providing a coherent, portable package of practices you can take with you and apply anywhere, anytime, so that you can rise to the very top of the Adversity Continuum. You will depart with your own Adversity Advantage Climbing Route, able to perform your own alchemy. Life's lead becomes gold, darkness becomes light, and normality turns into greatness. And you will emerge poised, if not anxious, for the advantage you will gain from each new adversity.

THE MOUNTAIN AS METAPHOR

Erik and I have chosen the mountain as our metaphor, not to represent a testosterone-induced, tackle-the-summit athletic feat, but as a universal symbol of inspiration and aspiration. People share a drive to ascend—to move forward and up in our lives; to gain, rather than lose, elevation. Don't worry. You certainly don't have to be a climber or an athlete to relate to all this. While Erik's stories from the world's top peaks may sound impossibly daunting, the lessons within those stories link quite practically to the more normal, often involuntary challenges and hardships we all face in the course of our various endeavors.

To be blunt, adversity is utterly heartless. It could not care less whether we succeed or fail. It doesn't care about our human definition of fairness or justice, and it would just as soon crush us as propel us through its gauntlet. Like a gale-force wind, it can do serious damage. Or, if harnessed, it can take you farther than you could otherwise go. The exciting news is that no matter how mundane or irritating your hassles may be, they can be used for dramatic gains. And it all begins with the first Summit, when you turn into the storm and take it on!

TAKE IT ON!

MOUNT MCKINLEY (DENALI)
Base Camp: 7,200 feet
Summit: 20,320 feet–tallest peak in North America

Kites rise highest against the wind, not with it.
–SIR WINSTON CHURCHILL

You probably don't wake up hoping for a day full of adversity. No one does, including me. In fact, I never consciously thought about adversity until it sought me out. Even then, like most people, I did everything in my power to avoid it, downplay it, and deny its existence. Not until I eventually embraced its full force did I begin to understand what I could do and who I could be. And when I look back on the whole painful process, I can hardly imagine my life unfolding in any other way.

The role that adversity plays in our lives was revealed to me most powerfully on the first of my Seven Summits, McKinley, the most notorious peak in North America. There I was, a blind guy, wedged into a tent at 7,200 feet. I lay there wondering what insanity had led me to believe I could take on a 20,000-foot mountain, let alone one so daunting. I slid deeper into my sleeping bag, gritting my teeth against the Arctic blasts, and remembered how the idea began.

One morning eighteen months earlier, I had sat at the top of a 100-foot desert rock pinnacle with my climbing pal, Sam. It had been a particularly gratifying climb up a crazy knife-edge arête. We were talking about all the cool routes we had tackled, and Sam remarked on how amazing it was that I could climb at all. Many people had told me this; and, frankly, I had grown kind of weary of the accolades. I had nothing against the kindhearted people who were affected by my efforts. It moved me to know I had influenced their mind-set. No—the fault wasn't theirs; it was mine.

I've always had a restless voice inside me, which seemed to speak loudest when my life felt a bit stagnant. Stepping into new and challenging situations has often created positive results for me. I remember—during my freshman year of high school—tapping my white cane down an empty hallway toward the wrestling room, to try a sport I had a hunch blind people could do. A few years later, I tried rock climbing for the first time; and after college, I moved alone across the country, from New England to the southwestern desert, a place I knew nothing about, to start a life as a fifth-grade teacher. I think we all have that voice inside us, haunting us in a good way, if we will only listen. Thank God for that voice. We'd never grow, and we could never make our enterprises grow, without it.

When I was a middle school English teacher, my students and I were reading one of my favorite short stories, "The Secret Life of Walter Mitty," by James Thurber. I felt a lot like Walter. He definitely has that little voice egging him on to do something great with his life. He imagines himself facing all sorts of adverse situations. First he is the captain of a U.S. navy hydroplane in the middle of a horrific storm, then a famous surgeon performing a lifesaving operation, and then a bomber pilot in the Royal Air Force flying a secret wartime mission over Germany. But we learn, sadly, that Walter's brave adventures are only daydreams.

For me, though, that little voice was getting louder and louder. I guess I longed for more than daydreams. At twenty-six, I had already gained a lot of attention as the "blind rock climber," and I knew that if I just kept pursuing the same level of challenges, no one would ever accuse me of being a slacker. Blindness could have been my ticket to taking it easy for the rest of my life, the bar set at the current level, my past becoming my greatest achievement, thus relieving me from ever having to stretch or face any further self-imposed hardships.

So, on top of that rock face, when Sam asked me, "What do you say we try something a little bigger?" I was intimidated but excited. As he began explaining all about this massive peak in Alaska, I immediately knew what he proposed involved immense pain, relentless training, and enormous adversity. I also sensed, though, with a gut-wrenching blend of anticipation and dread, that I was headed to Mount McKinley. I loved climbing, but—even more important—I burned to take on the impossible and, in the process, elevate my own life and maybe even the lives of others.

It may sound crazy, a blind novice taking on such a dangerous mountain; but in many ways, Denali was the perfect big peak on which to begin. Since all of McKinley is glaciated, crisscrossed by giant gaping crevasses, the only way to climb it is to be roped up with teammates. Even when the wind was howling and I wouldn't be able to hear footsteps crunching in front of me, I'd have the direction of the rope to follow. Also, although McKinley is steep, its snowy surface is pretty smooth, so most of my steps would be relatively consistent.

I eagerly plunged into all the preparation. There was so much to learn: how to throw yourself down on your ice ax in case a teammate slipped into a crevasse, how to pull the teammate out with a pulley and rope setup, how to put up tents with my thick gloves on, and how to cook freeze-dried meals on a camp stove by touch. I even read in Braille a stack of accident reports with the crystal-clear goal of not adding myself to McKinley's 198 fatalities. I saw each new obstacle as a way of fully confronting difficult issues before they had a chance to defeat us on Denali.

Finally the day arrived when Cessna planes, packed to the ceilings with gear, flew across the Alaska Range, their skis skidding onto the ice runway at Base Camp. Day after day, we lugged sixty-pound packs and pulled fifty-pound sleds up the glacier, often sinking in snow up to our knees and pushing through hammering blizzards. The days just kept getting harder.

Two weeks into the trip, as I kicked steps up a steep headwall, my colossal pack felt as if it were compressing my spine and mashing my internal organs. The strap around my chest was suffocating me as I gasped in the oxygen-poor air, and with each exhausting step, I seemed to gain a foot only to slide back two feet. On the way back down, after dropping off a load of gear at a higher camp, I found myself constantly sliding into the deep boot holes frozen in the trail, my ankles and knees being wrenched into bizarre angles. I staggered back into our camp at 14,500 feet and lay in the snow outside my tent, utterly spent. I was dizzy and nauseated, puking in the snow, tears welling up in my eyes. I honestly wasn't sure whether I had what it took to wake up the next morning and do all this over again.

Every day became a new education on just how far I could push myself. I struggled physically, and even more mentally. But nineteen days after flying in, we reached the summit, a little lump of snow in the sky. We learned later it was Helen Keller's birthday.

When we got down to Base Camp, my wife, Ellen, who had flown in to meet us, said I looked like a hunched-over old man. My face was scaly with windburn on top of sunburn. Afterward, a reporter asked me what I was going to climb next. I told him I was going to climb into bed for a long nap. Inwardly, however, something had changed. It was as though an internal reservoir of energy and purpose, which should have been completely dry, had actually grown fuller. My mind and spirit burned with a boundless vitality that I didn't know I possessed.

Then, unexpectedly, letters and cards began to pour in. There were bundles of them, and some were in Braille. They were from classrooms all over the world, as far away as India and Japan. Many were from parents of blind children who had almost lost hope. This entire adventure had begun with a small voice inside my head urging me on, but now this voice was being joined by an international chorus of blind children and their parents telling me to climb higher. It was then that I began to dream of the Seven Summits.

I never set out to climb a mountain as a way of breaking world records or becoming anyone's hero; but, probably like you, I've wanted to breathe in as much joy, fulfillment, and accomplishment as humanly possible. Despite our fears and our perceived limitations, we don't have to remain Walter Mittys, always dreaming with a hollow feeling inside. No matter how big or small our adversities may be, if we face the facts, turn into the storm, and *take it on,* the depth of meaning and richness of our lives are limitless!

Adversity happens. It doesn't play favorites, and it comes in all shapes and sizes. And your natural response might be "Take it away!" rather than "Take it on!"

In enterprise, the greatest inventions and advances are often spawned from or through adversity. It was Apple Computer's dismal market share in personal computers that unleashed the industry-defining iPod. Likewise, it was concern over global warming, oil dependency, and fuel costs that triggered the first hybrid automobiles. In Africa, the foot-pedal water pump that transforms parched villages into irrigated fields grew from horror over rampant disease and starvation. Worldwide, we see the greatest outpouring of kindness in the face of the worst disasters. Pain, fear, discomfort, and injustice are far more powerful motivators than their opposites.

But what about your own adversities? And I don't mean just the big stuff. What about your everyday adversities? Someone drops the ball on an important project, leaving you hanging out to dry; your e-mail crashes; the platters for the party aren't delivered to your client in time; your son's teacher just called you at work about "his recent behavior." You get sick when you can least afford to. Someone you love is down and out. Your classes get dropped. Your car's engine light goes on at the worst possible time—these are everyday happenings, or perhaps they all happen on the same day. The truth is that adversity makes up most days.

For a long time it had seemed to me
that life was about to begin—real life.
But there was always some obstacle in the way,
something to be gotten through first, some unfinished business,
time still to be served, a debt to be paid.

Then life would begin.
At last it dawned on me that these obstacles were my life.
—ALFRED D. SOUZA

Whether you are ultimately weakened or strengthened by each event, or by the accumulation of events, will depend on your first mastering the ability to *take it on*. This Summit will equip you to:

▶ Define and score adversity for yourself and your organization.
▶ Learn to cloud seed—recognize worthy challenges in your life that will help you to grow when you face facts.
▶ Step up to face the facts, as you
  • Pinpoint where you land on the Adversity Continuum.
  • Check your Adversity Assumptions.
  • Complete the Adversity Inventory to sort the adversities in your life for greatest possible advantage.
  • Pick your Summit Challenge—the one thing you've always wanted to do but haven't done (yet)—and pinpoint the related adversity, your Summit Adversity, that, if harnessed, would benefit you most.

Finally, armed with your discoveries and tools, you will turn into the storm and implement your Summit One Strategy.

ADVERSITY DEFINED AND SCORED

Defining adversity is the first step. What exactly are you supposed to take on? What exactly is adversity to you? Adversity is *personal*, and *relative*. It is also universal, in the sense that it affects everyone. It may be useful to categorize adversity into two areas, (1) *inner adversity* (internal, physical, mental, emotional, and spiritual states that cause you hardship) and (2) *outer adversity* (things that occur outside you that cause you difficulty). We each have varying degrees of both. In whatever manner, everyone—including you—faces life's tough stuff.

TWO CATEGORIES OF ADVERSITY: Examples

Inner Adversity	Outer Adversity
Lack of confidence	Someone violates your trust
Lethargy	Natural disasters
Fear, anxiety	Canceled flight
Uncertainty	Economic downturn
Depression	Best friend moves away
Self-loathing	Your new car gets scratched
Physical pain	Your computer crashes
Loneliness	Your coworker gets upset with you
Self-doubt	You fail a class
Fatigue	Your insurance rates double
Poor health	A loved one passes away unexpectedly
Insomnia	A noisy neighbor moves in next door

Most people think of adversity only as something serious or terrible. But it really encompasses the entire range of hassles, obstacles, difficulties, hardships, misfortunes, setbacks, and challenges, even those we willingly take on. So, for the purposes of this book, we will go by this powerful yet simple definition:

Scoring Your Adversity

How big is any particular adversity likely to be? The magnitude of adversity you experience is determined by (1) *impact*, its real or imagined, existing or potential severity; and (2) *importance*, how much it matters to you.

> Adversity occurs when something negatively affects, or is predicted to negatively affect, someone or something you care about.

People often disagree—even argue vehemently—over how big or serious a specific adversity may be. One person might see it as

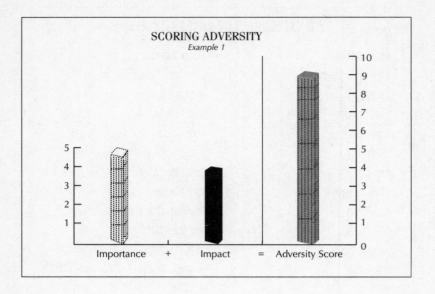

minor, while another perceives it as devastating. For your own clarity, and to reach clarity with others, the simple exercise of scoring the magnitude of any adversity is highly useful. This gives you something firm for comparison, since adversity is all relative.

If an event, like a stock market crash just before your retirement, has an impact on something that matters greatly, with a potentially disastrous affect, then that adversity might score nine on a ten-point scale. If it has a huge impact on something of less importance—this might be true of the same crash when you have only a few, minor "hobby" investments—then you might score it as, say, five or six. And, of course, if something minor happens to something you hardly care about, you might score it as one or two.

Scoring adversity this way can ease some common conflicts. If a given event scores ten for you and three for your teammates, that would explain why you may be so much more intense and urgent about the issue than they are. If the boss appears to be overly

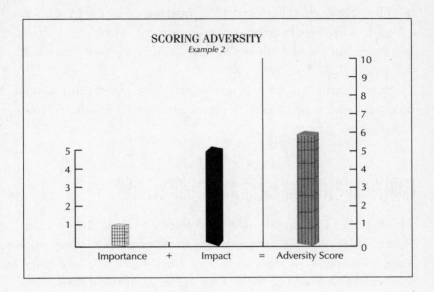

ramped up over an issue you consider minor, it's a likely indicator that he or she scores the adversity higher than you do. And if an adversity significantly affects someone important to you—such as your boss—it now, by definition, becomes an adversity to you. If your customer is going ballistic over a "silly thing," and you are not, chances are there's a scoring discrepancy. Getting to the heart of the matter—why your adversity scores are so far apart—can lead to real resolution and results. Of course, you're unlikely to pull out a scoring mechanism as each adversity arises, but there's nothing to stop you from asking this: "To help me understand where you're coming from, on a scale of one to ten, if ten is as bad as it can get, and one is nothing, how would you rate this situation?" Other people's scores, just like your score, which is based on your own perception, may be dramatically influenced by past experience. People who experienced their ten on the front lines of war or as victims of violent crime may rate nothing else higher than six or seven for the rest of their lives. But others who have faced little adversity might consider a long line at their favorite restaurant a most distressing setback. You might find it difficult not to judge this behavior as "spoiled," but it's all relative.

Scoring your adversity is one thing. What about those people you know who seem to seek or create adversity? I call them "emotional storm chasers."

EMOTIONAL STORM CHASERS AND CLOUD SEEDING

The Weather Channel on television features a special show called *Storm Chasers*, highlighting escapees from the asylum of common sense who somehow reached the conclusion that the best use of their vacations would be to track tornadoes or hurl themselves into hurricanes. The program usually showcases some lightning-fueled zealot racing across the American prairies, trying to catch the best-ever footage of a cyclone by anyone whose car is not suddenly tossed into a neighboring state. These people get their buzz from adverse weather. The worse it is, and the closer they get, the faster their veins pulse, and the higher their voices become.

The purpose of this book and this chapter is *not* to turn you into an emotional storm chaser. Certainly, there may be some adversities you seek, or clouds you choose to seed. But in most cases, bad weather will find you wherever you are—and there is nothing you can do to change it. If, however, like the skies on most days in southern California, your life is a little too calm and predictable, then you may wish to do some *cloud seeding*—stir up your skies. I regularly coach organizational leaders to do this, to awaken their people's inner strengths and unleash their higher potentials.

Cloud seeding usually involves picking the right clouds—that is, the right issues—to mess with. These are the ones you think may yield the greatest results. Given the calm that may come from a successful year or a recent winning streak, you may wish to stir up some adversity at work by confronting the one issue that is holding things back and preventing the achievement of the next level of success. Socially, you may decide to confront a friend who is living in denial or for whom a wake-up call may offer enormous potential benefit. Or you may seek to work through a festering misunderstanding that could renew your relationship with someone important. Personally, you may decide to take on some chronic shortcoming to free up miles of fresh trail.

It's wonderful when you see the people closest to you decide to seed some clouds. My son Sean had graduated from college with a double major and a world of promise. He decided to go to work at Starbucks as he sorted things out. He was paying his own bills and being fast-tracked for promotions. But as his paychecks rose, his sense of purpose sagged. So he decided to create some adversity.

He went to apply for a new one-year MBA program at Cal Poly. The school said admission to the program was closed. So he went to talk to the dean, who gave him a packet and a small glimmer of hope. Sean completed his packet in half a day, and kept after it until he was accepted. Suddenly he had a lot more stress—no paycheck and lots of bills. This was precisely the kind of adversity he sought. Sean intentionally raised his level of adversity from three at Starbucks to seven at Cal Poly. He was suddenly living with a chronic hardship—the fairly significant negative impact his choice made on his financial well-being, options, and lifestyle. Now he's on fire with the idea of pursuing a career as a business ethicist—helping leaders make principled decisions in the face of adversity. It's not important whether or not this becomes his ultimate career. What is important is the growth he, or you, will experience by seeding clouds filled with adversity.

Sometimes seeding clouds means intentionally trading one adversity for another. Shari is one of the best-liked administrative assistants for one of PEAK Learning's clients. As good as she is at her current job, her unfulfilled vision was to handle grant writing for her firm. Her adversity was inner disappointment and self-doubt—which averaged a score of four to six, depending on the day.

She woke up each day with a gnawing sense that she could be doing something more challenging and fulfilling, like writing grants, but unsure that she had what it took to do so. She just knew that she loved the idea of playing a role in winning funding for worthy environmental causes. But Sheri had two things holding her back.

First, while she typed reasonably fast, her speed was limited by the fact that she used only two fingers of each hand. It was her little dark secret, which she hid brilliantly by being just fast enough that no one paid attention to her technique. But for the past twenty years, cranking out big documents against tight deadlines had always caused Shari enormous stress.

Second, people always made good-natured fun of Shari's voice, which was very high and girlish. So the idea of making grant presentations to the powers that be in the federal government was excruciating.

Although the option of putting her work life on cruise control and simply accepting her fate was tempting, Shari decided this was the time to take it on. So she did some strategic cloud seeding by forcing herself to struggle through a beginners' typing program during lunch breaks. It was painstaking, if not embarrassing, to feel so completely incompetent, like being back in seventh grade. A couple of coworkers even asked, "Why are you putting yourself through this? It's not like you have to, right?" In fact, Shari was often tempted to fall back into the old speed-pecking method. But gradually, over a few weeks, she found that she could whip out documents typing the new way as fast as she could the old way, with only slightly more mistakes; and soon she was zipping along at a confidence-building pace.

Meanwhile, Shari announced to her husband over dinner one night that she wanted to invest in voice lessons. And despite his protestations and loving pleas not to mess with "your adorable little voice," Shari went to a voice coach every Tuesday evening for several months. She was scared that the people who knew her best might think she was weird for talking differently. But she began to carefully experiment with speaking more from her diaphragm, and less through her head and nose, especially at work. In the process, she had to confront and work through a lot of unexpected issues about her femininity and power. She even lost sleep over some of the turmoil. On days when her adversity felt more like a nine, she was tempted more than once to turn off the noise these issues created in her head by simply walking away from the lessons. Ultimately, though, she found the struggle invigorating.

Within three weeks she started to notice a real difference. In her second month, Shari took a deep breath, set her jaw, and decided to volunteer to do the "brown-bagger" lunch presentation to the staff on some of the new grant writing requirements. She used her newly evolved voice and was greeted with a few good-hearted imitations, but received mostly amazed praise from her colleagues. Not surprisingly, she was finding it easier and easier to spring out of bed for another day of work. Shari had been comfortable in her competence, living with her chronic mid-level adversity. But she knew that to fulfill her vision, she would have to make some uncomfortable changes. So she seeded a couple of clouds, made some rain, and was on her way. She incurred some necessary suffering to achieve her goal. In some ways her new reality was more challenging than her previous one. But by swapping one set of adversities for another, Shari was more fulfilled.

What clouds might you seed to help you reach your goals? Or do you think cloud seeding is only for people like Erik—titans of adversity?

The Big Stuff versus the Small Stuff

I need to address a reaction you may be having after reading Erik's story at the opening of this chapter. Sometimes when we hear these amazing tales of people who face the really big stuff and do extraordinary things, it's hard to relate. Our stuff may seem so small in comparison that we don't even think their example may apply to us, so we think, "They're different." Quite the contrary. The truth is that you can learn to perform the same sort of alchemy with your adversities as Erik did with his.

Have you noticed that you respond to some adversities more effectively than to others? It turns out that taking on the small stuff can actually be tougher than taking on the big stuff. In our *Adversity Advantage* programs we have had countless people come up to us perplexed. They usually say something like, "I just don't get it. When something really bad happens, like when my teenager was in a car accident, I am incredibly strong. But my computer crashing can just debilitate me! Why is that?"

There is a scientifically grounded reason why people are often more effective at taking on the big stuff. You are constructed, through the flight-fight response, to draw forth previously unknown powers when the big stuff hits. Earthquake? Tornado? Subway strike? You can rally. A torrent of high-octane chemicals inside you fortifies you with powers you never knew you had. But what about a slow, constant drizzle? Or a gray, overcast chill? It turns out that we humans do not have a similar protective mechanism for bringing out our best in these less dramatic conditions. The good news is that you can craft and install a new mechanism for shining forth in gray weather by mastering the first Summit, and each of the remaining six Summits offered in this book.

FACE THE FACTS: THE ADVERSITY CONTINUUM

The Adversity Continuum is designed to help you gain utter clarity on how you interact with adversity. In this section you will come to grips with your foundational relationship with adversity. You will learn how, by ascending farther up the Adversity Continuum, you can increase your energy, along with your everyday greatness. Approach this next section as an exercise, not just an insight. Do it rather than just read it.

The Adversity Continuum—Overview

This is the true joy in life . . . being used for a purpose recognized
by yourself as a mighty one . . . being thoroughly worn out
before you are thrown on the scrap heap . . . being a
force of Nature instead of a feverish selfish little clod of ailments
and grievances complaining that the world will not
devote itself to making you happy.

—GEORGE BERNARD SHAW, *MAN AND SUPERMAN*,
EPISTLE DEDICATORY

From your own experience you know there are at least two kinds of fatigue. Over the course of your day, year, and life, you can be used up in a *good* way, or you can be used up in a *bad* way. Being used up in a good way means pouring forth your finest effort toward an engaging, elevating cause. Being used up in a bad way happens when you expend your precious life force being pummeled by adversity, suffering real loss, with little if any gain.

The cause makes all the difference. And many of the most exciting or important causes require the most torturous tasks. It's one thing to be required to navigate the constant, often wearing hassles of filling out reams of paperwork and reasoning with banks or bureaucrats in an effort to secure scholarship funding for your dream of attending medical school. That can be both frustrating and exhausting, but the reason transcends the requirements. The same could be said of doing such tasks to help your ailing mother enroll in Medicare. Tough, but important. It's quite another thing to have to face the same sort of wasted hours at work just to get the most mundane requests—like a new stapler or parking permit—approved for a job you're not that crazy about in the first place.

In our research, the vast majority of folks (87 percent of more than 150,000 respondents) reported that, more often than not, they were fatigued in a bad way—consumed by adversity—ending the day and spending much of their lives drained and unfulfilled. Holidays and their anticipated retirement—their fantasies for an adversity-free life—were the only hoped-for escapes from the cycle.

It's true. Adversity can sap your life force. But it needn't do that. Why spend your best effort fighting the very wind that can fill your sails and take you to otherwise unreachable lands?

> *I firmly believe that any man's finest hour,*
> *his greatest fulfillment of all he holds dear,*
> *is the moment when he has worked his heart out in a good cause*
> *and lies exhausted on the field of battle—victorious.*
>
> —VINCE LOMBARDI

The Adversity Continuum depicts the range of our approaches to life's tough stuff. It is a steep climb that few complete. As with most mountains, the lower elevations are where you find the crowds. But the higher you go, the better life gets.

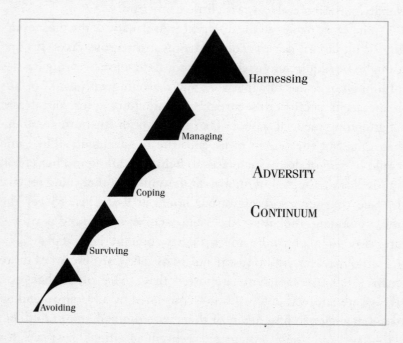

AVOIDING ADVERSITY

At the bottom of the continuum resides one of our most natural and instinctive responses to any adversity—*avoiding it*. And a classic avoidance mechanism is *denial*. While denial has its place and can buy you time, it prevents you from taking adversity on. As a result, the potential benefit that adversity might bring is delayed, or even denied to you.

Erik went through this stage in his young life as he was going blind. Many know Erik as the amazing blind guy who climbed Everest and the rest of the Seven Summits, but his relationship with adversity has been more complex than any sound bite can capture. When he was a boy diagnosed with a rare degenerative retinal condition, his fear and dread of going blind were so overwhelming that he just could not accept this adversity, let alone take it on. That's the real story, which he explains vividly.

Denial protected me from both pain and possibility. Even as I was slowly losing my sight, week by week, bit by bit, the idea of total blindness loomed like some vague nightmare way out there in the future. Amazingly, I was able to convince myself that it wasn't happening. I had placed myself in a state of suspended animation, unable to go forward, unable to go back, trapped in an isolated cell of complete stagnation. Doctors had clearly told me and my family that I'd be blind by my early teens, but, although this sounds hard to believe, I convinced myself that their diagnosis had been a mistake, that there were other reasons why I couldn't see as well as I did the day before. I had an explanation for everything: "The sun is right in my eyes. The lighting in this room is terrible. Words look smaller in books because publishers are squeezing more words onto the page to save money." When something happened so overwhelmingly clear that I couldn't explain it away, contemplating the prospect of blindness was so frightening that I'd pull away from the thought, block it off as if slamming a prison door shut around me.

Some have told me that my brain's brilliant con job seems almost ridiculous. How could you have turned away from the obvious facts of the situation? My answer is simple: the mind is an enormously powerful machine. No matter what the facts, no matter what the overwhelming evidence, it has a remarkable capacity to convince us of whatever we want to believe.

If this sounds unlikely, consider the alcoholic who is unable to see his dependency despite the devastating effect it has on his life and family. Or consider the chronically poor performer who is genuinely shocked when he gets fired, even after many serious discussions with his boss. So, surprisingly, when I woke up one morning just before my freshman year in high school completely blind, it came as a massive blow for which I was totally unprepared.

As Erik found, avoiding adversity—denying it—can be exhausting, like endlessly hiking the entire way around the base of a mountain, rather than taking it on. People who actively try to downplay adversity tend to be haunted by an insidious fear that the thing they're working so hard to avoid will forever remain, or worse yet, mutate, come back to life, and strike again.

Avoiding adversity can create cancerous emotions like self-doubt and even self-loathing. A morbidly obese man who wakes up each day fully aware that he needs to lose weight, and who happens to be equipped with all the knowledge and tools to actually do so, does not tend to enjoy a boost to his self-esteem each day he ignores or postpones the hard work it would take to regain his health. So why do people avoid adversity? The benefit comes from preserving an easier, more comfortable state. It's often a heck of a lot easier—at least for the moment—to stay where you are than to climb to a better place.

Avoidance is unique, because it is a negative. It is based not on what you do but on what you choose *not* to do. A sure sign that you are avoiding adversity, therefore, is feeling sapped—not by something you experienced but by something you chose *not* to experience. If you've ever spent considerable effort escaping a situation you may have been dreading, then you know that, ironically, the energy one expends avoiding an adversity may ultimately exceed the energy required to take it on!

However, avoidance has its purpose. For example, if you are utterly spent, having just survived a flood, and you know that the first floor of your house is filled with mud and vermin from the floodwater, you may consciously decide to avoid that adversity, for now, and put your family up in a hotel. When the onslaught of adversities is potentially overwhelming, your values define your priorities, and you strategically decide which hardships to sidestep, and which ones to take on first.

SURVIVING ADVERSITY

Likewise, *surviving* adversity can be downright arduous—the goal being simply to come through still standing, or at least alive. Sometimes, given dismal enough circumstances, survival is exceptionally noble, even inspiring, and is all one can hope for, at least temporarily. Hanging on tenaciously for another day without food or water while pinned under earthquake rubble is elevating behavior. Slogging off to a job you hate, day after day, year after year, just because it's easier than bettering your circumstances, is not.

It's not difficult to tell when you are in survival mode as opposed to avoidance mode. In general, avoidance, such as procrastinating on doing your taxes, only staves off the inevitable, whereas survival can bring relief—the release of coming out the other side or, in the case of your taxes, finally getting it all done. With avoidance you go

around; with survival, you go through. With survival you often experience completion. With avoidance you do not. Ideally, survival is
only a temporary stopping point on the way to higher elevations.
Being stuck in survival mode, like avoidance, tends to be grueling,
because you invest enormous energy, and you gain little if any
ground. Most people are not at their best in survival mode. They
desperately lash out in an effort to preserve themselves, often at the
expense of others. If your motto is, "Every day above ground is a
good one," you are probably spending too much time in survival
mode. Too many change-battered people I see in our clients' organizations seem to be living by this creed.

COPING WITH ADVERSITY

You've surely witnessed people applying all sorts of common strategies in an effort to cope with the adversity—or get by—in both constructive and destructive ways. Among the more destructive ways
are drinking, complaining, blaming, and playing political games of
one-upmanship to out-position others in the eyes of the decision
makers. More constructive coping methods include venting to
friends, blowing off steam at a gym, and taking occasional breaks,
such as going for a walk to get some fresh air. Erik, for example,
coped with total blindness by telling himself that he'd simply have
to navigate as best he could despite his diminished abilities and expectations.

I coped with going blind by telling myself that, although I'd never be the
same, I'd just have to live with it—as a person lives with a debilitating disease.
I begrudgingly took the long white cane that the professionals gave me and
went through the motions, but I still felt helpless, unable to affect the direc-

tion of my life, like a dried leaf blowing in a storm. Wherever I'd land, I'd try to react, usually badly and often with visceral anger. My response was primitive, like a cornered badger baring his teeth and lashing out at the world.

I tried to accept the fact that I could no longer do many of the things I loved: riding my bike, watching movies, and horsing around with friends. I was coping as best I could, but some days I'd sit in the cafeteria listening to the excitement, laughter, and food fights passing me by, and I'd see my life through a rearview mirror, looking into the past, looking at all the things I once could do and had lost. I wasn't afraid of going blind and seeing darkness, but I was terrified of being swept to the sidelines and forgotten, afraid that at the ripe old age of fourteen I'd be a nonfactor, unimportant, and forgotten. My hopes for the future had been snatched away. By coping, I was barely keeping my head above water, but I was still slowly drowning.

Adversity deserves whatever time and energy are required to glean the fullest possible benefit. Many people get stuck in coping mode because the perceived impact of the adversity is so great that it takes all they have just to stay even or prevent a downslide. The problem arises when you expend tremendous resources but experience more detriment than advantage. That's why, even if you are enormously successful at any of the lower elevations of the Adversity Continuum, the best you can hope for is restoring yourself to your earlier form. You emerge at best unscathed, but you've lost precious time, energy, and opportunities in the process.

MANAGING ADVERSITY

When you manage adversity, you are trying to minimize its downside and its potential impact on other facets of your life or organization. We've been raised to believe that effective leaders and individuals manage adversity well. Managing adversity is like operating a moderately effective furnace. It's more productive than coping, surviving, or avoiding, but it still has a price.

People with chronic pain and illness often manage their adversity in elevating ways. Deborah Weist's doctor found a lump in her breast and expressed serious concern, calling for immediate tests. So, the day before receiving her test results, Deb, training director at DIRECTV, decided to fortify herself against potentially devastating news. She walked the Race to Robie Creek, a half marathon in Boise, Idaho, which features an eight-mile uphill trek, earning its billing as the "toughest race in the Northwest." During the race she thought, "OK, if I do have cancer, I'm going to do all I can to manage this thing, so I can come back one day and *run* this hill!"

The tests came back positive, and, true to plan, Deb dug in and managed her situation as best she could, day by day, by taking charge of her education, treatment, and recovery all the way through her rigorous chemotherapy and alternative therapies. She created a plan, with timelines and goals, examining the odds and doing all she could to strategically minimize the downsides and increase the chances of a full recovery. Five years to the day after receiving her diagnosis, Deb *ran* Robie Creek. Later that year, she went on to fulfill another goal—to run a full marathon before her fiftieth birthday.

When you work to affect your adversity in some positive way, you are managing it. Done right, proactively managing adversity can be an effective way to keep it in check. When Erik uses a talking computer, a guide dog, or a Braille writer, he is managing his adversity by working with it more effectively. But whether for Erik or for you, merely managing your hardships is only half the battle. Everyday greatness requires more.

HARNESSING ADVERSITY

It is only at this level—*harnessing*—that your "furnace" produces more energy than it uses. I saw Erik speak to the top 150 global executives at Baxter International. When I saw the way he touched, moved, and inspired these leaders with his amazing story and example, I knew that he had shattered their perceptions of what's possible. And on hearing the chairman and CEO, Bob Parkinson, comment to his people, "This shows all of us how little of our *real* potential we ever *really* tap," I knew that their conversations the next day, and their forward planning for their enterprise from this moment on, would be dramatically elevated. When you use adversity to elevate yourself and others, or for some tangible gain, that's *harnessing* adversity.

And make no mistake—it's not as though you flick a switch or swallow a magic pill and—voilà!—you are suddenly impervious to tragedy. Whenever you face something exceptionally tough, it's only natural, and in some ways healthy, to bemoan all that can be lost.

It is much, much harder to ponder, let alone comprehend, what can be potentially *gained*. Three days into the nightmarish aftermath of hurricane Katrina—arguably the worst natural disaster to hit the United States—a local resident, who lost everything to the storm, was interviewed on national TV. When asked about how he felt, knowing that his city was completely destroyed, John DuBois replied, "New Orleans is gone. But it always has had some serious problems. . . . I know this may not be a popular time to say this but . . . maybe this is our golden opportunity to make her better for everyone." The interviewer was stunned, and instantly shifted the conversation back to death, looting, and chaos, or something more befitting the mind-set of most people. Too bad. John was on to something.

The truth is that most of us spend time moving between levels of the continuum. The key is to minimize the time spent in the lower levels and maximize the time spent at the top.

EXPERIENCING THE ADVERSITY CONTINUUM

Level	Upside	Downside
Avoiding	Spares you pain Buys you time	Significant energy drain Can sap self-esteem Does not deal with the issue Often fear-based
Surviving	Staying alive Remaining mostly intact	The longer it lasts, the tougher it gets Can be emotionally damaging Often intensely draining
Coping	Can feel productive Limits the downside	Holding, but usually not gaining ground Ranges from demanding to all-consuming Can become the main focus
Managing	Working with adversity Keeps adversity contained	Requires substantial energy and effort Can be a full-time job Does not unleash the potential gains
Harnessing	Big energy boost Accelerates progress Drives innovation Boosts confidence Strengthens morale Builds momentum Creates competitive gains Produces fuel for your dreams	

The Starting Point

Now that you understand the different levels of the continuum, you can answer the opening question. In general, how do you relate to adversity? When it strikes, where on this continuum do you spend most of your time? The most effective way to gauge your relationship is to indicate on the diagram below (or jot down on a separate sheet of paper) the percentage of your adversity-related effort you tend to spend at each level of the continuum. You may find yourself at different spots on the continuum, depending on the hardship. The purpose is to reflect, and assess how much time you spend at each level.

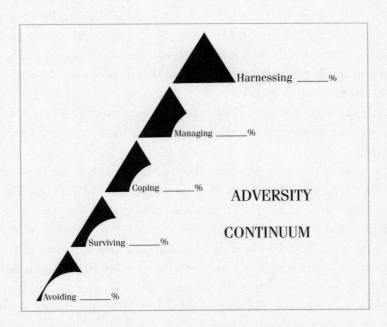

FACE THE FACTS: YOUR ADVERSITY ASSUMPTIONS

Erik inspires us with his glowing example of how one person, even with initial reluctance, can transform the relationship with adversity. But to do so, he had to come to grips with his underlying Adversity Assumptions: that blindness would make him obsolete and that denying it would make it go away.

Adversity can provide the challenge, the kick in the pants, that helps you grow. My son Chase, on the cusp of graduating from law school, was denied a job he wanted quite badly. It would have been a big boost for his career and eased the strain on his and his wife Katie's household income, which had become more stretched after the birth of their first child. Chase had given the application process his all and had made the first cut of interviews, but he was not hired. When we spoke, his disappointment was palpable. And he needed to vent his frustration. So I listened. Then I asked him, "As much as this hurts now, Chase, let me ask you a strange question. How do you think getting denied now might influence your happiness and engagement in your *next* job?" He paused.

"Oh, huge! I mean, I'll be so much more into it and grateful to be getting some real experience, knowing how tough it is out there."

Most people's assumptions about adversity run along the lines of "less is more." Many of us think of retirement, or "the good life," as a life that is simpler, calmer, more predictable, and easier. We build gated communities where we attempt to keep chaos out, and calm predictability within. We take vacations to escape adversity, if only for a few days. Following the philosophy of "less is better," parents commonly do all they can to reduce children's adversity, instead of allowing the children to contend with some adversity on their own. Overall, "less adversity is better" drives much of our financial planning, and many of our choices about how we live.

Check your own assumptions. Since you are reading this book, you probably agree with the premise that we can gain some advantage from difficulties if we use them properly. Most of the time, however, people miss the opportunity to gain real advantage when adversity strikes. Why is that? The problem stems from one's Adversity Assumptions.

I worked with a client recently to unearth his deeper Adversity Assumptions. In his own words, they included:

1. "It is *my* job to shoulder it, and to protect my loved ones from adversity."
2. " 'Success' can be gauged by how effectively you eliminate adversity from your life."

MY ADVERSITY ASSUMPTIONS

What are your assumptions about adversity? To get yourself started, write down your two predominant assumptions about adversity. What would the people who see you most and know you best guess your assumptions about adversity to be?

Now that you have defined adversity, considered where you fall on the Adversity Continuum, and gauged your Adversity Assumptions, the next step is to determine from which challenges you can gain the greatest fuel. Which lead do you want to turn into gold?

FACE THE FACTS: THE ADVERSITY INVENTORY

The purpose of this exercise is to identify your aspirations and pinpoint your Summit Challenge—the one thing you have not done, but always wanted to do—as well as the related adversity or adversities that can offer you the greatest potential power, if harnessed. We will call this your Summit Adversity.

You can complete this activity using the Adversity Inventory provided on page 39, or using a blank sheet of paper, whichever you prefer.

Note: You will be using your Summit Challenge and Summit Adversity throughout this book, and beyond.

It takes a certain degree of courage to make an inventory of your adversities. But all worthy ascents begin with coming to grips with where you are, so you can move forward and up. Two sample inventories, Tanya's and Erik's, are provided to help you think through your own.

STEP ONE: *CATEGORIZE YOUR LIFE*

List all the categories of life that matter to you, including family, work, friends, community, health, hobbies, and others. Go through the list and double-check your items. It is amazing how easily we can let something significant temporarily slip out of our consciousness. In a recent program of ours, a fairly stressed-out corporate manager and mother of three innocently forgot the category "children," even though she remembered to list her leadership position in her condominium association. Her head was in the professional mode, and it took her several moments to consider the full panorama of her life.

STEP TWO: *DECLARE YOUR ASPIRATIONS*

Beyond mundane goals, list your top two or three aspirations for each category of your life. These are things which you have not yet accomplished, but which you aspire to achieve in the short or long term.

STEP THREE: *PRIORITIZE YOUR PAIN*

Thoughtfully consider and then list the top two or three adversities that are causing you the most pain or discomfort within each cate-

Your Adversity Inventory

Step 1	Categorize Your Life						
Step 2	Declare Your Aspirations						
Step 3	Prioritize Your Pain						
Step 4	Pick Your Adversities						
Step 5	Summit Challenge						
Step 6	Summit Adversity						
Step 7	Clear the Trail						

gory. Your initial thought may not reveal the true source of pain. We often cite the symptom rather than the cause. Think about the pain beneath the pain, and enter *that* on your list.

For example, Tanya is a college student who recently completed our program. Her academic aspiration is to graduate. For her, procrastination hurts, but hating her major hurts more. That is the pain beneath the pain. Double-check your own depth and honesty. Did you get to the pain beneath the pain, or did you remain on the surface?

Notice in Tanya's example that there are some seemingly superficial answers like "I always come home smelly" from her restaurant job. And there are those that are brutally honest, such as "I feel like I am failing my parents." Usually, the pain beneath the pain tends to be a fear. In Tanya's case, the fear is of letting down her parents in a time of need. The more the real pain remains unrecognized, the tougher it is to unleash its force. Minimizing pain is one way people avoid adversity.

STEP FOUR: *PICK YOUR ADVERSITIES*

Within each category, scrutinize the adversities you listed in Step Three and pick the one that, if you took it on, would unleash the greatest energy in your life. Did you pick the easiest or the most important? Did you pick the one most important to others, or to you? Go for heft. Being bigger, tougher, and deeper, these adversities carry more force. Remember, the tougher the adversity, the richer the ore to perform your alchemy.

STEP FIVE: *PINPOINT YOUR SUMMIT CHALLENGE*

Let's rise above your aspirations to your overarching Summit Challenge. What percolates inside you when you ponder the word *challenge*? Does it induce trepidation or make you sit up a little straighter? Does it tie your gut in knots or infuse you with determination? The dictionary defines a challenge as "a situation that tests

Tanya's Adversity Inventory

	School	Mom's family	Dad's family	Friends	Rowing team	Restaurant job	Tutoring
Step 1 Categorize Your Life							
Step 2 Declare Your Aspirations	Graduate on dean's list / Have major be my passion	Help turn things around / Create deeper conversation / Genuinely love each other	Help turn things around / Have one happy holiday / Rejuvenate the relationship	Be lifelong friends with Nikki / Have three real friends	Become captain / Win "one man" race	Get a new job / Work up to manager	Hire people to help / Start my own business
Step 3 Prioritize Your Pain	I feel like I'm failing my parents / I hate my major, and it's too late / Procrastination, I feel like a wimp	Rick disciplining me like I'm twelve / We never talk about important stuff / Being a fake big sister stinks	His new girlfriends steal our time / Brandon's drug problem is worse / I hate being in that house	They use me for my car / Nikki and I have lost touch / I feel super lonely/no one to talk to	Kills my sleep / Coach is a real jerk / We never win	I always come home smelly / Lack of appreciation, significance / Other people flake out, I pay for it	I sometimes come unprepared / My heart isn't in it / It's too far away
Step 4 Pick Your Adversities	I hate my major, and it's too late	We never talk about important stuff	I hate being in that house	I feel super lonely/no one to talk to	Coach is a real jerk	Lack of appreciation, significance	My heart isn't in it
Step 5 Summit Challenge	Graduate with a degree I actually love						
Step 6 Summit Adversity	I worry that I'm too far along in my major to change courses now						
Step 7 Clear the Trail	I will stop wasting my time and energy on worrying about the extra money and time it will take to change my major. Instead, I will make an appointment with my advisor and together we can go over my options and see what the real costs will be						

ERIK'S ADVERSITY INVENTORY

Categorize Your Life	Family	Adventuring	Nonprofit work	Work: keynotes, media, writing	Friends	Overall health
Step 1 Categorize Your Life						
Step 2 Declare Your Aspirations	Spend more time at home Adopt a child	Climb the Eiger Guide 10 blind students on Inca Trail Climb Carstenz	No Barriers, expose disabled to outdoors World Team Sports, take kids climbing Create opportunity for third world blind kids	Complete this book Create films that inspire, instruct Improve lives through keynotes and adventure	More outdoor quality time Reconnect with specific folks	Remain injury-free Adventure for decades more Balanced training regimen, two hrs/day
Step 3 Prioritize Your Pain	Balancing competing interests Sometimes Ellen worries Missing big moments with Emma	Training insufficiently Endless coordination of details	Feeling like not doing enough Huge time commitment	Balancing it with training Pressure to keep it fresh Knowing when to say no	Never enough time together Separating work from fun Drifting apart	Plaguing injuries/wear and tear Finding moments to just be, relax Keeping it consistent
Step 4 Pick Your Adversities	Sometimes Ellen worries	Endless coordination of details	Huge time commitment	Knowing when to say no	Separating work from fun	Finding moments to just be, relax
Step 5 Summit Challenge	To help as many people as possible to strengthen their relationship with adversity					
Step 6 Summit Adversity	Finding or making the time to do it right					
Step 7 Clear the Trail	Say no and help my team say no to the things that are less "climb-critical"					

somebody's abilities in a stimulating way." I might add, "and that includes a certain dose of adversity along the way."

You will want to make sure your Summit Challenge is stated in a way that:

- *Excites*, maybe even frightens you
- *Enriches* you deeply
- *Inspires* your strongest will
- *Connects* to your highest "why"
- *Improves* you—makes you better
- *Benefits others* (ultimately) in some meaningful way, if successful
- *Builds capacity*—demonstrates and strengthens your capacity for future challenges
- *Fuels greatness*—demonstrates and strengthens your everyday greatness

So, Step Five is to select from your list of aspirations the most compelling thing you've always wanted to do, but have not yet done (or completed), for any reason. Write your Summit Challenge on your inventory in a way that fits as many of these criteria as possible, since you will work with it throughout the remainder of this book.

YOUR SUMMIT CHALLENGE

The one most compelling thing that you've always wanted to do, but have not yet done.

STEP SIX: *SELECT YOUR SUMMIT ADVERSITY*

In order to achieve your Summit Challenge, you will surely face some adversities. The next step is to select the one adversity (obstacle, hardship, difficulty, hassle, setback) that: (1) You are sure to face as you take on your Summit Challenge. (2) If harnessed, would offer the greatest potential energy or breakthrough.

This is your Summit Adversity. Think of it as a "fuel cell." For decades scientists have been attempting to create free energy—something that generates more energy than it consumes. This is the holy grail of energy research. Obviously such a discovery could transform society. And on a personal level, converting adversity into fuel could transform your life. As you well know, adversity is readily available!

This adversity may be the most daunting, most impossible, or most worrisome. But whatever the case, step up and select the one adversity that has the greatest potential upside, once you perform your alchemy. Erik's issue has to do with the dynamic tension between his time limitations and the quality he produces. So his Summit Adversity is "Finding or making the time to do it right." Insert your own answer at the bottom of your Adversity Inventory.

STEP SEVEN: *CLEAR THE TRAIL*

What's your excuse? To take it on, you must learn to unleash the fuel embedded in your Summit Adversity. Energy is depleted by impurities. To harness it best you must purify your adversity by coming to grips with the excuses and reasons that prevent action—anything that dilutes its potential force. With the same courage it took to face the facts, the next step is to take a cold, hard look at what gets in the way, and clear the trail.

Excuses sometimes get a bad rap. We tend to label people who make excuses as weak or evasive. But everyone makes excuses, and excuses serve a vital purpose. Excuses are reasons made personal. Excuses are your mechanism for keeping your self-concept—even your *self*—intact, especially when you are under attack. If we confronted you in the hallway and asked you why you are not the number one, undisputed best in the world at what you do, chances are you have some pretty good reasons.

> Excuses are reasons made personal.

Thankfully, you are not living in a state of soul-crushing anguish over your status as less than the best in the world. That allows you to get on with your life, including your effort to become even better. That's the upside.

The obvious downside of excuses is they become a refuge for doing less than we are capable of doing, often on issues of extreme importance. Hiding behind our excuses, no matter how valid they are, is the *opposite* of taking it on. Excuses diminish the potential power of your Summit Adversity, in the same way that overexplaining things dilutes the main point.

If you completed your Adversity Inventory you already know what your Summit Adversity is. If so, revisit your current level on the Adversity Continuum and your Adversity Assumptions, and be honest about your reasons for why you have not been harnessing your Summit Adversity so far. Use the following questions to hone your thinking. Then, based on those thoughts, insert your answer to the Clear the Trail challenge on the inventory.

- ► What are the primary reasons you have *not* optimized that adversity so far? Is it because the adversity makes you uncomfortable or requires extra effort, or because you just don't know how?
- ► What are the *real* excuses? What are the excuses *beneath* the excuses? What's really at the heart of the matter? Do you blame lack of time, when in fact the deeper reason is the potential discomfort the adversity might bring?

Clear the Trail Challenge: If your best friend in the whole world had the ability to see right through you, what would he or she see and pinpoint as the *real* reason you have not harnessed your adversity so far? Would your friend tell you that you are taking the easy way out?

OK. Now that you have given some serious thought to clearing the trail so that you can tap into your Summit Adversity, you are ready to hit the road toward your Summit Challenge. Consider what life will be like when you really take it on.

You are ready for the final step in taking it on, which is to *turn into the storm.*

TURN INTO THE STORM

It was actually through confronting some serious adversity that I finally decided to turn into the storm. One day, I was walking down a dock near my house, only halfheartedly swinging my cane in front of me, and accidentally stepped right off the side. I did a flip in the air and landed on my back on the deck of a boat. It was amazing that I didn't break my back or crack my head open. I crawled back onto the dock, stunned and terrified. For the first time my fear of actually dying overwhelmed my hatred of blindness. I could no longer deny it, circumvent it, or wish it away. No amount of positive attitude training was going to help either. Blindness was real and it had happened, and if I continued to turn away and ignore the facts, it would eventually kill me.

So I committed myself to learning how to navigate with my cane and how to read Braille, and the results were surprising. By walking down the hallway using the cane properly, I wasn't embarrassing myself by bumping into walls and I could actually carry on a conversation with friends. By reading aloud my Brailled essay in class, I felt connected with the other kids. The tools I had loathed because of my fear that they would make me different were the very tools which allowed me to reconnect with my classmates.

I had lived in denial and then tried to cope, because of my overriding assumption that blindness and the techniques that came with it would isolate me and make me feel unfulfilled; but only through facing it head-on, even embracing it, was I able to glimpse the pathway forward.

A few months later, when I got a newsletter about a rock climbing program for blind kids, I ran my hand up the wall of my room and thought to my-self, "Who would be crazy enough to take blind kids rock climbing?" How-ever, I couldn't walk with my eyes, but I could use a cane; I couldn't read with my eyes either, but I could read with my fingers. So I asked myself, what else might be possible if I could gather up the courage to turn into the storm?

If I hadn't fallen off the dock and scared myself into action, I might have gone on merely existing in the lower stages of the continuum. But thankfully that scare was the beginning of a long journey toward taking on my adversity, toward fueling a higher level of contribution and a more productive life.

How many of us live in that state of suspended animation? Sometimes adversity permeates the air around us like oppressive moisture in a coming storm, and we are unable to act. Like some of the people who refuse to evac-uate before a hurricane, we squeeze our eyes shut and refuse to look at the dark clouds bearing down on us. Even when we can't help looking, we come up with plausible excuses about why it is impossible to act—"If I were a little younger, things would be different. If others hadn't done those horrible things to me. If I had been born taller, smarter, stronger." All these are defense mech-anisms that we use to avoid action, barricades summoned up by the mind to protect us from confronting a difficult and painful truth. The only way to really harness the full force of your adversity is to turn into the storm, and bring it on.

Although you wouldn't wish blindness on anyone, you may be thinking that in one strange way, Erik was fortunate. Because he could not escape his blindness, he was *forced* to deal with it. And from that mandate, he grew and gained enormously. You may be thinking, "Sure, if I had to deal with some tragedy, I would. I'd rise to the challenge, and my heroism would shine through. But it's the daily mundane muck that weighs me down." There is another way.

When you turn into the storm, you are consciously deciding to grab the wheel and enter the weather, and *not* wait for a wake-up call that forces you into action. As a result, you confront the naked truth of your reality, rather than sugarcoating it to make yourself feel better. If your doctor says, "You're carrying a little extra padding and that will hurt your heart over time," you might think, "I really should exercise more, when the opportunities arise." In contrast, you might take immediate action if your physician said, "You're a walking time bomb. You're fat, out of shape, and killing yourself as we speak. I'm serious. Your heart could blow at any moment. If that's what you want, just do nothing."

YOUR TAKE IT ON STRATEGY

"Take it on!" is my favorite battle cry for attacking a barrage of adversity. If you know that tough weather is coming, you can drive yourself nuts hoping it doesn't hit, or worrying about what happens when it does. Or you can gear up, turn into the onslaught, and say, "Take it on!" The idea, as Erik learned, is to do so not just when you are forced, but proactively, by choice, because this provides the energy you can harness, the lead you can turn to gold.

As for Tanya, our disenchanted student, her Take It On strategy looked like this:

1. Her Summit Challenge? *To graduate with a degree I actually love.*
2. Summit Adversity? *My major.*
3. How will I take it on? *Request an appointment and have a heartfelt talk with my adviser about my current concerns. Together, come up with some solutions to my situation.*
4. When will I do it? *Today I will call for the appointment, which I hope will happen by the end of the week.*
5. What benefits might I enjoy? *I could get this weight off my shoulders; express my unhappiness; and come up with something new, better, and more exciting for me, and for my future.*
6. Who needs to know? *My parents and my roommate.*

YOUR TAKE IT ON STRATEGY

This step-by-step exercise will lead you to your strategy for turning into the storm and beginning to harness the force and benefits of your Summit Adversity, for starters—and all
your other adversities, over time.

1. Refer back to your Adversity Inventory, your aspirations, your adversities, and your
   Summit Challenge.
   ► Of all of your aspirations, is the one you chose for your Summit Challenge the
     one thing you are most compelled to do, but have never done?
2. Check your Summit Adversity.
   ► Is it the one difficulty related to your Summit Challenge that, if harnessed, would
     unleash the most potential energy and lead to the most significant positive
     breakthrough?
3. Think through the following questions to begin to shape your strategy for taking it on.
   ► If you were to turn into the storm with your Summit Adversity, how would you
     do it?
   ► If you were to ask for or welcome the full force of the adversity, how would you
     do it?
   ► What protections do you need to strip away to experience it fully and harness its
     force?
   ► What courageous conversation do you need to have with yourself or others in
     order to "bring it on" and take it on?
4. Devise your strategy by writing down your answers—which are now refined—to these
   final questions.
   ► Specifically, *how* will you turn into the storm and take it on? Describe your strat-
     egy or approach.
   ► For your Summit Adversity—by *when* will you begin to take it on?
   ► *What* are the specific benefits you expect to enjoy once you do?
   ► *Who* needs to know about the commitments you have made through this
     exercise?

As so often happens, by turning into the storm and implementing her Take It On Strategy, Tanya actually enjoyed some unexpected advantages. Her conversation with her adviser led to an internship with an international aid agency that Tanya converted into an exciting and meaningful first job on graduation. Without the adversity and her decision to turn into the storm, Tanya may never have found her path.

Congratulations. You have completed the first of our Seven Summits—the journey to glean meaning and advantage from the inevitable hassles and hardships that we all face. The tools presented in this Summit are difficult, involving painstaking soul-searching. Keep in mind that to find lasting value in the Adversity Advantage, you have to dig deep. If you haven't sincerely addressed these exercises, but have just skimmed through, go back and do them diligently before moving on to Summit Two.

When we step into the storm, the path will almost always get tougher, involve more pain, and take longer than we predicted. When the path seems hardest, it will be tremendously tempting to fall back into old habits of denial, coping, and minimizing—those defenses that have failed us time and time again.

Years ago, this happened to me during an attempt of Mount Kenya, a 17,058-foot volcanic rock monolith, jutting vertically out of the East African plains. As always, my climbing partner Charley and I prepared diligently, planning our climb for September, in the middle of the warm dry season. We ecstatically envisioned pulling our way up 3,000 feet of finger-width cracks in sunny equatorial Africa, wearing sticky rubber climbing shoes, helmets, T-shirts, and shorts—in other words, we envisioned climbers' heaven.

But after a three-day approach in the completely unexpected pouring rain, Charley looked up at the face and was silent for a long time before saying, "E, it's totally different from the pictures. It looks more like a peak in Alaska. The whole face is completely covered in snow and ice." His voice revealed astonishment and disappointment. I turned to our local guide. "I thought this was the dry season," I said. "It is," he insisted, "but with global warming, everything is changing—snow during dry season, drought during rainy season. The farmers don't even know when to plant their crops anymore."

So our expectations for a quick and pleasant rock climb were dashed. Instead, while the face remained shrouded in mist, we waited out a week of relentless snowfall, hoping the conditions would improve. When they didn't, we sat down to have a frank discussion about our options. The ascent would now be a lot tougher than we had hoped. To have a chance to summit, we'd need to abandon our plan for a fast one-day ascent. It would now take us at least two days. Rather than scurrying up with minimal gear, we would need to schlep heavy packs crammed with stoves, sleeping bags, and a tent, and spend a night squeezed on a tiny ledge halfway up the face. We'd also need to be more painstakingly methodical as we placed our boots on ledges covered with ice and jammed our hands into cracks choked with snow. Sections that were easy when dry would require double the effort.

By the end of our conversation, Charley and I were reeling under all the new realities. The idea of totally changing our plan, our approach, and our expectations was overwhelming. Maybe the face wouldn't be as difficult as we thought. Maybe we'd climb faster than we anticipated. Maybe we'd get a perfect, bluebird day. Wasn't it supposed to be the dry season? In the end, despite all the facts thrown up in our faces, I found myself packing for a one-day attempt.

So when the night sky actually appeared clear, we left at three AM and committed ourselves to an all-out push. We tried to feel positive and optimistic. I remember actually thinking that with a little luck, we might just make it. However, it's not often adversity throws you a bone.

About halfway up, the face began to change. As predicted, the cracks were choked with ice, and the lower-angled faces were totally covered in snow—slowing us down to a crawl. We shouldn't have been surprised when, about noontime, it started snowing and hailing.

We tried to hang tough, putting in an unbelievable effort to keep going;

but two hours later, with the snow melting on the face and pouring icy water into our upturned sleeves, we were exhausted and getting cold fast. We knew we were beaten. Shivering, we made the long, demoralizing rappel down to camp and called off the climb.

The good news is that Mount Kenya is but one climb and will always be there, waiting for another attempt. At the same time, we all want to achieve what we've set out to do. It isn't always good enough to try but to fail nobly in the effort.

Looking back, I realize that what defeated us was being unable to summon the resolve to take it on. The prospect of heavy packs weighing us down, the thought of a miserable night out on a ledge and starting the next morning with cold hands and feet, the contemplation of a ten-hour rappel through the cold and dark—all this was more than we could handle. If we had adjusted our course appropriately and been able to climb the entire face in those tough conditions, our sense of accomplishment would have been off the chart. Instead, not only did we go home empty-handed, but we also went home empty, knowing that we had not engaged the mountain with the best parts of ourselves. Since then, I've learned a valuable lesson: it's not enough to face the facts. We need to act on them and follow them where they lead us. By stepping into adversity, I've gained a whole new understanding. From the moment I begin an ascent, I know that if I fully take it on, I grow and deepen as a person, but it's hardly ever an easy climb.

The greatest people, teams, and organizations step into the storm, when others step back. Rising to the occasion once or twice is admirable, but doing so over and over again, adjusting agilely with each and every adversity, requires more. It requires both immense will and sufficient skill, as well as developing new capabilities to rise up to the next challenge. And, ultimately, harnessing adversity requires you to dig deep and Summon Your Strengths.

SUMMIT ONE—TAKE IT ON!

GUIDING PRINCIPLE
People who glean the greatest advantage from their adversities learn to *take it on*.
We need to rethink our relationship with and assumptions about adversity—and life.

Adversity Defined and Scored
Adversity occurs when something negatively affects, or is predicted to negatively affect, something or someone you care about. *Key elements* are how much you care, and how big the impact might be.

Big versus Small
You're more naturally equipped to respond to the big stuff. But you can deliberately install the mechanism you need to optimize the small stuff too.

Face the Facts: Adversity Continuum
Most people *avoid, survive, cope with,* or *manage* adversity—consuming their life force in the process. *Harnessing* adversity feeds your life force.

Face the Facts: Adversity Assumptions
Most people assume that adversity is bad and that less is better. You now know that adversity is not only potentially good but *essential* for everyday greatness.

Face the Facts: Your Adversity Inventory, Summit Challenge, and Summit Adversity
List and sort adversities, and pinpoint the one thing you've always wanted to do but have not yet done, as well as the related adversity from which you can gain the greatest advantage.

Turn into the Storm
Instead of turning away from your adversity, you turn into it and bring it on, so you can devise your Take It On Strategy.

Take It On Strategy
Your personalized approach to taking it on and beginning to turn adversity to your advantage.

SUMMON YOUR STRENGTHS

ACONCAGUA

Base Camp: 14,000 feet
Summit: 22,834 feet–tallest peak in South America

Whatever does not destroy me makes me stronger.

—FRIEDRICH NIETZSCHE

A lot of people buy into the idea that the best way to optimize your potential is to assess your natural strengths (they often refer to these strengths as talents or gifts) and then build your pursuits around them. Sure, natural strengths matter, but relying on them solely can be tragically limiting.

Beethoven wrote his best music, including his great Fifth Symphony, while he was deaf. I wonder what he would have ended up doing if a strengths coach had told him to pick a job "more befitting a deaf person." Van Gogh was told he was an awful painter. What if he had listened to the naysayers, instead of using the criticism to fuel his passion? Would Einstein, labeled "academically ungifted" as a child, have pursued science if his school counselor had persuaded him to stick with manual labor? What if the countless business leaders with dyslexia—Richard Branson of Virgin and John Chambers of Cisco among them—had accepted the "known limitations" of their diagnoses? And, speaking personally, I wonder just how many blind climbers there would be. Consider all the masters who were once maladroit. Consider all the strengths lying dormant within each of us, waiting to be summoned.

Often, the best things in life do not come naturally. Therefore, you should boldly decide what you want to do, why it's important, and whether you have the will to persevere. Next, figure out what strengths you have or might be able to develop—from scratch, if necessary—to make it happen. Then you need to try, struggle, fail, and fail again, until you get the results you're after. From that experience of learning to smelt the primary elements— skill and will—your strengths will emerge. Let adversity be the flame in which your strengths are forged.

Focusing exclusively on what you're good at can actually be a subconscious way of copping out of the adversity that is implicit in every effort. Instead, you want to use adversity to help you grow entirely new strengths and sharpen existing ones. Think of the times you faced a tough situation and, unintentionally, emerged with new confidence, a new insight, or perhaps a deeper connection with the magnitude of your own resilience. My bet is you wouldn't trade those moments for anything. Neither would I.

Just as you can develop strengths through adversity, you've also got to be able to use them best when adversity hurts the most. An impressive list of strengths means little unless you can deliver those strengths in the face of real hardship. Do this, and they are truly yours.

But regardless of how many strengths you can build and use effectively, it's almost impossible to achieve greatness alone. Linking with the right people can elevate the breadth and scope of your impact. However, the formula for picking your rope team is much more complex than simply inserting people into their proper spots on the basis of their current abilities, like a snaptogether puzzle.

Summit Two will help you do what I had to do on Aconcagua: confront the brutal truth about what you currently are and are not good at in the face of your highest aspirations, as well as what strengths you and your team need to build in order to get where you want to go. It will equip you to rethink this notion of strengths so that you and your team can bring forth your best in the toughest moments. Last, you will apply all you've learned to building team strengths together. Instead of being an impediment, adversity will become the pathway through which your strengths grow and ultimately shine.

Aconcagua, the tallest peak in the southern hemisphere, highlighted all my weaknesses and few of my strengths. On McKinley, I could hear my climbing partners' footsteps crunching in the snow and ice in front of me, and we were all roped together, so that following was easier. Aconcagua, though, is one of the windiest places on earth and consists mostly of rock and scree—the loose, floating gravel that makes solid footing nearly impossible. In the howling wind and across rock, the sound of footsteps would be completely lost.

Also, McKinley was a smooth steep plane of snow: since I could predict my next steps, I was able to get into a good rhythm and save a lot of energy. But on Aconcagua I'd need to constantly negotiate treacherous fields of boulders of all sizes, and lethal ice pinnacles called *penitentes,* which rise up five or six feet from the ground like twisted fangs. On trails, I'd use long trekking poles to keep my balance and to feel my way; but on top of uneven boulders and penitentes, with huge deep zigzagging cracks between steps, I'd move at half the speed while putting forth double the effort. The consequences of a misstep would be a broken leg or worse.

The first time my team and I attempted Aconcagua, we failed to summit. We encountered extremely cold, blustery weather, and so we stayed put at a lower camp. As a result, when the one clear windless day finally came to the mountain, we weren't in position at our high camp and couldn't take advantage of it. The difficult terrain had also taken its toll on me. By the sixteenth day, when we finally went for the summit, I was exhausted and moving way too slowly. At 21,000 feet, with fierce winds blasting us back, I couldn't hear my climbing partner Chris Morris in front of me anymore. I felt disoriented and a little panicky—not just blind but now deaf. Chris gathered us together to shout that the climb was over. The mountain's barricade was just too much for our collective abilities. It was such a difficult and miserable trip that most of my friends weren't interested in trying again. Also, their blind partner's slowing them down probably didn't provide much incentive for another attempt.

But I was determined to use this adversity—our failure—to our advantage, although my will alone would not be enough. I needed to evolve new skills for negotiating in this hostile terrain. So during the intervening year, I set about developing the skills that I lacked—and that I knew I needed if we were ever going to succeed on Aconcagua. I practiced on the slopes of Colorado's "fourteeners"—14,000-foot peaks—which have a rocky terrain similar to Aconcagua. I honed my pole work to balance more effectively in precarious spots. Also, I created a new technique: I'd stand on a boulder and, while putting my weight on my back leg in a deep knee bend, would probe out with the other foot to find the next boulder. Then, I'd reach my poles across the large gap and plant them where I wanted to step. I trained hard with extra weight in my pack so we could really push strongly if we had to. Chris and I developed a new mode of communication with a bear bell, which Chris would jingle to the left and right, helping me to follow through wind and rock.

We practiced over and over and over, knowing it wouldn't be enough to master these new skills in calm conditions. We had to make them work in the worst weather. And we got our chance. The ferocious Colorado winds repeatedly blasted away at us as our dress rehearsal, and I worked hard to calm my mind in the midst of their fury as we pushed toward different summits on exposed ridges. I was still working harder and having to concentrate more than the others, but no one ever guaranteed me that life was going to be fair or easy, and I didn't really care. I was just grateful that I could find a way to be doing the thing I loved.

Then we regrouped and took on Aconcagua a second time. Right out of base camp, Chris and I lost our only other teammate, who descended because of acute altitude sickness. It was just the two of us; and as Chris so clearly stated, "Now we cannot afford to make *any* mistakes."

As had happened the year before, the weather was marginal, but we kept pushing our camps up the mountain, knowing that this time we had to be in position for the summit when the weather turned fair. One day we felt so strong that we skipped an intermediate camp and climbed almost 4,000 feet to the next camp.

On summit day at 21,000 feet, we encountered even worse winds than the year before: sixty miles per hour. The previous year, I had started the morning very overdressed, so when I hit the wind and became wet with sweat, I was instantly cold. This time I dressed lightly and had all my extra clothes organized and ready. We huddled behind a rock and put on everything we had to fend off the wind, with only limited success.

As we struggled up the ridge, Chris's bell, which had been working great until then, must have frozen, because I could no longer hear it—just when I needed it most. We were being blown back and contemplated retreating. But we had trained enough and had become skilled enough to keep pushing on, with an idea that if we could break through the wind, we'd enter a calmer zone around the leeward side of the mountain.

Chris knew I couldn't hear his yells, so for three hours he continually turned around, banging his pole against rocks and putting his bare fingers in his mouth to whistle at the top of his lungs. All that training with extra weight was paying off. At 21,500 feet, the wind abated, but the cold intensified. When I stumbled onto the rocky summit, the extreme altitude, along with my complete exhaustion, made my connection with the earth feel tenuous, as if I were perceiving reality through a distant pinhole. But we were on top, finally, after two years of trying.

When I eventually got back to "high camp," I collapsed in the frozen dirt, lying there with half of me convinced that I wasn't cut out for this life. I wasn't tough enough. I wasn't resilient enough. And besides, what a ridiculous pursuit for a guy who couldn't see! But the other half of me couldn't imagine doing anything else with my life. I wanted to climb forever.

I once had a college professor who said that human beings are probably the only species in the entire animal kingdom who dream beyond their limitations. I find this an admirable quality. To settle into our obvious strengths and the paths where they lead us is to slash from our psyches our deepest yearnings, our highest aspirations, and those transformative qualities that define our lives.

A year earlier, in better weather, I couldn't make it to the summit. This time, we used the adversity of that failure to grow stronger and more adept.

The tougher it got, the better we got. Together, our will and our skill forged new strengths that overwhelmed my weaknesses and got us to a place most people thought we'd never experience. Through adversity, we equipped ourselves for bigger challenges to come. And through Summit Two, you can do the same.

Where would you be and where can you go without the ability to summon *your* strengths? And what role have you let adversity play? How effectively do you boldly decide what you want to do and why you want to do it, and then figure out what skills you have, can adapt, or might be able to develop—from scratch if necessary—to make it happen? Do you, like Erik, use adversity to forge new strengths, or do you typically rely on what you naturally have?

Equally important, *when* do you summon your strengths? Which strengths come through when the weather is calm as opposed to when the weather is rough? When do you feel strongest? How does your behavior when the pressure is on affect the degree to which others trust and respect you? When adversity strikes, what can people count on you to deliver?

In order to get the best results you cannot possibly go it alone, so what about your *team*? Do the team members build and bring forth their strengths through adversity? Do they all bring out their best when it matters most? Or do people slip into a default mode, resorting to protective, safer, smaller, less effective behavior when the pressure is on? What would you and your team like to take on, but haven't taken on, maybe because you're not convinced that you possess the strengths it would take to get there? What if you could achieve this? And how effectively do you weave your individual strengths with others to create collective greatness?

Summit Two is not, therefore, just about harnessing the

strengths you have. It is also about developing new strengths that you can bring forth in times of adversity to accomplish what you set out to do. In Summit One you learned how to use adversity as fuel. Research indicates that "high AQ" people don't just rely on their existing strengths. They constantly and relentlessly develop new strengths, expanding their capabilities—developing additional capacities that can directly contradict what others once labeled as weaknesses. They recognize that evolving new strengths gives them traction, momentum, and options. But having, forging, and then bringing forth the right strengths is both difficult and insufficient. Once you have the right strengths, you must also learn to summon them at the right times. More specifically, you turn adversity to your advantage by bringing out your best in the toughest situations.

Every business I work with, regardless of the industry, struggles to consistently and effectively rely on its employees' strengths in order to move toward its vision, mission, and strategic plan. Business leaders know that doing this determines the fate of their enterprises. But some leaders definitely call out these strengths better than others. And the great ones are not always headline stories in the *Wall Street Journal*.

For instance, consider a privately held regional oil company with convenience stores equipped with gas pumps, and home heating oil terminals, scattered through New England, eastern Canada, and Newfoundland. How can it hold its own against the global brand titans who dominate the industry? The leaders at Irving Oil know they can't possibly compete on scale, resources, or political heft. But they can compete on strengths, especially when adversity strikes.

The climate within this company is exceptionally warm. But it's not enough to deliver the company's unique brand of authenticity and integrity when everything's running smoothly and the sun is shining. Almost anyone can do that. Together, Irving Oil's leaders have come to realize that as global events create unprecedented swings in oil prices, and as the the energy business gets more complex and uncertain, they must forge some new strengths—like agility, mastery of change, innovation, and systems thinking—to secure their future. And developing these strengths only keeps Irving Oil in the game. It must turn its new and existing strengths into what I call Adversity Strengths—what it does and delivers in the toughest moments—in order to create genuine competitive immunity.

So in 2005, when a hurricane nearly crippled the oil industry, Irving's leaders sprang into action. They immediately foresaw the skyrocketing prices at the pumps and in the home, although they didn't fully envision the fierce criticism and government inquiries that were unleashed as a result of record-breaking industry profits.

Mike Crosby, COO of Irving Oil, and his leadership team decided what they wanted—to achieve healthy profits while improving customers' satisfaction. This goal was an exact fit with their mission. Then they set out to accomplish it. The urgency of the situation forced them to think quickly and systematically about all the moving parts. Together, they strategized about the potential downside to the unprecedented price fluctuations, and they reached out proactively to the customers. They called their customers, one by one, to reassure them that although the storm was fierce, there would be fuel, and that Irving was doing everything in its power to keep home heating oil as inexpensive as possible. Customers' satisfaction went up and the bottom line smiled, while their competitors' top leaders were put on the defensive on national television in front of an increasingly outraged public.

Decide what you want to do, and clarify why you want to do it. Then bring forth and nurture the strengths required to make it happen. Most important, summon the right strengths when adversity strikes, and you, as well as the people around you, will win. Summit Two will equip you to do exactly that. Specifically, you will learn to:

- ▶ Decide what you want to do—revisit your Summit Challenge.
- ▶ Apply the Strength Formula to discern why you want to do it, and what is needed to make it happen.
- ▶ Forge and summon your Summit Strengths—those required to fulfill your Summit Challenge.
- ▶ Bring out your best in the toughest situations—applying the powerful difference between your Adversity Strengths and your Regular Strengths.
- ▶ Create a Team Advantage—a team of highly interdependent individuals that forges and summons its strengths through adversity to create breakthrough results.

As Erik says, "You don't have to be the best. You just have to be darn good when it really counts."

STRENGTH FORMULA

Let's begin with your Summit Challenge and apply the Strength Formula to these questions: (1) *Why* do you want to undertake your Summit Challenge? (2) To make it happen, what strengths do you need to develop and bring out?

In this section you will assess where you are on each dimension of the Strength Formula. You will build on your position as you move through each section in Summit Two.

Adversity Tools

Summit Two offers a series of interactive exercises. To glean the greatest benefit from your investment in these pages, you will want a pad of paper or a blank document so that you can thoughtfully work through each exercise in sequence.

Skills, Talents, and Strengths

Let's begin by clarifying three common terms—*skills, talents,* and *strengths*—in ways that will ultimately help you turn your adversities to better advantage. Perhaps you think of these three terms as the same thing. That is because today's popular business books often confuse them by using them interchangeably. Given the importance of these facets of human endeavor, the confusion is unfortunate. We view these terms differently.

For our purposes, we define *skills* as those things you're relatively good at, whether innate or learned. *Talents* are skills that you have a natural ability to do well. They still may have to be refined and developed further, but you have a natural ability to do them with relative ease. In many books and articles, it's popular to distinguish learned skills from innate skills (talents). While there is much discussion on the difference between talents and skills, for the purposes of this Summit and this book, the argument is unimportant. When Erik forms a climbing team, he does not care if the abilities people possess are innate or learned. He only needs proof that they exist. If you're relatively good at it, it's a skill, which is the term we will use going forward.

To confuse matters more, it's common for people to throw the word *strengths* into this discussion. This is where we see the real difference. Strengths are a different order of magnitude. Strengths are grander and deeper than skills. They are more overarching and sometimes less specific than skills are to a given task. Our dictionary defines *strength* as "an extremely valuable or useful ability, asset or quality." In other words, strengths are portable qualities that may encompass or be a result of several skills. Notice they are not minor abilities of slight benefit, but assets of tremendous value. Skills are therefore a subset of strengths. Strengths go deep.

Skills build the house; strengths hold it together, especially when the wind blows.

For example, asking good, probing questions to learn what a customer needs is a skill. Using the answers to those questions to shape customer-centered solutions is a strength. For Erik, boulder hopping became a skill. Balance and agility emerged as his overarching strengths. And finally, knowing how to pack your backpack and knowing how to dress for subzero temperatures are skills, but the organization and discipline it takes to do these things are strengths. Notice that Erik's strengths make him stronger for all his future endeavors, as yours will make you stronger in yours.

For you, or someone you know, working on your computer may be a skill. But over several years of practice, especially in the face of adversity, technical problem solving may have emerged as a strength. One example is a passenger I saw in an airport lounge, who spun around in her chair to cheerfully help an older, frustrated businesswoman reconnect the wireless broadband card in a laptop. The passenger's skill was getting an Internet connection using current technology. Her strengths, which may have emerged from years of helping others in similar situations, were troubleshooting, problem solving, and communicating in a calm, clear, and helpful manner.

Will

> *Strength does not come from physical capacity.*
> *It comes from an indomitable will.*
> — MAHATMA GANDHI

Of Erik's many qualities, it is his sheer human will to do the thing he sets out to do that most people find incredibly inspiring. Seeing it in action, whether on a television special or in one of his award-winning films, or better yet in person, is truly humbling. A common response to meeting Erik and hearing his story is, "It pretty much kills any excuses I have for not . . ." When your will is stoked, that's what it does. It overpowers excuses with conviction, effort, and action. Will can drive everyday greatness, because it spurs you to do the right but difficult thing that others might back down from doing. And it takes significant will to accomplish your Summit Challenge.

At any level, *will* is one part *determination*, one part *desire*, one part *decisiveness*, and one part *effort*. Will takes and consists of all these elements. Altogether, will may prove a formidable force that can overcome, even overpower, other winning traits such as intelligence, charisma, and curiosity. To be strong-willed about something is to put your force of conviction and effort behind it— to want it, focus on it, decide it must be done, and then do it.

Yet people hedge their bets every day. They believe that to show conviction is to risk disappointment or ridicule if they fail. I believe that to withhold conviction is to sacrifice everyday greatness. Will plays a major role in developing new strengths, especially Adversity Strengths, as it does in most worthy endeavors.

> When it comes to doing anything worthwhile, if you don't have the will, you won't.

Will is also a matter of relentless effort. If you've ever raised a child or been close to someone who has, you know this is true. Let's assume the aspiration is to raise a happy, healthy, good person. Taking on that obligation for eighteen years or more, beginning with years of around-the-clock work, energy, and creativity, is a fantastic everyday demonstration of will.

This also raises a question: the will to do *what*? Unfortunately, not all parents are good parents. Some parents are distracted when they face challenges, losing their will to do any more than survive parenthood. Others put tremendous will (effort, desire, and conviction) into parenting but end up doing things that are ineffective, or even damaging to their kids. Will has enormous power. That's why it is so vital to channel your will toward something that ultimately elevates you and others.

The same principle applies to anyone who has mastered a craft, or has simply risen to the level of being relatively good at something. Effective leaders *don't* tend to say "Good enough" or "Hey, close enough" in reference to people's efforts toward real priorities. Instead, they tend to engage people in working, often tenaciously, to make something good, even better. The quest to elevate and evolve fuels them.

Now that you have been introduced to the components, the formula for strengths is, we hope, both simple and practical.

Will + Skill ⇨ Strengths
Will combined with skill yields strength.

Will applied to using and developing skills yields strengths. To test this formula, remove either factor from the left side, and see what happens. Let's say you have a skill (or talent), like imitating singers on the radio, but you have no will to use or develop it. How likely is performance or music to become a true strength? Likewise, if you had the will to do your best, but completely lacked any musical talent, would you be very likely to develop music as a true strength? No—you need both will and skill to evolve new strengths. Here is a simple way to think of it: *Skill without will remains still. And will without skill yields nil.*

The Why

> *He who has a strong enough why can bear almost any how.*
> —FRIEDRICH NIETZSCHE

A huge part of your will is your *why*. Having meaty aspirations is a good start. But it is the *why*—your highest, most compelling reason for an aspiration—that will help guide you through the cold, dark night of adversity. Mundane whys tend to evoke, at best, moderate will. Noble, elevating whys spur uncommon will. For example, how many miles would you run for a mere workout? Now, how many would you run if you knew that today, and only today, each additional mile would provide funds to immunize, feed, and save the lives of starving children in Africa? Would you let a little rain or wind stop you from your quest? For which one would you likely be willing to endure more pain?

When Chase Martin was in the Peace Corps in a remote village in South Africa, he met Beatrice, an astounding young Rwandan woman, who had hidden under her bed while she watched her family brutally tortured and murdered. Under the veil of darkness she escaped, village by village, country by country, until she showed up desperate and destitute in South Africa. All she wanted was to stay and go to school there, to be allowed to live. But the South African government was threatening to deport Beatrice, and soon.

All Chase wanted to do was help Beatrice avoid deportation and certain death. But he soon realized that the will to help was not enough. He needed the tools. He could have left well enough alone. He had a great wife, job, and future.

Instead, he decided that never again would he feel so useless when someone needed his help. He would go on to law school to get his degree and help the Beatrices of the world find a home. But there was one problem. Chase never did particularly well at, and never really loved, the academic side of school. It wasn't one of his strengths. But Chase knew he would have to endure three years of sometimes extreme adversity in order to achieve his goal. When we have the why, it's amazing how we can summon the strength to do what has to be done.

Stephen Covey, who so generously contributed the foreword to this book, suggests that we need to ground our efforts in our mission or purpose and in what he calls "universal principles." Over the years, through helping millions of people worldwide formulate their personal mission statements, Stephen discovered that, overall, people are naturally driven to contribute positively to others and to the world. We all want our brief time here to matter, to be significant. The more compelling your why, the more adversity you will weather for the cause, and the greater your *will* to make each aspiration come true. But, as you now know, will is not enough to achieve everyday greatness. It takes a certain degree of skill, too.

YOUR SUMMIT STRENGTHS

You are now ready to apply the Strength Formula to your own personal Summit Challenge. The following exercise will guide you, step by step, to arrive at the answers to some of your most important questions:

- ▶ What do I want to do?
- ▶ Why do I want to do it?
- ▶ What is the most significant adversity or obstacle I will face as I attempt to do it?
- ▶ What strengths do I have, and which strengths do I need to forge to make it happen?

As with all the exercises in this book, treat yourself to the full, rich value of the experience. Step away from other distractions. Give your answers serious thought. Record them in a way that will let you keep and reuse them. Engage fully, and enjoy.

YOUR SUMMIT STRENGTHS

Note: A blank form is provided on the following page to help guide you through this exercise.

1. Begin by restating separately your Summit Challenge and Summit Adversity, leaving ample space beneath each.
2. Next to each, draw a blank box, and fill in your Will Meter. On a scale of one to ten, indicate the amount of will you have to take on your Summit Challenge and Summit Adversity. Ten is the highest, one the lowest.
3. *Why* do you want to take on your Summit Challenge? What is the highest, deepest, most compelling reason for doing it? Write down your thoughts.
4. Do your best to list all the skills you think will be required to be successful with your Summit Challenge; then repeat this for your Summit Adversity. The lists may be similar or different, and they may include skills you do not yet possess.
5. Put a check mark (✓) next to those skills you need but do not yet possess.
6. Next, separately list the overarching strengths required to succeed with your Summit Challenge and Summit Adversity. These are bigger and more encompassing than skills.
7. Put a check mark next to those strengths you need but must improve on or do not yet possess.
8. Finally, think about and write your best answer to this question: Drawing from Erik's opening example, how can you use your Summit Adversity to develop each of your targeted or missing strengths? We'll call this your Adversity Strength Strategy.

YOUR SUMMIT STRENGTHS

WILL METER (1–10)

Summit Challenge _____

_____

_____

Why? _____

_____

_____

Skills

_____

_____

_____

_____

_____

_____

Strengths

_____

_____

_____

_____

_____

_____

WILL METER (1–10)

Summit Adversity_____

_____

Skills

_____
_____
_____
_____
_____
_____

Strengths

_____
_____
_____
_____
_____
_____

Adversity Strength Strategy_____

_____
_____
_____
_____
_____
_____

YOUR SUMMIT STRENGTHS—Erik's Example

WILL METER (1–10)

Summit Challenge   _To help as many people as possible_ | 10 |
strengthen their relationship with adversity.

Why? _Because it has a profound, enduring, and_
foundational impact on their lives. It would be incredibly
rewarding.

Skills

Research

Listening to people's stories

Coaching

Speaking/presentations

Writing

Media interviews

Strengths

Empathy √

Communicating/connecting with others

Teaching √

Learning √

Being purposeful about my Summit Challenge √

	WILL METER (1-10)
Summit Adversity _Competing demands_	9

Skills
Time management

Prioritizing

Calendar software

Saying "no"

Strengths
Efficiency √

Communicating values

Creativity (finding ways to live my Summit Challenge in any circumstances)

Adversity Strength Strategy I can refuse to accept any work that is not directly aligned with my Summit Challenge. Make sure I am true to my Summit Challenge in every presentation and outreach effort I do.

ADVERSITY STRENGTHS VERSUS REGULAR STRENGTHS

Now that you have thought through the Strength Formula—what strengths you need to forge and summon to succeed with your Summit Challenge—you are ready to explore one of the most important issues you will face in any endeavor. This issue is who you are and what you bring out not when times are calm, but when the world is turbulent and adversity rules the day.

Under what circumstances do you bring out your strengths? What do people count on you for when the pressure is on? How do you feel about who you are and how you behave when adversity strikes? As the example of Irving Oil points out, you, like most people, possess two kinds of strengths, Regular Strengths and Adversity Strengths. Regular Strengths are those qualities you regularly demonstrate under calm, normal conditions. They are what most people think of as strengths. For Irving Oil, they included relational strengths like authenticity and kindness.

Adversity Strengths, on the other hand, are what you summon when adversity strikes—those strengths that rise up and shine when you're under the gun or feeling the pressure, or when a situation goes south. These are the strengths that help you rise up to effectively take on each new challenge. And these are the strengths on which trust, respect, and integrity are largely built.

I was chatting with a teenager at the finish line of one of the biggest cross country ski races in Norway. I asked him who he was waiting for. "My mom," he explained in his impressive English. "She's pretty into it." When I complimented him on being such a thoughtful son, coming to watch his mother race, he said, "Yeah, well, my mother is about the most thoughtful, kind, and fun person you could

> What matters most is not who you are or what you bring forth when all is right, but rather who you are and what you bring forth when something goes wrong.

meet—well, most of the time. You just don't want to be around when she's stressed out. Then all of that goes away—faster than that skier who just flew by!"

How similar or different are your Regular Strengths and your Adversity Strengths? If you are like most people, or the teenager's mom, many of your strengths might glow under ideal conditions like a celebration or a vacation, or when life is clicking along. You may be a riot at parties, a joy on holidays, or an incredible leader as the company flourishes. These may be the times when you are the best at listening, being creative, making people laugh, connecting with others, being spontaneous, solving problems, getting things done, or just being a positive influence on others. But how apparent are these supposed strengths when you're under significant or extended pressure, strain, and adversity? For a leader, it's important to note that whenever you do something that very few others can do, the benefits are magnified.

For some people, their lists of Regular Strengths and Adversity Strengths are nearly identical. For others, the lists are completely distinct. In other words, the strengths—even the person—these people bring forth in calmer times are completely different from what they demonstrate when the wind is howling or the heat is on.

> Summon your strengths when adversity strikes, and its countless advantages are yours to harvest.

The problem with this separation of selves has to do with integrity. By *integrity*, we mean the state of being whole or complete, not the degree to which you are ethical. If you are two distinctly separate people depending on the circumstances, then there is no integrity between the parts. There is no real connection between the "calm you" and the "stressed you."

If there is complete overlap between your Regular Strengths and Adversity Strengths, then you have exceptional integrity. If, for example, you are compassionate in both calm times and tough times, then people trust you to be compassionate, no matter what.

If, however, your compassion is highly situational, then your efforts might become suspect, creating results less desirable than what you had intended.

You probably know people who demonstrate different qualities when they are calm and when they are stressed. The question is this: under which circumstances are they *better* and *more effective*? Unfortunately, it is quite common for people to split into separate selves when adversity strikes. Their Regular Strengths step back, and—assuming they actually possess some—their Adversity Strengths step up. If the contrast is extreme, other people can feel as if they are dealing with someone who is almost bipolar, and they remain on guard, wondering which self is going to appear, and when.

So one way to turn adversity to your advantage is to close the gap between your Regular Strengths and your Adversity Strengths by first completing this exercise, and then applying the principles and practices offered throughout this book. This pays huge dividends in all relationships and will heighten trust and respect, as well as integrity. And given that your Summit Challenge, by its very nature, includes a certain degree of adversity, which kind of strengths do you need to move forward? The next step is therefore to define any potential gap between your Regular Strengths and Adversity Strengths.

Like many of the challenges Erik and I present you with throughout this book, the following exercise is simple, but not easy. The first step requires you to list those things the people who know you best might say you do best under normal circumstances. Imagine yourself looking each person in the eye and asking, "What do you consider to be my strengths as a person (leader, son, friend . . .)?" Remember that strengths transcend skills. They tend to be more overarching and general. For example, asking questions is a skill. Connecting with people is a strength. So, think back on past conversations with the people who know you best, or comments from them, like, "You're always . . ." What are the words or themes they consistently use to describe you?

The second step asks you to list the things these same people would say you demonstrate best and most consistently under pressure. What strengths emerge when the heat is on? So, when my bride, Ronda, says to me, "Whenever something bad happens, you get incredibly focused," she's highlighting an Adversity Strength. It's something that is particularly noticeable to her when we face adversity. How would the people who know you best complete the sentence, "Whenever something bad happens, you always . . ."?

Once you've got these two lists—your Regular Strengths and your Adversity Strengths—you are ready to compare them, examine the gaps, and begin to consider how you will close those gaps so that you have ultimate integrity between who you are and who you are under pressure. Look for the gaps that cause you or others the most difficulty. It's easy to identify the most obvious ones. If you're nice when things are good and mean when things are bad, the contrast is unmistakable and impossible to ignore. But it is often the more subtle gaps, the ones that lie behind your blind spot, that offer the greatest opportunity.

It can be a wake-up call when you examine the gap between your Regular Strengths and Adversity Strengths. What strengths do you currently lack in the face of adversity—strengths that, if you demonstrated them, would fuel your everyday greatness? For example, I am capable of showing patience when everything is serene. But under pressure, like an urgent deadline, a missed flight, or a fleeting opportunity, I move fast, and then I have pathetically little patience for people or things that move slowly. I'm not proud of this, but it has been my default mode my whole life. This gap flourished in my blind spot, until I did this activity with my loved ones. At first, I rationalized their observations away, thinking privately, "I'm not being impatient. I'm just being appropriately intense, and effective." By the time the third

STRENGTH SORTER

List all those things the people who know you best would say are your Regular Strengths—
the strengths you actually demonstrate under fairly calm or normal circumstances.

Next, list your Adversity Strengths—those strengths the people who know you best
would say you demonstrate most consistently and effectively when you are under chronic
pressure or are faced with adversity.

Regular Strengths   Adversity Strengths
1. _____   _____
2. _____   _____
3. _____   _____
4. _____   _____
5. _____   _____
6. _____   _____
7. _____   _____

How do the two lists compare? How much, if any, overlap or difference do you find between the two lists?

What is the one Regular Strength that you are most compelled to turn into an Adversity
Strength? _____

Adversity Gap Strategy: How will you do it? _____
_____
_____
_____

person used the phrase "really impatient," I knew I had a gap that
needs addressing.

I know that if I could demonstrate greater patience when under
pressure, it would help me be more magnanimous and connected

STRENGTH SORTER MENU

Following is an abbreviated list of strengths derived from research in strengths theory.

Relationships—Strengths related to your ability to understand, connect with, form, and maintain relationships with other people.

Creativity (ingenuity, originality)—Strengths in the arts, invention, ideas, innovation, design, and more.

Attitude/Outlook—Strengths related to outlook, energy, optimism, perspective, open-mindedness.

Virtues—Strengths related to honesty, fairness, restraint, selflessness, courage, and more.

Thinking—Cognitive abilities related to how you think about things.

Physical—Strengths related to coordination, fine motor skills, stamina, flexibility, movement, and more.

Spiritual—Strengths related to sensing, connecting with, and tapping into the higher level of the world around you.

Other—Strengths you possess that do not fall neatly into any other category.

M. Seligman and C. Peterson, *Strengths, Virtue, and Character*, 2004.

with the people around me when magnanimity and connection really matter. How do we close the gap and create new Adversity Strengths? Once again, it's simple, but not easy. It's enriching and humbling, because you'll bump up against your very nature, and realize how your behavior ripples out across situations in ways you never intended. Like Ebenezer Scrooge in Dickens's *A Christmas Carol*, you may experience a wake-up call when you courageously come to grips with how what you do affects those you care about, whether or not you intend it to affect them. And that wake-up call can be cathartic and, of course, a great source of fuel. Greatness requires awareness, humility, and follow-through.

You need to find a way to close your strength gaps—a way that works for you. Personally, I engage the people around me who are most likely to be present at, if not directly involved with, the next adversity. I simply approach them directly with my request: "Listen, I recognize I'm not as patient as I would like to be with you and everyone else when we're under the gun. And I am really committed to doing better, but I would like to ask for your help. Next time I'm impatient with you or anyone else in a bad way, I'd really appreciate it if you'd alert me by saying something with the word *adversity*. That will be our code word indicating that I need to slow down and do better. And please know that while I may not appear pleased when you do it, and I may slip up, I *am* grateful, and I *will* listen."

The important thing when you are enrolling others in helping you close your strength gaps, of course, is to honor your commitments, and never, ever shoot the messenger. And it's always a nice gesture to thank people for their role, especially when you're least happy about being reminded. It's not always best to ask this of your subordinates, since you may unintentionally be putting them in a terrible predicament. Being able to pinpoint, address, and take action in an area in which you seek to improve is a sign of everyday greatness. Chances are you'll inspire others to do the same. That's good leadership. Closing the gap between your Regular Strengths and Adversity Strengths is a powerful step toward turning adversity into an advantage, by helping you bring out more of your best, especially when things go wrong. Take a moment now and insert your own Adversity Gap Strategy in the exercise above.

THE TEAM ADVANTAGE

All that you've done so far—sorting your Regular Strengths and Adversity Strengths, refining your Summit Challenge, pinpointing your Summit Strengths, and devising your initial strategy for summoning your personal strengths—can unleash tremendous energy. But the reality is that your individual strengths only go so far. And you can't possibly possess or develop every strength you need to tackle every important challenge in your life. That's why—whether at work, at school, at home, with friends, or in your community—most of your grandest aspirations will not be achieved alone.

With each new expedition, I turn to others for the missing strengths required for the challenge. In fact, one of the unexpected benefits of going blind was that it forced me to confront my limitations and to begin building around me people who could help me grow and make me better. In my early years, I strove to be independent; but when I began climbing mountains, I experienced an evolution far more beautiful and powerful than independence. That is interdependence.

A group of people assemble around a unified goal, and they form a "rope team" with everyone's fate becoming inextricably linked to everyone else's, especially in the face of adversity. And at a team level, they do what you've accomplished at an individual level. They begin with their Summit Challenge and Summit Adversity. Then they sort, assemble, and sometimes develop the strengths, mostly Adversity Strengths, they need to rise to the challenge.

One of the most inspiring facets of any climb is the complete and utter commitment demonstrated by forming that rope team. You are literally roped together, wriggling up the mountain like a snake, each of the parts of the team performing a distinct and vital function, yet with everyone in perfect sync. If one person goes down, you go down with him. If he falls, you fall on your ice ax and arrest his plummet, as he would yours. Such a commitment is based on enormous trust, the kind of trust that can emerge only from facing adversity together. Think about it. Whom do you trust more: someone with

enormous talent who has never faced any real adversity, or someone with
reasonable talent who shines every time adversity strikes?

As we apply these principles and tools, it's important for you to
know that Erik's teams have been some of the best in the world. On
Mount Everest, for instance, not only did Erik become the first
blind climber to reach the summit, but his team made history too.
Typically, ten percent of climbers reach the summit. Erik's team applied their Adversity Strengths to bring nineteen out of twenty-one
team members to the top. That's the most people from one team to
reach the top of Mount Everest in a single day. *Time* magazine
called Erik's team one of the greatest ever to climb the mountain.
The accomplishment serves as a perfect allegory for what is possible for your team. So how did they do it?

Remember the strength formula: Will + Skill ⇨ Strengths. It's
important to note that Erik's team had no superstar, no world-
renowned climbers. The team had normal people—including an
architect, two doctors, a physician's assistant, a teacher, and a geo-
physicist—all of whom had the will, including the compelling why,
as well as the Adversity Strengths to do something that far tran-
scended anything any of them had ever done before.

In contrast, think about all the teams you've encountered that
had enormous talent but fell short. A classic case of the hubris of
talent happened in 2004 when the United States' men's Olympic
basketball "dream team," made up of top-paid marquee-name professionals and the hottest college recruits in the nation, entered the
games in Greece as the overwhelming favorite. Each player was a
clear standout in his position, boasting incredible personal stats and
numerous team championships.

How could the "dream team" possibly lose? It had the top talent, and the United States had won the gold in twelve of the past

fourteen Olympics. For many Americans, this team was synony-
mous with gold. Imagine the crushing blow when the team lost by
nineteen points to Puerto Rico in the opening round, went on to
lose two more games, and had to settle for a bronze medal, standing
below two far less talented teams.

I can't even hear the words "dream team" without thinking of
the former number one accounting firm in the world, Arthur Andersen. Years ago, I was on a raft trip on the spectacular Colorado
River with a group of adventurers and guides. I was grateful that the
people were there mainly to enjoy the awesome scenery and the
epic journey. So I was a little annoyed when one of my fellow rafters
came right up to my face after a canyon hike and asked in his
most professionally modulated voice, "So, Paul, tell me, what do
you do?"

I paused and asked, "Bill, you first. What do *you* do?"

Bill lit up. He immediately poured forth an earful on how he
was on the partner track at Arthur Andersen, "the number one firm
in the world," with "partners' average yearly income in excess of
one million dollars." When I asked him what made this firm the
best, he responded, "It's simple, we have the dream team of the accounting world—all the brightest, most talented people want to
work for us. Who wouldn't?" I remember wondering what happened to Bill when I read of Andersen's indictment in the Enron
scandal, and its resulting fall from the throne. Apparently, some of
the "brightest, most talented people" did the wrong things in their
moments of truth. Assembling talented people helps, but it never
guarantees success.

So, if talent and smarts alone aren't the answer, how do you select a team that will win in the face of adversity? Go for AWE.

The A Factor–Adversity

The A Factor has to do with how people perform and what strengths they bring forth while facing adversity. The A Factor is a gauge of how effective, consistent, trustworthy, and dependable a person is when the pressure's on. You can probably imagine instantly how important the A Factor is to the people in your personal life. But what about its effect at work?

In business, I see our clients struggle terribly with the question of whom they should hire or "get on the bus," as the noted business author Jim Collins says. Do you go for talent? Well, clearly, as we've been discussing in this chapter, skills and talent matter. So do values. In fact, these factors can matter tremendously. But are they enough? We think not. You need to gauge the A Factor, or people's Adversity Strengths.

The good news is that you don't need to complete a profile to get at least an initial gauge of a person's A Factor. Just talk or think your way through the A Factor Snapshot, below.

And, of course, there are ways to at least partially gauge a person's A Factor with no profile at all. Erik takes potential new team members out on trail climbs and mini-adventures, where people are subtly checked out to see how well they handle the tough stuff, as an indication of their A Factor on a more serious climb. Likewise, you can put people into challenging situations, or take note when such situations happen to arise, and gauge their A Factor that way. Obviously, the more realistic the trial, the better the results.

Clearly, this is just a starting point. But if, as a result of reading this book, you become much more deliberate in assessing the A Factor of the people you invite to join your "rope team," then your time will have been richly invested.

THE A FACTOR SNAPSHOT: ASSESSING ADVERSITY STRENGTHS

You can apply the A Factor Snapshot to yourself or to others.

Instructions: Use this brief exercise to get an initial gauge of people's A Factor—who they are likely to be, and what they are likely to bring out under pressure. You can repeat the process with those who can offer additional insight about a person, and then compare their answers to see what common themes emerge. This exercise is also a way to gauge how well a person appears to know himself or herself.

BACKGROUND

We all carry two sets of strengths with us: our Regular Strengths (RS), which we draw from and demonstrate under normal circumstances; and our Adversity Strengths (AS), which tend to shine forth when something goes wrong, or when we're under real pressure. And sometimes the two lists are completely different.

STEP ONE

Using the modified Strengths Sorter on the following page, in the first column (RS) rate the person (or yourself) on each item on a scale of one to ten, ten being highest, using the question, "How effectively and consistently does the person demonstrate this strength under normal circumstances?" Or, if you prefer, how would the people who know the person best (at work or in life) rate these Regular Strengths—how effectively and consistently is each strength demonstrated under normal circumstances?

STEP TWO

Next, in the second column (AS), rate the person on each item using the question, "How effectively and consistently does the person demonstrate this strength under significant adversity or pressure?" What ratings would those who know the person best assign to each strength?

STEP THREE

Address these questions.

- ► Of this entire list, what Adversity Strength does the person most need to develop? Why?
- ► What are the things the person tends to do *best* when under real, even chronic, pressure and stress?
- ► What have other people commented on or noticed about the person's behavior when he or she is facing adversity? What are the common themes?

MODIFIED STRENGTH SORTER EXERCISE

RS   AS

Relationships—Strengths related to the ability to understand, connect with, form and maintain relationships with other people.

Creativity (ingenuity, originality)—Strengths in the arts, invention, ideas, innovation, design, and more.

Attitude/Outlook—Strengths related to outlook, energy, optimism, perspective, open-mindedness.

Virtues—Strengths related to honesty, fairness, restraint, selflessness, courage, and more.

Thinking—Cognitive abilities related to how you think about things.

Physical—Strengths related to coordination, fine motor skills, stamina, flexibility, movement, and more.

Spiritual—Strengths related to sensing, connecting with, and tapping into the higher level of the world around you.

Other—Strengths you possess that do not fall neatly into any other category.

RS = regular strengths
AS = adversity strengths
M. Seligman and C. Peterson, *Strengths, Virtue, and Character*, 2004.

Blind Spots

As we read Erik's amazing tales of harnessing adversity, we forget that we all tend to suffer our own form of blindness—blindness to our true strengths and our potential. Some people overestimate what they have to offer; others underestimate it. In either case, the blind spots—the gaps between how we see ourselves and how

others see us—can cause problems. I find that in using various pro-
files, and even in using the snapshot above, these blind spots are
common. There are usually discrepancies between how one sees
oneself and how others view one. And, as true as that may be regarding a person's Regular Strengths, the gap in perceptions is
often increased dramatically in assessing one's overall A Factor and
specific Adversity Strengths. In short, many people are blind to who
they are in the face of adversity, either overestimating or underesti-
mating their A Factor.

You can put yourself and your team in a much stronger position
the next time adversity hits by (1) gaining utter clarity and being
brutally honest about your own A Factor, (2) helping others to shed
light on theirs, and (3) working on developing the Adversity
Strengths you need.

The W Factor–Why

Practically every book about teams states the importance of having
a group of individuals commit to a single, unifying cause. I would
interject the word *elevating*. Earlier, you read that the *why*—the
W Factor—has a huge influence on one's will. We've all seen people
with tremendous ability rot away in an environment or in a pursuit
for which they have no W. It's simple but very informative to ask a
person, *"Why* do you want to be a part of this team?" Then come
back again: "Yes, I understand, but *why?"* I find that by my fourth or
fifth *why*, I get at the real why, the why beneath the why. The inten-
sity and content of the real why give you a gauge of where people
score on the W Factor.

Consider it a serious warning sign if a
person's why is anemic, self-centered, or
small. But if the why is authentic, uplifting,
heartfelt, and compelling, chances are that it

> People's will rarely exceeds
> their why.

will engage the deepest pools of the person's will. If someone asks you, "Why do you want to be a part of this team?" you might answer, "Because I want to be part of something gratifying or worthwhile." That's a perfect answer. You intuitively understand the opportunity to elevate yourself by becoming a part of the team. You aren't reduced. You're made *better*.

In our *Adversity Advantage* programs we do extensive exercises to get at the why. But, frankly, what's the quickest and best way to get at the W Factor? *Ask.* Ask people why they want to do the thing they want to do. Then ask again, until you get the answer that rings truest.

The E Factor—Ego

While humility is widely considered a virtue, Erik and I believe that in many ways, ego, or one's "idea of his or her own importance or worth," has gotten a bad rap. Sure, we're all put off by the person whose ego far exceeds his or her capabilities, can't fit through the doorway, or simply sucks the air out of the room. But Erik and I believe there are two kinds of ego: unsubstantiated and *substantiated*.

The question is this: what is the relationship between one's self-perception and one's actual strengths or potential contribution? If the former is bigger than the latter, then people have an unsubstantiated ego. They think they're better or more than they are. But if people's self-perception, no matter how great, is smaller than their real strengths and capacity to contribute, then they have a substantiated ego. They may think highly of themselves, and for good reason. The point is not to be put off by someone with a substantiated ego. It just might prove vital to the cause.

As Erik points out, most of the great climbers he invites onto his rope team have substantial egos. They're amazing climbers, and they know it. To this Erik responds, "Thank goodness!" Imagine if they were overly humble, and failed to realize how capable they really are, especially in the face of adversity. As soon as the next unexpected challenge arose, they might back down, rather than rise up, when it matters most.

It turns out that the E Factor can play a big role when adversity strikes. A certain degree of ego, chutzpah, and moxie is needed to take full advantage of the adversities from which others back down. Ego can be what fortifies you with the belief in yourself to dare to take risks, take on the daunting and the impossible, step up when others step back, or even forge ahead through some pretty rough weather.

And ego can tie in closely to the W Factor, the why. I discovered that, in general, it takes a reasonable ego to even consider going after the higher whys. Those who perceive themselves as unworthy or incapable are likely to lower their sights to more pedestrian goals. Personally, I would not want anyone on my team at PEAK without a healthy, substantiated ego. Members of my team need it!

There are a few practical ways to get at the E Factor. The direct method is to ask people how good they think they are, overall, or at certain skills; how well they rank in certain strengths; and how important they feel their role is on their current team. Then compare the answers against the perceptions of others who witness these people firsthand, particularly members of their team. This simple approach can lead to some vital insights.

A more methodical approach is to use the A Factor Snapshot. Again, this can be straightforward and simple. If a person's self-assessment on the snapshot significantly exceeds the assessment of others, that's a sign of an unsubstantiated ego. If it is the other way around, depending on the size of the gap, the person may be partially hindered by humility. So, again, don't assume a positive sense of self to be a bad thing. When it comes to harnessing life's tough stuff, the term *healthy ego* certainly applies. Look for the E Factor in anyone you bring onto your rope team.

When I hear leaders speak about assembling a team for an

adversity-rich mission, I often hear them mention talent. But in fact, the more adverse or demanding the circumstances, the less talent—the traditional and widely accepted notion of strengths—may matter. It all comes together when you assemble your rope team.

When Erik decided to take on Everest, he had to look for AWE in the people he selected. He definitely could not afford people without an enormous A (adversity) Factor, the ability to deliver their best while under adversity. Nor could he afford anyone without the W (why) Factor—a clear, compelling reason for suffering through such an epic feat. It had to be about more than just conquering a mountain.

Finally, he had numerous superstar climbers with enormous talent who wanted to join him. But he couldn't afford people on his rope team whose E (ego) Factor was too weak, or exceeded their strengths. It would threaten the team fabric, and lead to potentially dangerous behavior. Erik's teammates turned down some of the most skilled climbers out there in order to create a team with AWE.

THE GIFT OF ADVERSITY

After I picked my team using the criteria I now know of as AWE, the next step was to test ourselves in a real Himalayan environment. So, my Everest team of thirteen attempted Ama Dablam, a steep, forbidding peak just a few miles from its taller, more famous cousin. When I look back, I realize that if my team had not faced significant adversity together a year before attempting Everest, chances are we never would have reached the summit. Adversity was the teacher that elevated us from a bunch of skilled friends, with the desire to climb together, to a true team capable of doing something great when it really mattered.

This talented group of individuals, assembled together for the first time, climbed pretty well as a team, with people gravitating toward their natural strengths, as they so often do. We had technical experts, or "rope guns," using their functional brilliance to get out in front fixing lines up the ridgeline and sheer faces. We had analytical experts using their knack for detail to plan all the moving parts of the ascent. And we had the "grunts," like me, using their endurance and strength to slog heavy gear.

After three weeks in favorable conditions, we had made great time, setting up a camp at 21,000 feet. Looking back, I realize that we were using only what I call our calm weather strengths or Regular Strengths—those that are most obvious and easily accessed. But circumstances were about to change.

The next day the monsoons began to roar in, layering the mountain with snow and ice and giving us only a couple of hours of sunlight to climb in before the daily onslaught. But because we were experienced, none of us were fazed. If you want to climb, you have to expect to face some adverse weather.

So we made some adjustments. Because climbing up and down the steep rocky face was starting to beat me up, Eric Alexander and I chose to stay at the 21,000-foot camp while the rest of the team went back down to base camp to wait out the storms. Eric and I were stuck up there for eight days with snow and rock crashing down around our tent, with its right corner hanging precariously over a 5,000-foot cliff.

Finally, the rest of the team fought their way back up to us. We immediately drew on the expertise of our "rope guns" to set climbing lines up higher so we could continue our ascent, but the long wait had cut too far into our resources. We were running out of the food and fuel we had set aside for our summit push, and expecting no respite in the horrible weather, so PV, our team leader, made the difficult decision to turn us back.

Although we had bonded, and we knew that each of us possessed the will and skill to climb, the effort had done little to convince us that this gang had—or lacked—what it took to succeed on Everest as a team. How many teams give it "our best shot," but faced with some "understandable obstacles," or "lack of resources," throw in the towel and say, "Well, we did what we could," without ever tapping the deeper strengths that they need to win?

How often is adversity the excuse for falling short or being less, rather than the impetus for becoming something more? For us, our real chance to harness adversity was about to arrive.

As the team carefully rappelled downward, everything was now covered in ice, even our ropes. We named one particularly scary section Abject Terror; it was a fifty-foot traverse across vertical rock on a fixed line, our fifty-pound packs pulling us backward over thousands of feet of space with no handholds or footholds. And another afternoon storm swept in, the wind now picking us up and slamming us back against the rocks.

Far below me, Eric, judging himself to be in a safe spot, disconnected himself from the line and stepped on a rock, which immediately dislodged and sent him careening 150 feet down a rock face. He was banged up badly, and everyone breathed a sigh of relief when he waved to signal that he was OK. However, the fall had dramatically shocked his system, and soon his lungs began gurgling with each breath, a sign of severe altitude illness, which can quickly kill.

Getting Eric down the mountain under those conditions would be hazardous, demanding the team's very best. Calm weather strengths suddenly meant nothing in comparison with the Adversity Strengths we needed now.

Steve Gipe, our easygoing, slow-talking team doctor, always the last into camp, showed the most dramatic transformation. He sped up tenfold, as he rapidly rappelled down the face and scrambled across the boulder fields below to retrieve the oxygen bottles we had stashed for emergencies. In no time Steve had an oxygen mask over Eric's face and kept him moving, despite the fact that Eric was sitting down every ten feet, near collapse. Steve's Adversity Strengths became speed, focus, calm, and tenacity.

The rest of the team kicked into gear too, operating now as one cohesive unit, as we relayed heavy loads across Abject Terror. Later, team members took turns guiding me down the ice-coated face, as several friends stepped in to relieve each other without any prompting. Communication, endurance, focus, and interdependence surfaced as the team's Adversity Strengths.

It was about midnight when we straggled into base camp together, utterly spent. The adrenaline had long worn off, and all the team wanted was to pile into our sleeping bags, but there was much more work to do.

Steve Gipe had zipped Eric inside our "Gamhoff" bag, a hyperbaric chamber that brings you down to a simulated lower altitude, in hopes of helping Eric stabilize. But the pressure had to remain constant. So, despite our exhaustion, the team took shifts sitting outside the bag, consistently pumping air into it throughout the night and into the next day. Commitment became the last and most important Adversity Strength we added. Luckily, the next day there was a brief patch of clear weather, and we called in a helicopter that carried Eric down to safety.

Back in Kathmandu, we met with the statistician who keeps a record of Himalayan expeditions. After jotting down some notes, she turned to me and asked, "If you couldn't summit Ama Dablam, what makes you think you have a chance on Everest?" The question implied that we had tried something pretty bold, and had utterly and completely failed. But I thought differently.

If we had summited in perfect weather, we wouldn't have learned as much about each other's strengths or what we could achieve as a team. Instead, we had faced the perfect combination of adversity—terrible conditions, real danger, lack of resources, and utter exhaustion—to bring out our team's Adversity Strengths. The mountain had erected a powerful barricade in our path, and only by crossing through it did we become a real team. We had summoned the strengths that we knew might just carry us to the top of the world.

Aconcagua and Ama Dablam taught me that to be the best, you don't need to have an innate, freakish gift. There will always be people more talented than you or me. The question is not what you possess, but what you and your team bring forth, especially in the face of adversity.

My hope is that Summit Two has helped you rethink the whole notion of strengths, reassess your strengths, and approach the people you want on your rope team with fresh eyes and proven tools. Your footprint in life will depend on your ability to Take It On, Summon Your Strengths, and then—when adversity pummels you—apply the principles in Summit Three: Engage Your CORE. Turn the page and join me on Everest, as we engage our CORE together.

SUMMIT TWO—SUMMON YOUR STRENGTHS

GUIDING PRINCIPLE

To fulfill your Summit Challenge and use adversity to your advantage, you have to go beyond the traditional notion of strengths as natural gifts, or of assessing people's current strengths, matching them with the job requirements, and expecting great results. Harnessing adversity requires you and your team to pinpoint and develop your Adversity Strengths—those strengths you bring forth in the worst of times.

Summit Strengths

Those Regular Strengths and (mostly) Adversity Strengths you will need to have or develop in order to fulfill your Summit Challenge.

Strength Formula

Will + Skill $\Rightarrow$ Strengths (will combined with skill yields strengths).

Regular Strengths

Those strengths you bring out effectively and consistently under normal circumstances.

Adversity Strengths

Those strengths that shine forth under pressure or adversity.

Strength and Integrity

Your integrity, or wholeness of self, is determined in part by the degree to which your Regular Strengths and Adversity Strengths overlap. If you are two different people when times are calm and when times are adverse, then your integrity and trustworthiness are compromised.

The Team Advantage

Assemble people in your life and work with whom you can be completely interdependent, elevating everyone and everything you do along the way. For your rope team, look for AWE—the A Factor (who they are and how they behave under adversity), the W Factor (a clear, elevating, compelling why), and the E Factor (a healthy, substantiated ego that can carry them through rough times).

SUMMIT THREE

ENGAGE YOUR CORE

MOUNT EVEREST
Base Camp: 17,500 feet
Summit: 29,035 feet—tallest peak in the world

There is nothing either good or bad, but thinking makes it so.
—WILLIAM SHAKESPEARE

The first two summits taught you about facing adversity head-on and summoning your strengths when they truly matter most. You've got to dig in and take control when it counts.

On paper, this may sound easy, but what about when your "climb" is riddled with potentially paralyzing uncertainty? What do you do when some of the most important factors are completely out of your control, when the adversity is too big, when the level of hardship you have to endure renders the goal no longer worth pursuing, or when the goal you set out to achieve appears genuinely impossible? The reality is that anyone trying to achieve everyday greatness faces these moments of truth almost daily. Most people back down or break. But there are a rare few who prevail and emerge stronger and better as a result. I've always been intrigued by the difference.

What I've discovered through Paul's research is that there is a mechanism or switch, deep within you, which can be triggered whenever any type of adversity strikes. Engaging your CORE is about rewiring your response to adversity by using a new set of tools so you can take advantage of the hardships that accompany anything big and worthwhile. I've seen how this switch has sparked powers in me that I never knew I possessed, and I think it can do the same for you.

My CORE was truly tested when I faced the greatest challenge of my climbing career, right out of base camp on Mount Everest. The Khumbu Icefall is a blind person's worst nightmare, 2,000 vertical feet of jumbled-up ice boulders, ranging in size from baseballs to skyscrapers, all chaotically piled up. The Icefall is created by the glacier that pushes down the mountain ever so slowly and, on reaching a giant cliff, collapses under its own weight, tumbling and exploding like a river of ice.

Even before entering the Icefall, I could hear the looming, fragile ice towers shifting and cracking over my head like an army of grim reapers. The forces at play in the Icefall are enormous, and completely out of your control. It was chaos: with no two steps ever being the same, I had to climb up ice walls and down the other side, weaving along a trail a foot wide with a 1,000-foot drop to my right, jumping from ice boulder to ice boulder as they rocked under my feet.

To make matters worse, there were many cracks or crevasses zigzagging through the Icefall, and you had to either jump over them or walk a tightrope over narrow snow bridges. Sometimes the crevasses were so wide I couldn't feel the other side with my trekking poles. The only way across was a literal leap of faith. The members of my climbing team would tap their own poles on the opposite bank where they wanted me to land. Then I'd jump, knowing that if I was off by even a few inches, I'd shatter a kneecap or break an ankle.

To enhance the torture, there were dozens of crevasses so wide you couldn't cross them by jumping. For these, the Sherpas would lay aluminum construction ladders across the gap that the rest of the team needed to cross safely and efficiently. Sometimes there were five ladders lashed together with thin nylon rope or what I liked to call "Sherpa Kmart boat twine." I had practiced back home on ladders propped up on cinder blocks a foot off the ground; but when I stood on the real thing, with the ladders being buffeted by the wind and the middle bowing over a 100-foot chasm, it was a whole different world.

My first crossing of the Icefall took me thirteen hours. It was the hardest day of my life in the mountains. When I finally struggled above it and neared Camp One at 20,000 feet, I wasn't sure which was more trashed, my mind or my body. For those excruciating thirteen hours, I knew I could not make a mistake, yet I was never 100 percent sure my next step wouldn't drop off into space. Then, as I was nearing camp, I broke through the snow and sank into a tiny crevasse. A teammate reached out to grab me, but instead blasted me in the nose with the handle of his ice ax. So as I staggered into camp, not only was I green with nausea and about to pass out, but I had fat globs of blood dripping down my face.

Finally in my tent, I couldn't imagine crossing the Icefall once more, let alone the ten additional times required to acclimatize and to shuttle loads to the higher camps. I heard PV gathering the team outside to quietly tell them I was moving way too slowly. "If he takes thirteen hours instead of six, he has twice the chance of getting hit by falling ice, and so does anyone who is with him. And the odds increase in the afternoon heat. If he can't find a way to get through significantly faster, he'll have to go down."

As I fell asleep that night, I began hearing internal voices that I came to know as the "sirens." They called out to me and taunted me, saying, "If you can barely make it through the Icefall, you don't have a chance up higher. You gave it your best shot, but you're way outmatched. Go down while you still can. Besides, there are cheeseburgers and warm beds waiting for you."

In the *Odyssey,* the warrior, Odysseus, is sailing home from the Trojan War when he passes the island of the sirens—beautiful maidens who call out to Odysseus and his sailors with such alluring, melodious voices that the sailors become completely spellbound. They dive off the ship and swim furiously to the island, where they realize, to their horror, that the maidens are really monsters. The sailors are never seen or heard from again. Odysseus, knowing the power of the sirens, stuffs wax in his ears and has himself tied to the mast of the ship. Even then, their call is so seductive that he almost goes insane.

The adversity I faced on Everest seemed so big, terrible, and long-lasting that my brain simply pushed the panic button. I knew I had to take ownership, step up, and be a leader, by summoning my Adversity

Strengths—focus, tenacity, and mental toughness—now, when they mattered most. I told myself over and over that the sirens were my brain's defense mechanism gone haywire. They were monsters, lurking at the base of the mountain, waiting to gobble up my desire, my ambition, my very will.

What saved me was a beautiful Tibetan saying I had heard during our ceremony at Base Camp: "The nature of mind is like water. If you do not disturb it, it will become clear." I thought a lot about that. Whenever we face a great challenge, especially one racked with uncertainty, we contemplate the months of hard work, struggle, sacrifice, and risk, and all the dangers lurking around each corner, and it's easy to become overwhelmed.

I had been preparing for this climb half my life. I had trained for two years and had surrounded myself with the best people I could find. I knew what to do, but what was about to turn me back was my own mind, cloudy with fear and doubt. To give myself a chance, I needed to clear my mind, to still it like water. Everest, like all mountains, had to be climbed step by step, moment by moment. It was my job to focus on each step, on each moment, and to respond to each adversity along the way with clarity and resolve.

I knew there were many elements of the Icefall over which I had no influence, like the random collapses, the terrible terrain, and the immense distance; but there were many more things I could Control (C). I couldn't let my fate be determined by any outside force. I needed to take Ownership (O) of my own progress. I couldn't let today's adversity Reach (R) into every other aspect of the climb or allow it to contaminate the outlook of the whole team. The Icefall was just one stage, and I had to contain it. Last, I couldn't sucker myself into imagining that today's nightmare would Endure (E) for the rest of the climb. Although it was a mental wrestling match, I had to see the Icefall as a puzzle that could be solved.

On my second trip through the Icefall, Chris Morris asked me how I was feeling about the expedition so far. "Sometimes I honestly feel like I'm just going through the motions," I replied. "Sometimes I feel like I don't have a chance." "Then you don't!" Chris shot back and then was silent. Those three words affected me like a punch in the gut. After that, on rest days at Base Camp, I'd sit outside my tent and force myself to envision myself on the summit. I'd touch the snow under my gloves and hear the Sherpa flags blowing in the wind. I'd taste the empty air, void of oxygen and humidity. I'd feel the tears welling up as I celebrated with my teammates and would suddenly be energized by the triumph I believed would come.

With each subsequent crossing, I began discovering little systems to shave precious minutes off my time. My partners had seen me rally on earlier expeditions and thankfully stuck by me. On the ladders, I learned to judge the distance between steps so that I could balance my crampon points over the rungs. I began to memorize the sequences of the zigzagging foot-wide snow bridges over dozens of crevasses. For the open crevasses where I had to jump, teammates helped me by shouting out precisely when they were jumping and then landing, so I could gauge the distance and accurately copy their movements. I concentrated on pushing fast through the easier sections and on pacing myself through the tough parts. The minutes we saved added up to hours, and by my last trip up the Icefall, I had reduced my time from thirteen hours to less than five.

After two months on the mountain, we left on our final push for the summit. As I kicked up the face, my oxygen mask seemed to be suffocating me. Higher up, a lightning storm struck, stalling us out for an hour as snow and sleet blasted us sideways, built up on our down suits, and chilled us to the bone. Just below the summit, I inched my way across Knife Edge Ridge, fully aware of the drop of 8,000 feet to my left and 12,000 feet to my right. I jokingly thought to myself that the good news was that it wouldn't really matter which side I fell off. The challenges were formidable, but in comparison with the Icefall, none felt anywhere near as daunting. In fact, surviving the Icefall had given me more confidence than I ever thought possible.

We had been climbing for twelve hours when Chris Morris wrapped his now skinny arms around me and said, "Erik, we're about to stand on top of the world!" When there was no place else to go, I reached down and touched the hard snow through my gloves and listened to the Sherpa prayer flags blowing in the wind. I could even taste the air—just like I had envisioned. Day after day, I had worked myself to exhaustion; I had desperately fought against the uncertainty weighing me down like a mountain of doubt; a dozen times I had been on the verge of counting myself out. So even though my body stood on the summit, my brain hadn't yet caught up. Choked with tears, I pulled out my radio and sputtered to the Base Camp crew, "We're on the top. I can't believe it! We're standing on top of the world."

At the time, I didn't know how to neatly define my CORE dimensions; but it was on the side of Mount Everest that I learned the true power and benefits you can gain when you "Engage Your CORE." Engage yours, and your relationship with adversity will never be the same.

UNDERSTANDING YOUR AQ AND CORE—THE LANGUAGE OF ADVERSITY

Your CORE is derived from your Adversity Quotient (AQ), which is a measure of how you respond to adversity of all kinds, or—simply put—how you react to the world around you. It predicts and drives a host of factors that are critical to success. Here's the short list:

- Performance
- Resilience
- Engagement
- Innovation
- Attitude, morale, outlook
- Energy
- Problem solving
- Health
- Entrepreneurism
- Agility
- Longevity

Erik mentions in the introduction how my team and I formed the Global Resilience Project, in 2002, in order to build on the more than 1,500 studies that undergird the AQ theory. A collaboration of researchers worldwide, the Global Resilience Project is dedicated to exploring and expanding the applications of AQ to better equip people for an adversity-rich world. We wanted to better understand exactly what the differences are between those who harness adversity and those who are consumed by it.

The research has yielded some compelling findings. We've discovered, with mounting certainty, that when all other factors are held equal, high-AQ people rise to the top. They tend to outperform, outlast, outmaneuver, and outdo their low-AQ counterparts, in essentially any endeavor. And they tend to be energized by the same challenges that wear others down. We discovered that leaders of industry often have dramatically higher AQs than the people working for them; this explains much of top leaders' gut burn, and much of workers' stress. Leaders expect their people to demonstrate the same effectiveness under pressure that the leaders naturally possess. Fortunately, this ability can be learned. We discovered that not only can AQ be measured; it can be permanently improved. After hundreds of thousands of people have gone through our various AQ programs, every group's AQ goes up, and some AQs rise dramatically. After tracking some folks for more than a decade, we've found that once AQ goes up, it never sags back down. Measuring and improving AQ have been the sweet spot of our work for many years. And as the science evolves, so do our AQ tools. To get a preview of your AQ, go to www.AQ-Snapshot.com.

STANDING UP TO ADVERSITY

Now that you know you have an AQ, and that your AQ can often be a more robust predictor of success than your IQ, you may be wondering where your AQ and your CORE originated. Are they something you were just born with, like your fingers; or are they more like your posture, something you can consciously improve once you are made aware of it?

Posture is actually an apt analogy for AQ because your posture may appear genetic, but chances are you hold yourself in a way that may be eerily similar to a parent or another relative. Perhaps your entire family shares a distinctive posture—one all your friends can instantly recognize from a distance, even if it is based on just a silhouette.

The fact is that while posture is genetically influenced, it is largely determined by what you saw modeled and what you learned. And you most likely learned it subconsciously. Babies are profoundly observant. As an infant, you watched those around you stand, walk, sit, and engage in life, and you began to naturally model yourself on or mimic their posture. The more influential the person, the more you imitated him or her. So, by late childhood you had formed your posture, which became so natural that you could hardly imagine holding yourself any other way—unless someone came along, showed you some flaw in your current posture, gave you an enormously compelling reason to improve it, and coached you on exactly how to do so.

AQ is not very different from posture. Perhaps it is your posture with respect to adversity. To date, our best guess is that your AQ is roughly 10 percent genetic, but it is predominantly determined by what you learned or what was hardwired during your childhood. By watching the influential people in your life respond to adversity, you began to pick up and try out different pieces of their patterns of response, without consciously selecting those that would be best or worst.

The research on AQ and related response patterns dates back more than thirty-five years and was pioneered by Dr. Martin Seligman of the University of Pennsylvania, and a cadre of researchers from various additional sciences worldwide. In general this research indicates that at about age twelve, your AQ is highly formed. By age sixteen, or soon thereafter, it becomes hardwired for the rest of your life unless you are made aware of it and choose to change it.

So Erik and I want to help you see it; offer compelling reasons to change it; and, by sharing the practices of the highest-AQ people, help you improve it, so that you can not merely respond to but actually harness adversity.

INSIDE AQ–KNOW YOUR CORE

Your CORE—which resides in the center of your AQ—is the one thing you take with you into every battle. It ultimately determines whether you win or lose both at that moment and over the long haul. CORE is composed of *Control*, *Ownership*, *Reach*, and *Endurance*.

Control

One of the most timeless issues confronting people from top leaders in industry to the elderly in assisted living facilities is *control*. Whether it is the prerogative to choose how we spend our time, how we do our work, where we live, or what we eat, we all want some control. Yet control is an emotionally laden concept. On one hand, great evil has been unleashed in an effort to take control of people, property, belief systems, or resources. The most horrible authority figures are people who abuse their control. In complete contrast is the Serenity Prayer, rightly attributed in its lengthier entirety to Reinhold Niebuhr:

> God grant me the serenity
> to accept the things I cannot change,
> courage to change the things I can,
> and the wisdom to know the difference.

The aspect of control that matters most is *influence*. The most important question is not whether you are in complete control. The

vital question is this: when adversity strikes, *to what extent do you perceive you can influence whatever happens next?*

The stirring beauty, strength, and truth of the Serenity Prayer
are undeniable. So is the poem's utility as an inkblot test for AQ.
Your AQ determines your perceived control. High-AQ people perceive that they can always influence something, because even in dire
circumstances they can at least influence their own response.

When Erik crossed the Khumbu Icefall, he could not influence
his harsh surroundings or his blindness. But he could influence his
own mind—his focus and energy—so he could make it across, and
do it over and over again.

The lower one's AQ, the less control one perceives. Consider
several people facing the same adversity. The low-AQ people will
read the Serenity Prayer and interpret the adversity as something
beyond their control, so that they must "accept the things I cannot
change." By contrast, the higher-AQ people, in the identical situation, will be likely to find any number of factors they can influence
for the better, which give them the hope and energy to take it on!

Imagine that Erik had a lower AQ. Think how differently he
would have handled his blindness, how differently he would have
defined his sphere of control. Everest has epic forces you cannot
control. The winter jet stream at the top can reach 200 miles per
hour, and avalanches crush anything in their paths. In fact, when
Erik and his team were waiting at Camp Two for their push to the
summit, they could hear the winds on top "roaring like a bad vac-
uum cleaner." They had to wait a week for a respite, for the one or
two days in May when the winds calm down. Just as they were getting ready to go for the summit, it snowed for two weeks on the
Lhotse face, making the steep sides unclimbable for at least the next
week, and forcing Erik's team back down the mountain, crossing
the Icefall an excruciating and potentially demoralizing eighth
time. Anyone with a lower AQ would have quit, claiming that the
mountain had turned him back. But Erik focused on the things he

could control, like his fitness, supplies, strategy, and attitude, to get ready to give it another shot when the opportunity arose.

Perhaps this is why, of all four CORE dimensions, Control is the most robust in predicting health, and even longevity. A British study, roughly fifteen years ago, found that people who perceived low control over how they did their jobs died on average five years earlier than those with high levels of perceived control. Today a similar study reveals that the gap has nearly doubled, to a disturbing 9.8 years. So people who perceive more control over how they do what they do may live nearly a full decade longer than those who "accept" their lots in life.[1]

Engage your CORE by asking, with regard to Control, *"What facets of this situation or adversity can I potentially influence?"*—as opposed to those you may consider beyond your control. Even in dire circumstances, there is always something you can influence, even if it's just your own response. Most people dramatically underestimate what can be influenced when adversity hits, and this underestimation kills the majority of what's possible. Conversely, becoming utterly obsessed with what you *can* influence opens worlds of possibilities that others simply don't see. For a business, that creates competitive advantage, and for an individual, that means energy and engagement!

As powerful as Control is in determining your attitude toward adversity, it is when you take *Ownership* that the action unfolds.

Ownership

Ownership involves asking the question, "How likely are you to step up to do anything to improve the situation, regardless of your job description?" In other words, Ownership is not about shouldering the entire burden or wasting precious energy pinpointing blame. Rather, it is about the energizing tendency to do something, no matter how small, to make things better.

When two people are hiking, my guess is that the one who stoops down to pick up some unsightly trash is the one who feels better at that moment—even though cleaning the trail is clearly not his or her job. The same is true for the casual traveler who springs up to help an elderly couple stow their bag in the overhead bin on an airplane. We gain more energy and, yes, Control, when we demonstrate Ownership.

As you might guess, the higher one's AQ, the more likely one is to step up and engage. The lower one's AQ, the more likely one is to step back and disengage, probably since he or she is already overwhelmed!

In the business world, Ownership is one issue that brings tears to nearly every leader's eyes. Why? Because as the world gets more demanding, chaotic, complex, uncertain, and fast, people tend to focus more and more on what they need to do to survive, rather than stepping up to drive the next change, or innovate to get to the next level. But lack of Ownership means that important priorities remain unfulfilled, and that key tasks are someone else's job. The less Control you perceive and the less Ownership you take, the more weary you become, and the less likely you are to step up the next time a challenge or opportunity arises.

Ownership is one of the indisputable fibers of everyday greatness. Stepping up to help make things better elevates not only you but everyone around you. Question: *When should you do it?* Answer: *When you least feel like stepping up.* It gives you traction and Control.

Sometimes Ownership is about going beyond the strict confines of your day job or responsibilities, even when you're extremely busy. Michele Burkholder is head of Planning, Analysis, and Control at ING's Retail Annuity Business Group. You'll notice that her job title does not include training, leadership development, or talent management. In fact, like most leaders, she has a day (and evening) jam-packed with regular responsibilities. Nonetheless, when Harry Stout joined ING as president of the Retail Annuity Business Group, he quickly identified the need for more leadership development. Michele, who reports to Harry as a chief of staff, saw the challenges her colleagues had to take on to make the business tick. She stepped up to help devise a best-in-class leadership development program, amid the miring complexity of one of the biggest companies in the world; elevating herself and the whole business. Ownership is often about doing the right thing, even when it's not the required thing, or the thing for which you are evaluated.

Engage your CORE by asking, with regard to Ownership, *"What can I do to affect this situation or adversity immediately and positively?"* rather than worrying about who caused it, or who is responsible for figuring out the ultimate solution. Don't give away your precious power and momentum by waiting for others. Focus on *your* realm, *your* Ownership, and watch how you inspire others to do the same.

Reach

Do you know anyone who suffers from emotional oil spills? You know—this is the kind of person whose entire day is ruined when one thing goes wrong or whose entire project is destroyed by one minor mistake. Psychologists call this reaction to adversity *catastrophizing*. You get the point. The research on AQ reveals that *Reach*, or the perceived extent of adversity, plays a pivotal role. The lower one's AQ, the more likely one is to perceive any given setback as huge, massive, and all-consuming. The higher one's AQ, the more naturally one contains the fallout, not letting it become any bigger than necessary. "That was a tough meeting" and "Gee, I got disappointing grades this quarter" are very different from "We just lost our biggest customer—we're ruined!" and "I'm completely failing out of school!"

Reach influences the burden you carry in life. The better you become at containing difficulties, the lighter you feel. The bigger and worse everything appears, the more suffocating life becomes, crushing you under its mass, making it difficult for you to keep your footing. When you improve your Reach, you shrink the contamination, limit the downside, and expand the upside, unleashing new-found energy and possibilities.

As senior vice president of Human Resources and Communication at DIRECTV, Leigh Anne Nanci realized, after she measured her AQ and CORE, that her one weak spot was Reach. Despite her high AQ, she would suffer unnecessarily by perceiving events as bigger and more far-reaching than they needed to be. As a result, Leigh Anne would come home more fatigued, and sometimes bothered by more stuff, than was necessary. As she worked to improve her CORE by using the principles presented in this book, she began to see a dramatic difference. Specifically, when adversity hit, she learned to ask herself the CORE questions related to Reach: "How can I contain this adversity?" "How can I minimize the downside?" "What can I do to optimize the potential upside?" One day, someone on her team prematurely released a change-in-workforce announcement to the entire organization, setting off a wave of fear, anger, and confusion. It was a real mess. But instead of being overwhelmed by the disaster, Leigh Anne and her senior people paused, then immediately set about using the CORE process, listing ideas for containing the downside, and also trying to figure out some upside to the adversity. The situation, while tough, cooled off relatively quickly, and Leigh Anne actually found the whole process energizing.

Erik has to focus on his Reach practically every time he climbs. On Everest, and in life, one of the greatest challenges is not letting fear, doubt, and uncertainty gnaw at your resolve. On Everest, these are the forces that make up much of the lore of the mountain. The day before Erik's ascent from Camp Two to Camp Three, a twenty-year-old man slipped down the Lhotse face—an exceptionally steep ice slope. He spent the better part of the waning day lying there in the snow, abandoned for dead, before another climber was able to save him. Then, on the day before Erik's push to the summit, a Swiss man clipped his anchor onto the wrong rope, fell, and died. If

Erik had let these events start to root and spread in his psyche, they could easily have compromised if not ended his climb. But he contained the events and instead used them as a powerful reminder to stay absolutely focused all the way to the top.

Engage your CORE to limit the scope, size, and fallout of your adversities by asking, with regard to Reach, *"What can I do to minimize or contain the downside of this situation?"* and *"What can I do to optimize the potential upside of this situation?"* The second question may sound forced or strange. But one of the most compelling discoveries in our AQ research is that the higher your AQ, the more possibilities you perceive, and the more upside you see in even the most tragic situations.

When Erik assembles a climbing team, he absolutely avoids dreamy optimists. They're dangerous. He believes his teammates should possess a "healthy schizophrenia"—the capacity to hope for and have faith in the best, along with obsessing about, preparing for, and being brutally realistic about the worst.

This is the difference between disengaged optimism and engaged optimism. Disengaged optimists take refuge in their hope, giving up Ownership and Control and doing little to influence how long the adversity might endure. Engaged optimists are hopeful that their relentless, strategically focused efforts will increase the chance that things will turn out better over time. Especially in the toughest situations, you have to engage your CORE.

Endurance

When things get tough, how hopeful do you and the people around you feel? The final CORE dimension has to do with time, or duration. And it tends to either fuel or kill hope. When adversity strikes, Endurance involves asking: *How long do you predict it will last or endure?* People with higher AQs remain hopeful and optimistic. They can see past even the worst circumstances. People with lower AQs tend to see setbacks as long-term, if not permanent. This perception can crush the likelihood of coming out the other side, let alone the chance of benefiting as a direct result of adversity.

Endurance plays big with change. People who see a given change as temporary and something they can work through to accelerate the transition tend to be energized by change. People who perceive change as a grueling, horrible, long-drawn-out process tend to be crushed under its dark hulk.

When Erik took on Mount Everest, he knew that three months of relentless effort would take their toll. He and his team wouldn't be climbing the mountain just once; they'd need to go up and down several times to acclimatize and to supply their higher camps. They'd make multiple crossings through the Khumbu Icefall. They'd wait out countless storms. The local unrefrigerated Sherpa food would continually make the team sick with dysentery. To ponder the expedition as a whole was too intimidating.

To stay focused and sane, Erik broke the expedition into legs and created mini–finish lines. He'd concentrate on just getting to the next camp where he could rest and refuel his body. During long days, his teammates would help him envision the next rest stop, by saying things like, "Three hundred yards above us, we'll rest at the top of the Geneva Spur." His strategy was to envision and then work to get to the end of the next leg. You too can create your own mini–finish lines when the task you face is particularly daunting.

Engage your CORE by asking, with regard to Endurance, *"How can I get through this as quickly as possible?"* Address Endurance head-on by using this question to dispel the assumption that a specific setback must drag on and on.

THE SUMMIT GAME

One of my favorite devices for forging through the most brutal moments of a given challenge—the kind of moments when most people give up—is to play the Summit Game. It's a play off the Endurance element of your CORE. Here's how it works.

When I am being pounded by wind, ravaged by fatigue, pierced by cold, and stymied by countless crevasses, I simply envision what it will be like when I, and my teammates, stand on the summit. I vividly imagine us on top in full, living color. I walk through the final steps, the arrival, the shouts, high fives, congratulations, photos, smiles, hugs, and celebration—even the radio call back home to tell my family that I made it. And the more vividly I can imagine the moment of victory, the more energized I feel.

Paul calls this principle "Energy Lending." It's when you borrow or lend the energy from a future event to strengthen a current situation. But it's not like borrowing from your retirement fund to buy a car. When you lend yourself energy from a future event, there is no deficit, only upside. According to Paul's research, science supports this phenomenon. Vividly imagining an exhilarating event, like winning, achieving your goal, or summiting a mountain, can release the same neuropeptides in the body that the actual event would release. And the greater your imagination and immersion in the fantasy, the more energy, positive chemistry, and ultimate benefits you enjoy.

THE FAILURE FANTASY

Since both pleasure and pain are deeply motivating, the inverse of the Summit Game—the Failure Fantasy—is another one of my favorites and is also substantiated by Paul's CORE research. At first, the Reach of a particular adversity may seem so pervasive that one would be inclined to see it as insurmountable. So, through the Failure Fantasy, you allow the vivid and awful scenario of failure to scroll across your internal movie screen. All you have to do is fully im-

merse yourself in the painful fantasy of falling completely short of your objective, allowing yourself to pre-experience all the resulting consequences. Most
people can't bear to consider such moments. But doing so can be very compelling. Disappointment, frustration, regret, embarrassment, and anguish are
all excruciating emotions to suffer. And depending on the goal, if they are excruciating enough, the thought of having to live through the failure can be just
the kick-start you need to regroup, and redouble your efforts.

BUILDING YOUR CORE

On the basis of all our research, one thing is certain—you can begin
to make gratifying strides in your relationship with adversity *today*.
And given the number of adversities that strike each day, you will
have plenty of opportunities to practice building and strengthening
your CORE.

I've found that the most practical way to build your CORE is
through heightened awareness, with feedback, ideally, from multiple sources. One of the best ways is a 360-degree, or panoramic,
perspective. This provides each individual with powerful and helpful feedback, shining a light upon one's blind spots, so he or she can
grow stronger. Leaders gain particular value from this approach.
The solutions range from highly rigorous, formal instrumentation
to a more basic, commonsense approach.

The Self-Administered CORE Panorama

Derived from the Web-based panoramic AQ-360 instrument my
team and I developed, the first step in gaining heightened awareness
and feedback is to list those people who have the greatest opportunity

to see you respond to adversity, day in, day out. Members of your CORE team might include people at work—coworkers, your boss, customers, team members, or staff members—anyone who gets to see you in action. Or CORE team members might be people from outside work—children, partners, spouse, friends, parents, or siblings—

THE SELF-ADMINISTERED CORE PANORAMA

To gain a panoramic view of your CORE, ask these questions of the people who can give you the most accurate, reliable, and honest feedback.

1. On a scale of one to ten (ten being the highest), how effectively do you think I respond to adversity?
2. Am I more effective with certain kinds of adversities than others? If so, which ones am I better or worse at, typically? Am I better at dealing with big adversities or the small, day-to-day stuff? Any examples?
3. Are there certain times when I deal better with adversity than others? If so, when? What have you observed?
4. What is the most positive or negative example of how I dealt with adversity?
5. If I drew a line or continuum ranging from "helpless" on one end to "in control" on the other end, where do I typically fall when adversity strikes?
6. When the tough stuff hits, how likely am I to step up to do even the smallest thing to make the situation better?
7. How well do you think I do at keeping the adversity in its place? Do I contain the adversity, or do I tend to let it spill over into everything else?
8. If one is "It's over" and ten is "It'll last forever," how long do I tend to let adversities last? Where do most of my responses fall?
9. What do you like best about the way I handle adversity? What do you like least? Why?
10. What would be an example of a time when I have done what you just described?
11. If you were coaching me on how to handle adversity more effectively, what is the one thing you'd like me to do more, less, or differently?

anyone who has either regular opportunities or a long-standing opportunity to see how you respond to life's unexpected turns.

Next you will want to ask these people some simple questions. The CORE Panorama conversation often begins when you say, "I was just reading this book about how people respond to adversity, and I realized it is something I'd like to do better." Continue by defining *adversity* and asking the questions in the exercise on page 113.

Another way to get at your CORE Panorama feedback is to review the CORE dimensions (listed and described earlier); explain each; and then ask people to privately circle the one they think you do best, and put a check next to the one they think you do worst, or openly tell you their impressions.

The key is to be open and receptive to people's feedback. You can ask for responses in written or spoken form. The important thing is to go with whichever method gives you the most useful feedback.

Consider Your CORE

"What's my CORE?" can become your instant pulse check when difficulties strike. So perhaps the simplest, but possibly the most profound, way to build your CORE is to pay keen attention to what thoughts, words, emotions, and actions spark inside you the moment you face any kind of adversity.

C = How much control am I feeling or indicating? *(Control)*

O = To what extent am I stepping up or back in this situation? *(Ownership)*

R = How far am I letting this reach? How big am I letting it become? *(Reach)*

E = How long do I see it lasting? To what extent am I letting this drag on? *(Endurance)*

I have always been impressed by the stories people tell me about how tuning into their COREs made a world of difference for them, long after they attended an *Adversity Advantage* program. Whether in your relationships, job, health, or other pursuits, build your CORE each time a challenge arises in your path.

Recognizing CORE

Another way to build your CORE through heightened awareness is to use your CORE filter. Everywhere you go—in every conversation you hear, every movie you watch, every book you read, every newscast you hear, or every presentation you enjoy—listen for the CORE elements.

Immediately you'll hear facets of *Control*, as people say, "There's no reason we can't do this. We've tackled worse before." Or, "Well, this is out of our hands. There's nothing we can do about it now. It's too late."

You'll see people step back or step up, demonstrating the vital role *Ownership* plays in getting anything done and getting any problem resolved. You'll hear it when people make statements like "Well, I hope they figure out something" versus "I don't know all the answers, but I promise to get some of them for you right away."

You'll feel *Reach* in people's responses when they utter such classics as "This is a complete disaster. Just as our new product line is being launched, our supplier is cutting us off. We're doomed." Or, "We've taken a hit, but if we act quickly, we can more than recover in time for the end of the year. It'll be great to diversify our supply chain. It's long overdue."

You will be demoralized or inspired by *Endurance* as good people say things like, "We'll never get out of this one. Remember the good old days when . . ." Or, "We are just going through a tough phase. If we take decisive action now there is no reason we have to stay down for any longer than necessary."

Employ the CORE Strategy

Now we can put your CORE expertise to use with the most robust CORE tool we've developed to date. It is an extension of everything you have learned so far in this Summit, so you will see some of the same questions applied in a more complete framework. I call this your CORE Strategy.

Hundreds of organizations and thousands of individuals have come to PEAK Learning requesting our guidance in creating disaster response plans, executing strategic plans, dealing with market fluctuations, optimizing a potential opportunity, or simply working through a difficult situation. The CORE Strategy is the tool we teach organizations and people to use in order to respond better and faster than their competition, or simply to maximize the potential advantage of any specific adversity. It builds on the CORE questions, following a logical sequence. Here's how it works.

Begin with a particularly difficult challenge or goal. It can be personal or professional, organizational or private. In your case, begin with your Summit Challenge. Take out some blank paper, and write that challenge down, so you can work through this brief but powerful tool. Here's a tip. The CORE Strategy generates a lot of ideas. But as you come up with ideas, don't discuss, scrutinize, or judge them. Only *list* them. The scrutiny comes later.

Next, write your answers to each of these questions. Note that the questions can be asked of an individual or a group, of "you" or "us."

C = CONTROL

- What is everything beyond our control? What things do most people consider as beyond our control? (List them all.)
- Of those things, which ones are absolutely beyond our *influence*?
- Of the things you (or we) could potentially influence in this situation, which two are most important? (Circle them.)

O = OWNERSHIP

► Where and how can we step up to make the most immediate positive difference in this situation? (List your responses.)

R = REACH

► What is the *worst* thing that could happen?
► If we allowed ourselves to think outrageously, what is the *best* thing that could happen?
► What things can we do to minimize the potential downside of this situation? (List.)
► What things can we do to maximize the potential *upside* of this situation? (List.)

Tip: As soon as you begin working on building the upside of a given adversity, chances are you are already way ahead of everyone else!

E = ENDURANCE

► What do we *want* life to look like on the other side of this adversity? (Describe in detail.)
► What else can we do to get there as quickly and completely as possible? (List.)

THE ACTION FUNNEL

The final step in the CORE Strategy is to use The Action Funnel as a way to devise a specific, adversity-proof action plan so you can gain traction immediately. Post the entire list of potential actions, which you derived from the CORE Strategy, in plain view.

Again, it is best to record your answers, especially when there are multiple parties involved. You will know you succeeded when all parties have a clear sense of what they are to do, by when, and how. No one should leave empty-handed.

Below are two sample CORE Strategies. One is for a man whose grandfather had just suffered a minor stroke, and who woke

THE ACTION FUNNEL

Which action first?
By when?
How will you do it?

Most likely obstacle?
How will you
deal with it?

If the first action
fails or falls short,
then what?
By when?
How?

SAMPLE CORE STRATEGY

Summit Challenge—To bring my extended family together, one last time.

C = CONTROL

- ► What is everything beyond my control?
  - • *People's lives*
  - • *The weather*
  - • *Their desire to come*
  - • *Past history*
- ► Of those things, which ones are absolutely beyond my *influence*?
  - • *The weather (but I can influence how much the weather matters and choose dates when the weather is best)*
- ► Of the things I could potentially influence in this situation (including and beyond the preceding list), which two are most important?
  - • *Their desire to come*
  - • *The entire experience, how well it turns out*

O = OWNERSHIP

► Where and how can I step up to make the most immediate positive difference in this situation?
- *Contact people immediately*
- *Call around and see what are the real issues and obstacles*
- *Make reservations at a couple potential sites*
- *Send an e-survey to everyone on the invite list . . . (and more)*

R = REACH

► What is the *worst* thing that could happen? *No one comes*
► If I allowed myself to think outrageously, what is the *best* thing that could happen? *It becomes one of the best memories of people's lives*
► What can I do to minimize the potential downside of this situation?
- *Secure commitments early*
- *Get people on board, and commit their cash with mine*
- *Create a marketing campaign*
► What can I do to maximize the potential *upside* of this situation?
- *Pick an epic place that everyone wants to see and enjoy*
- *Ask around to see what other people have done that worked great*

E = ENDURANCE

► What do I *want* life to look like on the other side of this adversity? *For the rest of my life and theirs I want all those who attend to say this was one the best events of their lives, and that they are so glad they came and want to do it again*
► What else can I do to get there as quickly and completely as possible?
- *Ask people what it would take for that to happen . . . (and more)*

ACTION FUNNEL

► To which action do I want to commit first? *Call the six most influential and honest people on the list to ask their opinions and concerns. Gain their buy-in*
► When will I do it? *Call each person by the end of the week. Complete all calls by the end of the month*

ERIK'S CORE STRATEGY

Summit Challenge—To help as many people as possible strengthen their relationship with adversity.

C = CONTROL

- ► What is everything beyond my control?
  - *What people choose to focus on*
  - *Whether people buy and read my book*
  - *Whether or not people really apply my ideas and change their lives*
  - *All the stuff that gets in the way . . . (and more)*
- ► Of those things, which ones are absolutely beyond my *influence*?
  - *None*
- ► Of the things I could potentially influence in this situation, which two are most important?
  - *The quality and integrity of the message I bring*
  - *Working with Fireside/Simon & Schuster to conduct a fantastic marketing campaign*
  - *How effectively I lead my life in a way that inspires others*

O = OWNERSHIP

- ► Where and how can I step up to make the most immediate positive difference in this situation?
  - *Write this book*
  - *Continue to deliver keynote presentations at businesses and schools*
  - *Develop training videos that reinforce the message*

R = REACH

- ► What is the *worst* thing that could happen? *The book receives terrible reviews or is not read*
- ► If I allowed myself to think outrageously, what is the *best* thing that could happen? *This book becomes a global best-seller, setting Paul and me up to share and evolve our message for decades to come*

> ► What can I do to minimize the potential downside of this situation?
>   • *Do the best possible job on writing and marketing the book*
>   • *Marry my keynotes with the book content*
>   • *Create media opportunities to share these ideas*
> ► What can I do to maximize the potential *upside* of this situation?
>   • *Same stuff*
>   • *Have the book at film festivals and my other high-visibility activities*
>   • *Send the book to the right people*
>   • *Ask Stephen Covey to contribute the foreword to the book*
>
> ## E = ENDURANCE
> ► What do I *want* life to look like on the other side of the adversity that comes with writing this book? *Ideally, this book becomes a bestseller and a classic, something that stays on the shelves for years and years; and Paul and I continue to collaborate on both our mission and our approach*
> ► What else can I do to get there as quickly and completely as possible?
>   • *Work closely with Simon & Schuster to help them create the best possible final product, on time*
>
> ## ACTION FUNNEL
> ► Which action do I want to commit to first? *Clear the decks and complete this manuscript by our designated date*
>
> (And so on.)

up to the notion of doing something he always wanted to do, but had never done (for twenty-five years)—bringing his entire extended family together for a reunion. That was his Summit Challenge. The second CORE Strategy is Erik's, as it applies to his Summit Challenge.

Imagine the possibilities. As you are imagining and strategizing steps toward life on the other side of a given difficulty, others are still reeling. As you generate hope, others are mired in despair. Your energy ramps up while others remain deflated. This puts you in the ideal position both to win personally and hopefully to help others in your life to engage their COREs so that they can win too.

Sealy, the mattress company, had just launched a new product line, was in the throes of going public, and had aggressive growth goals to reach, when a major hurricane wiped out the production of TDI, the chemical ingredient used to produce the foam for its mattresses. When its main supplier called to inform Sealy's leaders that they were going to receive, at best, 50 percent of their foam requirements for the next ninety days, and possibly longer, Sealy knew that its entire year, not to mention its public offering and dealer relationships, was on the line. The good news was that its competitors were facing the same adversity.

So, Sealy's CEO, Dave McIlquham, pulled his top leaders together for an emergency meeting, applied the CORE Strategy for how to handle the crisis, and turned it into an immediate advantage. The leaders emerged with a plan that included rerouting some material from South Korea, getting some rougher form of material from South America, and gearing up for *more* sales than they had originally forecast. They knew they could not control the weather, but they could *influence* all the necessary factors to drive growth, improve relationships, and finish with a record year. While they were working on growing the upside, all their competitors were mired in the downside. While Sealy was the first to call its distributors, informing them of the crisis and how Sealy was going to fix it, the competitors were still denying the crisis, and ended up with egg on their faces. While Sealy was figuring out how to make the rougher material work, its competitors were empty-handed.

Al Boulden, Sealy's senior vice president of field sales, absolutely glowed as he explained, "So imagine calling all of our dealers a second time, a few weeks into the national crisis, and apologizing because we could only fulfill orders that were for twenty percent *more* than their normal run rates!" Sealy used the CORE Strategy to perform its own alchemy—converting the adversity of a natural disaster to its genuine advantage. And its customers and suppliers loved the results. Imagine the long-term financial value of that one CORE Strategy.

Understanding, building, and engaging your CORE will equip you with the capacity to perform your own brand of alchemy. A devastating tornado becomes a genuine opportunity to rebuild, start afresh, and reconnect to what matters most. A downturn in the market is an opportunity to refocus, retrench, and reinvest so you come out on the upswing better and faster than your competitors. A brutal divorce is a powerful opportunity for introspection, growth, and self-improvement. A failed stint at school becomes the galvanizing event for doing your best going forward. A bankruptcy clears the decks to reinvent your life. And while some people eventually are able to benefit from their adversities, your CORE determines how much you benefit, how soon you benefit, and how much you do or don't suffer unnecessarily in between, even in the most extreme circumstances.

In my opinion, there is perhaps no better example of overcoming adversity by engaging your CORE than the survival story of my hero, Sir Ernest Shackleton. The story has been told many times and has become a popular way to teach leadership and teamwork, but I have always looked at it differently.

To me, the hardships and suffering Shackleton and the crew of the *Endurance* faced when they became stranded near Antarctica defy comprehension. For nearly two years, and through the most brutal conditions known to man, Shackleton kept his men motivated, confident, and alive. He fully faced his situation, summoned crucial team strengths, and built a CORE Strategy.

Shackleton's original goal was to make a full traverse of Antarctica. He left the island of South Georgia in early December 1914, passed the South Sandwich Islands, and plowed through 1,000 miles of ice-encrusted waters.

A month into the voyage, however, the *Endurance* experienced an unexpected deep-freeze and became lodged in a polar ice pack. The men were
just one day from their destination at Vahsel Bay on the Antarctic continent.
Still, Shackleton and his crew were stranded more than 1,200 miles from the
closest settlement, and they had only one another to rely on for survival.

In the months that followed, they could do little to improve their situation; they could only wait until the spring thaw. Several times, they thought
they'd be set free, only to have their hopes dashed. For ten months, the moving ice dragged their ship until it was ultimately crushed. They salvaged only
enough items necessary for survival, plus a banjo and personal journals for
the twenty-seven members of the crew. Although they spent five more
months camped on the moving ice in flimsy tents and had to ration their mea-
ger food, they remained optimistic and energetic. Often, they played soccer,
performed music, and danced on the empty ice floes.

Finally, as the ice began to break, the crew set sail in three small
lifeboats, with the hope of coming into contact with the whaling ships along
the northern tip of the continent. Instead, the currents took them to Elephant
Island, where they came ashore on a barren land raked by intense storms.
Nevertheless, they had reached solid ground. And on landing, Shackleton
took eight men and sailed 800 miles in one small lifeboat, miraculously making it back to the island of South Georgia in late April 1916.

Reaching a familiar land, they were struck with a final blow. They had
come ashore on the opposite, uninhabited side of the island and, on top
of everything else, they then had to trek for a week over rugged, glaciated
mountains to finally arrive at a tiny whaling station. For many people, this final
obstacle alone would have been enough to cause abandonment and failure,
but to Shackleton, it was simply another adversity he needed to attack.
Finally, when the rescue party returned for the men left behind on Elephant
Island, they found the crew emaciated but, amazingly, all alive. Shackleton
hadn't lost a single man.

What seems most remarkable to me is that throughout the two-year
ordeal, although the reach of the adversity must have felt massive and the
endurance never-ending, Shackleton never stopped trying to affect the

outcome. The men never once gave up control over their destiny. They continued to be proactive, demonstrating intense responsibility, loyalty to one another, and ownership for keeping the team alive. A crew member, Frank Hurley, later wrote, "I always found Shackleton rising to his best and inspiring confidence when things were at their blackest."

In my opinion, although Shackleton failed at his original objective, he succeeded at something even more unimaginable. In the face of unbelievably low odds, he infused in his men the belief that they had the capacity to prevail. As Shackleton put it, "By endurance, we conquer."

Many years after surviving the expedition, a crew member stated that he was a better person for having lived through the ordeal. As for me, I don't know who I'd be today without my adversities. And while I'd never wish them on anyone, I am grateful for all the ways in which they have made me better, stronger, and more alive.

I now realize that I engage my CORE every time I face a challenge on a mountain and in life. By focusing on what I can influence, taking action to make the best of tough situations, working to minimize the potential downside and maximize the upside, and working relentlessly to get through the suffering, I have been able to shatter my own perceptions of what's possible.

I hope you will now employ the same strategies that propelled me to the top of Everest and drove Shackleton's crew to persevere. As you do, you'll go beyond what might have been, and begin to pioneer what's possible, unleashing enormous energy and opportunity along the way. In Summit Four, you will learn to become a Possibility Pioneer.

SUMMIT THREE—ENGAGE YOUR CORE

GUIDING PRINCIPLE

To turn adversity to your advantage you need to understand, build, and engage your CORE. You can use your CORE in any situation and for any challenge, setback, or opportunity. Top leaders and people in many walks of life use the CORE tools to respond better and faster to adverse events.

Understanding Your AQ and CORE

Your Adversity Quotient (AQ) is your hardwired pattern of response to adversity. Like posture, it may appear genetic, but it is learned, and it can be permanently improved. Control, Ownership, Reach, and Endurance are the four CORE dimensions that make up your AQ.

Building Your CORE

1. The CORE questions can be asked in any order, in any situation, and of anyone to rethink and strengthen your response to adversity.
2. The Summit Game and Failure Fantasy are CORE-based methods for Energy Lending—borrowing energy from the future to strengthen you now.

Engaging Your CORE

The CORE Strategy is used by industry-leading companies and by individuals worldwide to tackle everything from disaster plans and optimizing opportunities to resolving everyday challenges.

SUMMIT FOUR

PIONEER POSSIBILITIES

MOUNT ELBRUS
Base Camp: 9,000 feet
Summit: 18,510 feet—tallest peak in Europe

I dream things that never were and say why not?
—GEORGE BERNARD SHAW

How many times in your life has someone told you that something you wanted to do was impossible? Have you ever noticed that it's generally your associates, friends, and loved ones who try to "talk some sense" into you whenever you get some "harebrained scheme" to try something new, or to take a risk that they perceive as foolish? Be grateful that these people care enough to say something about it. They think they're doing you a favor, and maybe they are. But, what if . . . ?

What if they were caring but wrong? What if that thing you've always dreamed of doing is possible? How would it feel to be the one who made it happen? And what if, by making the impossible possible, you opened a whole new world of opportunities for yourself, your organization, and the people around you?

When I saw that in Paul's research, people who scored higher on his AQ scale delivered measurably more innovation, it made perfect sense. Whenever people create a groundbreaking system or do anything new of any real consequence, they usually take on a significant amount of adversity.

So it follows that almost everyone who works effectively through big-time adversity is likely to be a pioneer. Adversity simply spawns innovation.

When a person uses ingenuity and tenacity to do something different and better than other people, Paul and I call it "possibility pioneering." The dictionary says that a "pioneer" is "a person who is the first to do something, or who is a forerunner in creating or developing something new." I can't think of a person who wouldn't find that exciting.

Many people have told me that the days of pioneering are over, that all the great discoveries on earth have already been made, but their outlook is horribly limited. Consider how much of science, technology, and society itself is still veiled by darkness. It is only by attacking our personal challenges with a pioneering spirit that we can drive our own lives forward and even shape the destinies of our organizations, our communities, and the larger society.

Being driven by your own personal sense of pioneering doesn't mean you have to undertake scary first ascents or discover a cure for cancer. But it does mean being motivated from within. In the face of great challenges, it means asking this question: how can I do what I want to do with the resources I have or can build around me? The answer might require you to reach much farther than you thought possible.

What about all the parents, friends, teachers, and professionals—everyday people—who, in the face of real deadlines, dilemmas, and limitations, uncover new ways to do what they want to do. Think of all the organizations that live or die by their ability to pioneer possibilities.

How can you use your everyday adversities to make the undoable doable, to pioneer new possibilities so that you continue to grow and flourish?

The first step is to select an adversity-rich, worthy challenge. It should stretch you in new ways and represent new possibilities, if achieved. It should be something that involves some kind of risk or resistance, and just the idea of completing it should make you tingle with excitement.

The second step is to create a plan and then engineer the systems that will be the key to helping you get there.

The third step is to "Practice to Perfect" so you can make those systems work when they count most.

When I decided to climb Mount Elbrus, I had already climbed Everest, which is 11,000 feet higher and a whole lot tougher, less than a year earlier. I suppose my team and I could have approached Elbrus as just another of the Seven Summits to check on the scorecard, but instead my climbing partner Eric Alexander and I asked, "How can we stretch ourselves to make this more exciting and meaningful?"

We decided that the most compelling challenge would be not only to climb to the top, but also to ski the 10,000 feet from summit to Base Camp. No blind person had ever skied a major world peak. Climbing up through steep snow, ice, and rock with twenty extra pounds of ski gear and then skiing back down through that rugged, unforgiving terrain introduced an entirely new set of problems. That was actually part of the appeal—to create a plan, work through a process rife with difficulties, and see whether it could be done.

Eric and I would need to apply our ingenuity to overcome some major hurdles. Sometimes that means employing known methods in new ways. At other times the challenge requires an entirely new approach. To succeed at our quest, we would have to invent new systems to communicate, navigate, and function as one cohesive unit.

Eric and I trained for an entire year, devising new ways to communicate while speeding down a mountain together with only one ski length between us. Every word out of Eric's mouth had to translate to a precise and predictable action on my part. Ski turns have three sequential steps—getting the skis up on edges to initiate the turn, facing straight down the fall line, and bringing the skis around for the finish. So Eric learned to call out turns in three syllables, "Turn a left!" or "Turn a right." With each syllable, I'd know exactly where I needed to be in the maneuver. He could also elongate or shorten the call to indicate what size turn to make. A gradual turn would sound like, "Tuuuuuuuurn aaaaaaaa leeeeeeeeft." On a severe angle where I had to get my skis around quickly, he'd drop the middle syllable and yell, "Hard left."

One of the exciting, or terrifying, parts of skiing blind is that you're able to react to variables, like sudden drops, only as you feel them under your skis. So to ease the transitions, Eric learned to call, "Steeper" or "Flatter." In the narrower sections, where we wanted to cruise, Eric could extend a pole to me, enabling me to stay in sync with him on each turn. Eric and I even practiced with a new high-tech radio that let us communicate the turns when gale-force winds kicked in.

The element of speed, combined with a lack of sight, leaves no room for error. My worst nightmare was tumbling into oblivion or hitting a rock at thirty miles per hour. We practiced relentlessly to get the new systems hardwired so we could count on them to work in any conditions.

When the day of our summit push finally arrived, it took everything I had to get to the top. I was completely spent, and my legs were rubbery with the weight of the extra gear. I turned to Eric and admitted, "I don't know if I can do this." He paused, smacked me on the side of the head, and said, "We trained for a year. We are going to ski this mountain." So I wobbled to my feet, clicked into my skis, and—rubbery legs and all—careened down the ridge.

The fear inspired by hanging from my fingertips high up on a rock face is nothing compared with hurtling blind down a high-altitude peak. The conditions would go instantly from deep powder to rock-hard snow, frozen into waves by the wind. Although Eric did his best to avoid drop-offs, I was surprised by more than a few. After every five jolting turns, I'd hang over my ski poles, gasping for air.

On the long traversing sections, Eric took my pole and we skied side by side, our skis only six inches apart. Later, he stayed right behind me, navigating us down icy gullies, past cliff bands, and around rocks. When the afternoon winds kicked up, we had our high-tech radios ready to go.

Later in the descent, Eric and I became immersed in a whiteout. In these conditions, it's hard for sighted folks to distinguish the ground from the sky; everything loses its contrast. Eric didn't skip a beat as he called turns from behind me, but later he admitted he had used the bright red contrast of my jacket several times to tell him where the drop-offs were. Some things are better learned after the experience.

When we were 3,000 feet above camp, with the most difficult sections behind us, Eric said, "It's wide-open in front of you—nothing to hit even if you tried." So I tucked my body and leaned forward. The strength in my legs rebounded as I picked up speed. With the wind in my face and the blood pulsing in my ears, I began to lose the sensation of soft powder beneath my skis. It was easy to imagine that Eric and I had lifted up off the earth and were skiing through the clouds.

Almost a year later we learned that our system of oral ski commands was actually not novel: it was the same system the Blue Angels use to fly their F-18 Hornets in their renowned six-jet delta formation, often with only twenty-four inches between wingtips. In hindsight, I can say that if it worked for them, it was going to work for us. In fact, at a few points on the run I felt as if my descent were approaching the speed of sound.

A pioneer takes other people's beliefs about what is possible and shatters those beliefs into a million pieces. Each time those perceptions are rebuilt, they get bigger and more expansive. So you have the rare chance to blast through barriers and expand opportunities for those who come after you.

There is nothing about my story of skiing down Elbrus blind that you can't replicate with your own creative, gutsy approach to your challenges. Complete Summit Four, and you will use adversity to pioneer possibilities.

WHAT IS PIONEERING?

As we thought about sharing our ideas on pioneering with you, Erik and I learned something ourselves. Since Summit Four is about *creating systems* and *developing new ways to accomplish tasks*, we realized that Erik's personal experiences with creating systems would be more powerful and instructive than a bunch of my research. As a result, this Summit will take on a slightly different format and tone from the others. Erik will share his examples of pioneering throughout the chapter, and I'll share others, to communicate these principles in the most effective way we know—through real life.

Over the course of your life and career, has your perception of what's possible grown or shrunk? In other words, today as compared with years past, do you tend to believe that more or less is really possible? Do you spend most of your time doing what's tried and true, or do you continually invent new ways to get things done? How do you and your colleagues respond when someone comes to you with the question, "What if . . . ?"

Plato said, "The true creator is necessity, which is the mother of our invention." I would modify that aphorism and say, *"Adversity is the parent of our possibilities."* This natural human ingenuity can come out in the most basic ways. How many broken-down cars have limped to a service station on a makeshift repair of duct tape, bailing wire, or chewing gum? How many restaurants have invented a specialty of the house when they ran out of the standard menu items? How many enterprises have engineered major breakthroughs when faced with a supply shortage, too much inventory, or the prospect of going bankrupt? How many entrepreneurs became entrepreneurs to pioneer new ways to balance the demands of family and work, or in response to something they found outrageously unacceptable? How many times have you found a way when there was no way?

Nothing to Sneeze At:
Victoria Knight-McDowell, Airborne, Inc.

Victoria Knight-McDowell was a second-grade teacher who kept catching colds from her students. Instead of accepting her colds as "just part of the job," she came up with her own preventive remedy (including vitamins A, C, and E; seven herbal extracts; antioxidants; electrolytes; and amino acids) and called it Airborne. It now brings in over $100 million annually. She stopped teaching to run the company with her husband, Rider, and care for their son, Errol.

"The formula I developed was working for my husband and me, and for teacher friends. Rider and I were talking over dinner one night, and it just sort of flowed until we said, 'Let's put it on the market and see what happens.' Probably the most important thing we did was research a way to get it to effervesce in less than two minutes, since Americans like things that happen quickly. Then we cashed in our 12,000 tubes [packages of her tablets]. We put the labels on by hand, and I made sales calls at all the local drugstores after school."

Victoria's friends told her that she was crazy, and that she should use her and Rider's money to buy a house instead. She and Rider had to ignore the naysayers, and the aisles full of competition found in any grocery or drugstore, and pioneer their possibility.[1]

In Summit Four you will learn to pioneer possibilities in your work and life, as you cover the same three steps Erik used to pioneer possibilities on Mount Elbrus:

1. Pick a Worthy Goal.
2. Devise Signature Systems.
3. Practice to Perfect.

To survive, every organization must innovate. The relationship between adversity and innovation was substantiated through groundbreaking research[2] performed by Dr. Gideon Markman, assistant professor of strategy, innovation, and entrepreneurship at the University of Georgia. Markman discovered that those people who responded to adversity most effectively, as measured by their Adversity Quotient (AQ), generated the most innovation. Those who scored the lowest on AQ tended to innovate least.

Since Markman's study, my team and I have seen adversity spawn innovation time and time again. We see nonprofit organizations embark on new fund-raising approaches when faced with slashed budgets. We see sales teams reassemble the value package they bring to clients when faced with a crumbling economy. We see entire workforces step up to new challenges they must take on in order to stay alive, let alone win. In fact, we constantly rediscover that without adversity, many possibilities would remain, well, impossible.

Doing Better with Less

Today, we see this relationship between adversity and innovation all around us. John Suranyi, president of DIRECTV Sales and Service, has the classic profile of a high-AQ leader, someone who scores exceptionally high in response to adversity. On a scale of forty to 200, he scored 190, *before* the AQ training—a score that put him in the top 2 percent. He has natural optimism and is undaunted when faced with challenges. In fact, the tougher it gets, the more fired up John gets. He's an alchemist. You can see it in his eyes. He honestly considers bad news good news, because he knows the secret of *The Adversity Advantage*—that those who take on and convert their adversities better and faster win!

So, John wakes up each day, gets in his predawn workout, and contemplates how his team is going to use its ingenuity to make DIRECTV not just the best in the industry, but the best in the world at innovation, content, and customer service. This is DIRECTV's worthy goal. A classic comment by John: "Sure we're good, but we're still not there. We've *got to* be the best!" He is relentless, never says "if," and always asks "how." You can imagine the effect John's mind-set and leadership have on his team. Shifting the question is one of the Signature Systems John has honed to challenge and lead his team. And he gets to practice it daily. He puts constant "positive pressure" on his top executives to improve. Let's just say their lives are never, ever dull.

Scott Brown, senior vice president at DIRECTV, reports to John and oversees a world of 20,000 "techs" who install and service satellite TV in millions of homes each year. Adding to the complexity, the installers are employees of many independently owned companies contracted by DIRECTV to do the work. Scott saw the competition with the cable companies and telcos heating up. To remain competitive he had to reduce his cost per installation—the amount he paid to the installation companies—and improve customers' satisfaction at the same time. With skyrocketing fuel costs, and having just recently absorbed the cost of the newly mandated DIRECTV trucks and uniforms, the installers were in no mood for any revenue cuts. Scott was told flat-out by some of his biggest partners, "It's impossible." He heard that over and over. They were adamant, and the pressure was immense.

So Scott brought his team and the installation company leaders together for a four-day do-or-die session that we called "Partnering Possibilities." He asked, "What if it *were* possible? How would we do it?" He literally sat down at the table with these potential adversaries; and through a carefully crafted session, using some of the same principles presented in this Summit, they worked together to come up with the promised cuts, along with a plan to improve service and strengthen their businesses in the process. It became clear that reducing wasted service calls, along with improving the installer technicians' training to "do it right the first time," would achieve all three objectives. They actually thanked Scott and his team as they left, with comments like, "I came in asking myself whether I even wanted to do business with DIRECTV anymore, and I left feeling stronger about our relationship than ever before!"

Adversity *is* the parent of our possibilities. At work, when budgets get tightened and the goals are raised, what do *you* do? Do you throw up your hands and declare, "This is impossible!" Or do you work on finding a way to make the impossible possible? Guess which approach gets you promoted? When there are competing, important demands, and there is "simply no way" to get everything done, how do you respond? Do you get stymied or stressed and push back, or do you reassemble the pieces in a way that makes it all happen, even better than it otherwise would? When you get a grim diagnosis, when you are faced with the hardships of raising your children by yourself, when the employee you most rely on leaves for another opportunity, do you succumb to your fate, or do you focus your best energies on rallying around a Worthy Goal, devising and perfecting some Signature Systems for gaining traction, and finding a way to make the impossible possible?

Hands-Free Rolling Luggage

When you go through an airport, what do you see? Everywhere there are streams of people pulling their rolling luggage from place to place. A problem remains, however: when you are cranking through an airport, you have at best one hand free. This can be severely limiting; and as chiropractors will tell you, pulling one-sided for long distances is good for business—*their* business. I'm sure I'm not the only traveler who would love to have both hands free to make calls, grab a snack, or multitask to get more done.

Just last week, I saw a young professional-looking woman, probably in her early thirties, working with both hands on her wireless PDA while pulling her luggage. How? She had created a simple belt-and-hook system, which enabled her to smoothly pull her roll-on bag hands-free behind her like a rickshaw, rather than the standard way. It was so simple. Everyone schlepping heavy bags was envious and amazed.

Her alchemical formula was clear. She (1) had a goal or challenge; she (2) created what Erik and I call a Signature System— a personalized, customized, original way to make it work—and then she (3) practiced to perfect it, so it would work when it counted.

Imagine applying that same sort of ingenuity to something

that's really important to you, the thing you always wanted to do but never thought possible.

Stressed parents often become amazingly effective possibility pioneers. A challenge for many parents today is getting their children to want to read and learn, when distractions—video games and more—seduce the children's attention. When our boys were younger, my wife, Ronda, deivised an ingenious approach to helping them become avid readers. That was the worthy goal. Understanding the realities, Ronda decided to make reading fun by inventing "Read and Feed." It was originally pretty basic, and the first couple of attempts were mildly successful. She made improvements, and then we all got the new system down pat. It became an event.

Here's how it worked. If the boys did their homework and chores, they earned the right to do a Read and Feed on a weekend night. This meant they could read anything they wanted, including comic books (parental control involved, of course) and stay up to read as late as they wanted. In anticipation they would help shop for what they wanted to read and eat. We would prepare a special, personalized bowl of their favorite munchies and set them up in their reading spots. I'll never forget their smiles—"We're getting away with something really cool"—when they would nestle into their reading forts with the bowl of snacks. The boys would get pretty inventive in creating the perfect setup, adjusting the lighting, seating, and so on to devise little caves or alcoves. We're convinced that our now adult boys' passion for books started with Read and Feed.

A WORTHY GOAL

Deep inside, nearly everyone wants to do or be something more. Worldwide, we hear people express this personal sense of destiny, declaring, "I just feel like I'm meant to do something big, or something important." We all share the desire to demonstrate some modicum of greatness, no matter how small, in the time we have.

So, the first step you need to take to pioneer possibilities is to pick a worthy goal. This sounds simple, but it can be a meaty challenge. For your purpose here, we'll select your Summit Challenge. For an organization or an individual, any worthy goal usually flows from the question, "What if . . . ? Those two words inspired Erik to take on the challenge he describes in the beginning of this Summit.

When I set the goal of climbing down Elbrus, Eric and I asked the question, "What if we could do something that has never been done before?"

In choosing this Worthy Goal, Erik included some subtle factors, which you can explore by asking the following questions.

1. *Motivation:* Why do you want to do it? Is it tied to a higher, grander purpose, or is it purely for your own enjoyment? Can you make it accomplish both purpose and pleasure? Are you being driven by negative emotions, like a sense of, "Oh, yeah, I'll show you!" to prove something to someone? Or are you motivated by more positive, uplifting reasons? Are you motivated to reduce existing pain or to make something more enjoyable? Or both?

    When I conduct full-day programs in different corners of the globe, the travel can get arduous, and every session requires tremendous energy. I realize that for the people in the room that day, this is their first session, and they deserve my absolute best. But at the end of an intense day, I'm often asked, "Isn't it exhausting?" or "Do you ever get sick of it?" I always answer pretty much the same way: "Sure, sometimes I get worn down; the travel can get old;

but, truthfully, having this kind of effect on people's lives and our clients' businesses is so important and energizing that I could never get sick of what I do."

The *why* which we discussed in Summit Two, and which we're reintroducing here, adds great fuel to everything I do. Hopefully it does for you too.

2. *Strengths:* You will recall that Will + Skill ⇨ Strengths. To what extent would this goal leverage existing strengths, or does it require forging entirely new ones? Do you have the sheer will it may take to achieve this goal?

3. *Excitement:* Where does the idea of achieving this goal score on your excitement meter? Does it make you "tingle with excitement"?

The idea of skiing down Elbrus after an arduous climb, feeling the wind in my face and the speed beneath my feet, was exhilarating. Breaking new ground is always fun. But nudging other people to rethink what's possible for them is also deeply gratifying. Skiing down Elbrus, my Worthy Goal, was a direct hit in terms of all three of Paul's criteria—motivation, strengths, and excitement.

Notice what's *not* on the list. We did not list most of the typical criteria for setting goals—something specific, realistic, achievable, and measurable that you can do in a timely manner. These are excellent criteria for everyday goals. But, while important, they alone are not gutsy enough for your *Worthy* Goal—for pioneering possibilities. They're too limiting. That's why we begin with your Summit Challenge.

If, instead, you take on purely short-term, realistic, achievable, specific challenges, you may already have killed the top five most exciting possibilities you could pioneer. There is always someone who considers the big ones impossible, unachievable, and pie-in-the-sky. Ask John Suranyi, Scott Brown, or the rest of their DIRECTV team. They hear this sort of thing every day. While everyone is sitting around talking about what can't be done, someone is out there doing it. So, they go and do it. We don't tend to associate the word *pioneer* with mundane tasks easily done by anyone.

Take our hands-free traveler. Consider how well she worked with the timeless motivators—pain and pleasure. We can make the following guesses. Chances are she was a frequent traveler suffering the usual frustrations of wheeling her luggage from place to place. That was the pain. The pleasure might have been the uplifting vision of zipping through any airport hands-free, or even someday seeing her idea transform how people travel!

Among the existing strengths she may have needed to summon could have been her mechanical aptitude, creativity, and tenacity to keep working on her solution until it succeeded. Among the strengths she needed to develop might have been financial acumen to calculate how to make such an invention a potentially profitable venture.

Chances are she encountered plenty of naysayers who told her all the practical reasons why her rickshaw-style attachment would never work or would never catch on, especially when she was in the concept stage. You could hear them saying, "It'll hit you in the heels. It's not very classy. No one wants to pull around luggage like a workhorse with a plow! How will you stop without it hitting you? The last thing anyone wants to wear is some dorky-looking belt." And so on.

However, the excitement generated by the vision of making airport excursions so much easier and more efficient, while creating something genuinely new that could transform our concept of travel, must have been immense. And one could see how her excitement was fueled by the positive attention her ingenious device drew from admiring and maybe even envious onlookers.

PIONEER POSSIBILITIES

STEP ONE—PICK A WORTHY GOAL

To pioneer possibilities you must begin with a Worthy Goal. For the purpose of this exercise, you will begin with your Summit Challenge. You will then list additional options, to practice creating Worthy Goals at work and in life.

On a sheet of paper, list your Summit Challenge, and beneath it write three additional goals—three things you've always wanted to do but may never have thought possible—which you think would score highest on motivation, strengths, and excitement.

Go beyond the traditional New Year's resolutions—go to those goals which light you up when you imagine fulfilling them, but which may have always seemed beyond the realm of reality.

1. "What if I could . . . ?
2. "What if I tried . . . ?
3. "What if . . . ?

DEVISE YOUR SIGNATURE SYSTEMS

Once you or your organization have decided what to accomplish—your Summit Challenge—the next question is how you are going to do it. This is where the creative juices can really kick in, because pioneering possibilities may mean that you need to invent new ways of doing something, ways that are customized to your style or needs. The good news is that you don't have to be a creative genius to play this game. If, as in the case of your Summit Challenge, your goal is worthy and you want it badly enough, solutions will emerge.

> If necessity is the mother of invention, then adversity is the parent of our possibilities.

Paul and I call these customized solutions your Signature Systems. Like your signature, they become uniquely yours, and people associate a Signature System with you once they've seen it implemented.

Climbing Blind

A pioneer looks for solutions to every situation, and looks to tap into every bit of unrealized potential. But I don't see myself as a crazy Evel Knievel, taking an enormous amount of risk to do something miraculous, and hoping to live through it now and then. Being blind is one thing, but being blind and stupid is a fatal combination. I'm a calculated risk taker, more of a problem solver, an innovator who looks at things the world sees as impossible and tries to figure out a way forward.

A blind person gets pretty good at developing lots of signature strategies, tools, and systems which help him or her accomplish things a sighted person takes for granted. I match my socks by putting safety pins on the toes if they're black, on the heels if they're blue, and on the tops if they're brown. I can tell how big a room is by the echo, by the way sound vibrations bounce off the walls and ceiling. And when I was a shallow student, in college, girls in bars would often tell me, "I feel so comfortable with you because you aren't judging me by my surface beauty. You're seeing me for my inner beauty." What they didn't know was that I had invented a secret handshake with my male friends. By the way the men shook my hand, I knew what each girl looked like and if she was someone they thought I would like.

On a big mountain or a vertical face, developing and honing new strategies, tools, and systems is essential. Those Signature Systems make your team safer, more productive, and more efficient; and many times, they are the difference between success and failure. There are a dozen types of knots to be tied depending on the situation; there's a specific way to put crampons on so you don't trip over a loose strap and cartwheel down the mountain; choosing the right layering system at midnight when you are squeezed into a tiny tent determines whether you'll become hypothermic in your twentieth hour on the go; and the way you organize the gear in your pack, so you can easily get to the most important equipment, makes the difference between success and frostbite.

So often in our daily lives, there is a solution, if we can only create it. Sometimes, there's a book to read, a procedure in place, or a manual to follow. But more often, we're on our own. How often do we write something off as impossible when we haven't taken the time, haven't gone through the pain and failure, to figure out the way? When there is no book, no manual, and no procedure; and we have to engineer our own strategies, tools, and systems from the ground up, that's where adventure lies.

When I thought about ice climbing—climbing frozen waterfalls—many experts told me that it wasn't a smart idea. "It's not like rock climbing," one person said. "Ice is unstable. You have big, heavy, sharp metal tools in your hands and you have to know exactly where to strike the face. If you swing your tool in the wrong spot, you'll knock down a giant chunk of ice, the size of a refrigerator. It will come down and crush you, or even worse, your partner." That seemed pretty bad to me.

I knew I couldn't ascend the way sighted climbers do, by swinging at the healthy blue ice and not at the rotten white ice. So I learned how to climb in a different way. Using my hearing instead of my sight, I learned to use my ice tools as extensions of my hands and feel through the tips. When I find a weak spot in the ice or a concave dish above a bulge, I tap my tools, feeling the vibration through the ice and listening for the auditory pitch of the tap. If I hear a "dong!"—the sound of ringing a big hollow bell—that means big ice coming down on top of me; do not swing there! If I hear a tinny sound like tapping a dinner plate with a spoon, that means sharp shattering ice exploding in my face. The sound I'm listening for is a deep rich "thunk," a sound like hitting frozen peanut butter with a sledgehammer. When I hear that, I know I can swing, and it will hold my weight.

So, given these examples, what are the common characteristics of Signature Systems that you can replicate with your challenges and goals? Pioneers carry good PROPS.

The best solutions are generally:

1. **P**ortable. Most Signature Systems can be taken from place to place.
2. **R**eplicable or **R**epeatable or both. They can be readily rebuilt, reused, or repeated.

3. **O**riginal. They tend to be clever and unique.
4. **P**ersonal. They fit and are adapted to you—your unique style and needs.
5. **S**imple. They require a minimum of steps, hassles, and resources. They are not burdened by complexity, which only creates more things that can go wrong. It is not always easy to create something simple.

When you think of Erik's ice climbing, his "thunk" approach is portable, replicable, and repeatable: he can take it to any ice face; any properly skilled blind person can learn it; and he can use it over and over. It's also both original and personal. He invented it, and it fits both his needs and his style. Finally, his system is simple. It requires one movement and sound. Good PROPS. And when you're trying to create agility, simplicity, and efficiency, PROPS can really help.

Our hands-free traveler developed great PROPS. Her system was portable; and she could unhook it, put it in her purse or case, and take it anywhere. It was easily repeatable with similar parts. It was entirely original, personal, and extremely simple. That's why it drew instant admiration. Great Signature System.

PRACTICE TO PERFECT

Notice that with all the examples listed above, Signature Systems were not perfected in an instant, or even in the first few attempts. In fact, most started like a prototype, pretty rough, and needing some serious polish. Remember, what you think is the answer is usually the beginning of an accelerated road of discovery that may take you somewhere else entirely.

Don't get discouraged. It may appear that the people in these examples each had a flash of brilliance resulting in an elegantly de-

PIONEER POSSIBILITIES

STEP TWO—DEVISE SIGNATURE SYSTEMS

Begin with your Summit Challenge, your first worthy goal. Then, ask these questions to spark your thinking, and list *all* possible solutions.

1. How could I achieve this goal? How *else*? (Repeat until you have an exhaustive list of ideas written down.)
2. What is the best way to make this happen, given the resources I already have?
3. How would the most creative person I know attack this challenge?
4. What creative solutions have I seen in other, totally unrelated situations that could be modified to fit this goal?
5. What systems or approaches could I devise to accomplish this goal that would make good PROPS?
   - **P**ortable
   - **R**eplicable or **R**epeatable
   - **O**riginal
   - **P**ersonal
   - **S**imple
6. Of the ideas I've listed, which one is most viable or likely to work?
7. Of the ideas I've listed, which ones are the most exciting to ponder and potentially develop?
8. Which one would an expert in this area most likely endorse?
9. For which one do I have the will to keep at it until it actually works?

signed solution, which worked instantly. Quite the contrary. Most ingenious Signature Systems are as much a result of tenacity and relentlessness as they are of brilliance. As with the Wright brothers' first plane, most possibility pioneers have secret stockrooms packed with failed versions. Leaders have to recognize this and nurture strategic trials and early failures within their organizations, if they ever hope to own the kind of Signature Systems that could differentiate their organizations in the marketplace.

Flying Blind

When I decided to try my hand at paragliding, I was immediately apprised of all the reasons why this was impossible for a blind guy. But my instructor, Bill, thought differently. He said, "I'm not exactly sure how you'd do it, but I bet there's a way. If you're willing to try, I'll help you."

As we began to train, we found that many parts of paragliding were tactile, not visual. I learned to memorize each of the lines running from my harness to the wing, so I could feel any tangles before a flight. Taking off entailed running like crazy down a steep slope, directly into the wind. Paragliders use thermals, columns of heat rising up from the ground, to get lift. I found that I could feel when I came into contact with a thermal by the way the front of my wing lifted up and tipped me backward.

However, as Bill put it succinctly, "For you, the biggest obstacles will be steering and landing." For steering, Bill would talk me down from the base of the hill using two radios that hung from my neck. There were two in case the first one failed. If they both failed, Bill had a bullhorn.

As you come in for a landing, you've got to flare and slow yourself down dramatically by pulling the toggles that you hold in front of you. Otherwise, you can smack the ground at fifty miles per hour. Bill could tell me when to flare over the radio, but if he got hurt or I had to make an emergency landing, I needed to be able to do it independently.

We discussed high-tech solutions like a talking altimeter, but it wasn't reliable or precise enough. We finally settled on the idea of attaching a long string, hanging from my harness, with a bell tied to the end. If everything went right, the bell would ring when it hit the ground and tell me when to flare. The early landings were pretty rough as we experimented with different-size bells and different lengths of string. The first bells were too small; I never heard them. So we attached a giant cowbell that I not only could hear but also could feel through my body as it thunked the ground. I learned that you descend much faster at higher elevations. So the string needed to be lengthened. With the wind blowing toward you, you descend more slowly. So the string needed to be shortened. With all these systems working together, even a blind guy manages to execute a perfect stand-up landing every now and then.

As with so many other pioneering attempts, when Erik wanted to paraglide and was told he couldn't or shouldn't, and then succeeded, the reward was grudging respect. He didn't make speeches before or after about it—"Watch this," or "Told you so!" He didn't need to. Actions silence a lot of words. Results resound, while words whisper.

> Results resound, while words whisper.

The key point is that the rough systems you and your team devise will take a lot of relentless work to become smooth, elegant, dependable, and perfect.

Contagious Possibilities

One of the deepest benefits of pioneering possibilities is how readily it spreads from one area of your life to another. My wife, Ellen, and I have a lovely daughter, Emma.

Before Emma was born, I worried a lot about how I would raise a child when I couldn't catch a ball, play board games, or even change diapers. Actually, with diapers, I tried to convince Ellie that I couldn't do it because I was blind. Unfortunately, I had just returned from Mount Everest, and she wasn't buying that excuse.

Anyway, given the Worthy Goal—to be completely involved in raising Emma—I devised, and then practiced, some Signature Systems. A friend helped me adapt board games like Candy Land, so that each step on the path to Candy Castle is labeled with distinct tactile squares of material. I found children's books in Braille, so I can read Emma her bedtime stories. I found big inflatable balls that we could play catch with and that don't hurt so much when she pegs me in the head. I installed a big wrestling mat in our basement so Emma and I can tumble around without getting hurt. Together Ellie and I devised a system for locating her when she's nearby. The rule is that whenever I ask, "Where are you?" she has to say, "Right here, Dad," right away. Hiding or playing silent is not allowed.

Over the years, we have refined these systems to the point where I now feel reasonably confident as a dad. It turns out I like parenthood so much that Ellen and I decided to enhance our lives with an even bigger challenge and blessing. We decided to give Emma a sibling and adopt a little boy from Guatemala, to hopefully give him a good life. When our new addition arrives, I'll be ready with some new systems to handle the chaos of two.

PIONEER POSSIBILITIES

STEP THREE—PRACTICE TO PERFECT

Drawing from the other examples, and given your Worthy Goal and your first attempt at Signature Systems, what do you need to do to practice and perfect your approach so that you have effective PROPS?

- ► *What* are the criteria for an effective Signature System or solution?
- ► *Where and how* can you practice with the new system?
- ► *What* will you try first?
- ► *How* will you refine your solution?
- ► *Where* or *how* else might you try it?
- ► *Who* can give you helpful feedback?
- ► *When* or how soon can you begin?
- ► *How long* do you need to figure it out?

Now that you have a *Worthy Goal*—your *Summit Challenge*—and some initial thoughts on your *Signature Systems* and how you will *Practice to Perfect*—you are ready to begin to write the first draft of your Pioneer Story.

PIONEER STORIES

In every walk of life, pioneers have the most amazing stories, and they share a common plot. Pioneers and pioneering organizations, first, have a Worthy Goal (motivation, strengths, excitement). Pioneers meet adversity. Second, rather than be stopped, pioneers struggle to devise some way (Signature System) to use the available resources (PROPS) to move forward and make the impossible possible. Third, pioneers Practice to Perfect. They fail, rework the system, and then practice more, until the solution works and can be confidently applied, making them more sure-footed for future potholes and boulders in their path.

Given the components of the plot, what would you like your Pioneer Story to be? And don't think you have to be a superhuman genius to make it happen. Consider the following examples, and then Erik's narrative.

Fueling Hope

In the last decade, reductions in school funding and declining populations have threatened, gutted, or killed many rural school systems. As one of thousands, Wray, a town of slightly over 2,000 in the northeast corner of Colorado, was forced to slash nearly $750,000 from the District RD-2 school budget. Twenty people lost their jobs, and the district found itself in a real crisis.

In 2002, desperate to offset continued shortfalls, the superintendent of Wray challenged his staff to identify new revenue sources and redefine their ways of conducting business. They had a

Worthy Goal. He hoped to both save the system from financial ruin and enhance the quality of the educational experience for the district's 700 K–12 students at the same time. By framing their crisis in a positive way, the superintendent challenged his employees to become pioneers.

Jay Clapper, a vocational and agricultural technology teacher at Wray High School, saw the potential advantage in their adversity— viewing the challenge as a green light for an idea he had been considering for some time. He saw the answer "blowing in the wind." For a school rural district, his idea would represent a real Signature System. It would require using the district's resources in a new way to generate possibilities and abundance for the community. It would have to be portable (something he could take to other districts if he wanted to) and replicable, as well as original (never done this way before), personal (something that fit him and his style), and simple (not easy, but elegant and clean).

Outside his classroom was a large, barren hill that he believed would be an ideal location for a wind turbine. Clapper proposed to the superintendent that the school build a wind turbine on the site as a way to offset the school's electricity bill, which was approximately $80,000 per year. At the time, he knew only the basics of wind power; but he believed in his idea and had the determination and curiosity to explore its possibilities. He knew it would take tremendous work and practice to get the idea right.

Jay began by learning as much as possible about the feasibility of the project. He spent his free time outside the classroom researching various wind turbine systems, making contacts, and building allies along the way. His first breakthrough came when he finally won the support of the Rocky Mountain Farmers Union, which awarded him a grant of $3,000 to help him establish a pilot project. The school system then helped him obtain a larger grant.

But at each step along the way, Clapper faced new resistance. In fact, more than once he thought the idea was dead, but he remained determined to resuscitate it and see it through. Jay Clapper always saw the project as something greater than himself. He did not want to spend the rest of his life wondering what could have been. Most pioneers struggle with moments of truth—thoughts of simply quitting—but use their Worthy Goal and the adversity they face along the way as fuel to redouble their efforts and stay on course.

As the project progressed and the logistics began to fall into place, Clapper was faced with the question of where to plug in the generator. The most logical choices seemed to arouse the most opposition. He looked at plugging into the city and county grids but was faced with difficult regulations. "Why not plug the turbine into the school first and sell the extra power at wholesale?" he thought. But even here he had difficulty getting support. The major shift occurred when Clapper found supporters outside his town who expressed interest in his turbine-generated power. That tipped the scale. The town woke up and realized the real risk—that it might not be the beneficiary of the project—and their attitude toward Clapper began to change.

Ultimately, Clapper raised over $1 million to develop and install a 1.5-megawatt wind turbine, which will supply a quarter of the town's electrical needs and provide an estimated $180,000 a year in new revenue to the school district. Through relentless tenacity and refinement, Clapper accomplished what he wanted, leaving behind the rich tapestry of a pioneer's legacy—the stuff of local lore. Beyond the immediate economic benefits, Wray's students saw firsthand what happens when an individual pioneers possibilities in pursuit of a Worthy Goal. For decades to come, students will learn about sustainability and clean energy. And as other communities around the country face their own adversities, they can turn to Jay Clapper's wind turbine as an example of what's possible. For his remaining years, Clapper will be deeply gratified by the contribution he has made to his community.[3]

Pioneering Possibilities

A few years ago I got the opportunity of a lifetime, to climb a 1,000-foot tower in Moab, Utah, with two amazing pioneers. Together, we formed a one-of-a-kind team.

My first partner was Mark Wellman. When Mark was nineteen years old, he fell down a peak in the Sierra Nevada and broke his back. The news that he would never walk again shook the very foundation of his spirit, but that didn't deter him from going through painful rehabilitation; building up his shoulders, back, and arms; and eventually learning to climb again.

Mark invented an ingenious climbing system in which he wore a body harness attached to an ascender, a mechanical device that bit into the rope like teeth, making it possible to slide up the rope, but not down. Above, he attached a modified pull-up bar to the rope, also by an ascender. Mark would then slide the bar up the rope as far as his arms would reach. When it locked off, he would hang from it and do a pull-up to its base. Afterward, he would rest for a second and then repeat the whole process. With the stretchy rope and the wobbly bar, each pull-up gained Mark only about eight inches. Five years after his accident, Mark climbed the infamous 3,300-foot rock face of El Capitan with this same Signature System. It was estimated that he did about 7,000 pull-ups in seven days.

Hugh Herr was our second partner. Seventeen years old and already a brilliant rock and ice climber, Hugh summitted Mount Washington in a blizzard, became disoriented, and lay in a hole for three days, while his legs froze. After losing his legs below the knees, Hugh went on to get a doctorate in engineering at the Massachusetts Institute of Technology, where he developed extremely lightweight prosthetic legs and special, innovative detachable climbing feet. He had two kinds, both much smaller than adult human feet, that he made from the same sticky rubber used in climbing shoes. One pair was attached vertically and was used to wedge into cracks; the other was a horizontal pair, used to stand on ledges as small as the width of a dime. Five years after Hugh's accident, he was a better climber than he had been before. For a time, he was ranked in the top ten climbers in the country. Magazines called him the first "six-million-dollar man." Hugh jokingly attributes his success to being twenty pounds lighter than he used to be.

Along the two-mile trail to the base of the climb, I got the privilege of carrying Mark piggyback, his legs resting on my curled arms as I strained to jab my trekking poles out in front of us. With all 165 pounds of him on my back, his muscular arms clutching my neck, we were like an out-of-control video game. Mark desperately called out directions. "Deep ruts in the trail!" I jerked to the left to avoid them. "Cliff on the left!" I jerked back right and bounced jarringly through the ruts.

Hugh led the five-pitch climb. I came second, followed by Mark. The day was growing colder, and it was beginning to snow. I yelled down to Mark, "You got an extra pair of gloves? It's so freaking cold, Hugh can't even feel his legs." Hugh only grunted. At the summit, we sat together. The wind blew, and it snowed even more heavily. Mark finally broke the silence: "Not bad for three gimps, huh?"

From that experience, Hugh, Mark, and I conceived the idea for No Barriers, a nonprofit endeavor designed to blast open doors of opportunity for disabled people and help them access the beautiful, rugged open spaces of the world. The three of us had each struggled to develop the Signature Systems to climb. It was time to reach out and help others find ways to accomplish their own dreams, no matter what it took.

We held our first festival in Cortina, Italy, in the heart of the Dolomites. Several hundred amputees, paraplegics, and blind people converged on Cortina, where they interacted with scientists and researchers who were designing the latest assistive technologies. Participants were able to check out the latest and greatest wheelchairs as well as high-tech prosthetic legs with computerized knees, which are enabling above-the-knee amputees to walk, often for the first time since losing their legs. A blind technologist led blind people on hikes solely with the use of a talking Global Positioning System to guide their route.

Athletes like me led clinics on blind rock climbing. Mark led a hand cycling tour for paraplegics. At the end of No Barriers, Hugh, Mark, and I completed another climb together to demonstrate what was possible. Italian TV called our team the "wonder of the Alps." In June 2007, we'll hold our third festival in Squaw Valley, California.

Wouldn't all of us love a deeply confident voice in our heads telling us which direction to take—which path is credible and which is folly? But that's never the case. I'm often drawn by an outcome that I believe is attainable. It usually starts with a nagging feeling, which gets stronger by the day. I think to myself that under the right conditions, with the right systems, and with the right team around me, I believe it can be done. It's exciting to set myself on a course and try to turn my belief into reality.

One of the most pervasive forms of adversity is the inevitable uncertainty that confronts us when we attempt something new and untested. To put it simply, as pioneers we're always climbing blind. I've been rock climbing for more than twenty years, and one thing hasn't changed since the very first time. That is the *reach*.

As pioneers, we reach out into the darkness, predicting, calculating, hoping, and praying that we'll find what we are looking for, while understanding that there are no guarantees. We commit our minds and bodies to the reach, knowing that it is virtually impossible to reverse course. This kind of fear is overwhelming—the fear of flopping on our faces, the fear of looking stupid in front of our friends and colleagues, the fear of learning that we aren't as good at something as we thought we might be, or the fear that we've peaked and can't climb any higher. All those fears can conspire against us and paralyze us, so we decide to stop reaching, or we never reach out at all.

However, life is an ongoing, never-ending process of reaching out into the darkness when we don't know what we're going to find. We constantly reach out toward immense possibilities. They may be unseen, yet they are sensed. And it is in that *reach* that possibilities are pioneered and everyday greatness is realized.

To prepare for the pioneering journey ahead, you will need to pare down your life by making hard but rewarding choices about what you really need along the way. Summit Five will show you how to pack light and pack right.

SUMMIT FOUR—PIONEER POSSIBILITIES

GUIDING PRINCIPLE

To turn adversity to your advantage, you may need to go beyond the standard, tried-and-true approaches and solutions to pioneer new possibilities. Those who generate an upside while others are managing the downside tend to win.

Step One—Pick a Worthy Goal
- Motivation—*Why do you want to do it?*
- Strengths—*What skills and will does it require?*
- Excitement—*How jazzed up are you about taking it on?*

Step Two—Devise Signature Systems, Using PROPS
- **P**ortable—You can take it anywhere.
- **R**eplicable or **R**epeatable—It is something you can re-create or repeat or both.
- **O**riginal—It has never been done (quite this way).
- **P**ersonal—It suits you and your style.
- **S**imple—It is not easy, but stripped of any unnecessary complexity.

Step Three—Practice to Perfect
- *What* are the criteria for an effective Signature System or solution?
- *Where* and *how* can you practice with the new system?
- *What* will you try first?
- *How* will you refine your solution?
- *Where* or *how* else might you try it?
- *Who* can give you helpful feedback?
- *When* or *how soon* can you begin?
- *How long* do you need to figure it out?

Write your Pioneer Story
- What Worthy Goal—Summit Challenge—will you take on in the face of potential naysayers, relentlessly practicing to perfect? *What* kind of Signature Systems will make it happen?
- What will be the legacy of your breakthrough, when you pioneer your possibilities?
- Who will be enriched by what you've done?

PACK LIGHT, PACK RIGHT

VINSON MASSIF
Base Camp: 7,000 feet
Summit: 16,066 feet–tallest peak in Antarctica

It is not length of life, but depth of life.
–RALPH WALDO EMERSON

I've never heard anyone say, "I feel better about myself when I shrink in the face of adversity." However, I have heard countless heartfelt explanations from people about how—if only they had more time and energy, and fewer responsibilities and obligations—they would be more effective when adversity strikes. It's those "if onlys" that give me pause. More often than not, these rationalizations have to do with the real burdens of life. At some point even the stuff we own stops serving a meaningful purpose and begins to encumber us.

I discovered that it's tough to climb a mountain if you pack too much or if you pack incorrectly. Likewise, it's tough to be agile and effective at harnessing numerous adversities each day if you're weighed down by all the competing priorities vying for your focus. When this happens, everyday distractions bury the potential for everyday greatness.

Whenever I pack my gear for an expedition, I wrestle with similar issues. I have to ask myself what I need and what I don't. I think the same principles apply to life. Sometimes people have something worthwhile they want to do, but they don't know how to pack for their journey. It makes sense; the higher you climb, the more strategic and focused you must be with your planning and packing.

Summit Five will equip you with the principles and tools to pack light and pack right, so that everything, from your resources and time to your work and your health, is aligned properly for you to ratchet up the Adversity Continuum. Through Paul's lessons on packing for life, you will be able to benefit from life's tough stuff, and your alchemy will thrive.

For Chris Morris and me, just getting to Antarctica was a lesson in packing light and packing right. Only one old military cargo plane makes the arduous six-hour flight across the Drake Passage, attempting it when the nearly constant Antarctic winds die down enough for it to land. Since the plane can carry just enough fuel for the round-trip, every bit of weight counts. Each passenger has a strict 100-pound baggage limit, which includes personal gear plus a portion of team gear. One hundred pounds are plenty, but when you are contemplating a potential three-week expedition in which you will burn 5,000 calories a day and temperatures will drop to fifty below zero, the tendency is to overpack.

Also, since no one checks the body weight of passengers as they step onto the plane, some climbers, looking for ways to cheat the system, have discovered a loophole in the baggage limit. They stagger on board, dripping with sweat in the seventy-degree Chilean sun, dressed in their down suits and giant plastic boots, with espresso makers and satellite phones stuffed down their pants. Although I knew that the weight limit was a very serious matter, I couldn't resist cramming a five-pound bag of peanut M&Ms into my own down suit. Chris Morris had three giant sausages tucked away in his. Everyone was so weighed down that teammates were helping each other into and out of their seats.

Because Chris and I had sat at the tip of South America for nine days waiting out bad weather, we arrived in Antarctica way behind schedule. The pilot who dropped us at Base Camp now told us he'd be back to pick us up in one week—scarcely enough time for us to summit, and leaving absolutely no room for further weather delays. We'd need to move very fast. Typically, climbers on Mount Vinson have so much gear that they're forced to make double carries to each subsequent camp, but Chris and I no longer had this luxury. We'd have time for only single carries. We spent the next two hours reorganizing and paring down provisions, so we'd be able to haul everything up the glacier in one trip.

Arriving at Camp One that evening, we pitched our tent next to two teams who were heading down the mountain. To our right was an American team that had fallen short of the summit. The three Americans were lounging in a deluxe tent built for five, complete with high ceilings and plenty of room for gear. On the other side of us were five Polish climbers who had success-fully reached the summit. They were crammed into a tent for three. While the Americans feasted on gourmet meals like "Annie's All-Natural Pasta and Chicken Parmesano," the Poles had survived for weeks on instant mashed potatoes mixed with a bouillon cube for flavor.

Eastern Europeans have a reputation for being hard climbers. After the Berlin Wall came down in 1988 and the world's great mountains were opened to the Soviet-bloc countries, Eastern European climbers began dis-tinguishing themselves from their western counterparts. In the next ten years, they racked up a series of first ascents on the world's tallest peaks, on the most difficult faces and in the middle of winter. In their own countries, three generations of a family might live, sleep, and eat in a one-bedroom apartment, with the heat working only occasionally. So living in a tent on a mountain was viewed not as deprivation or a sacrifice but as a grand escape—the ultimate vacation.

Sharing some conversation with our Eastern European neighbors, I learned that their team had recently made the first ascent of a difficult face. They had spent an entire night up high, hanging in their harnesses. "How was it?" I asked one of them. He simply replied, "Cold, just like my apartment in Warsaw." Some people have marveled over these climbers' achieving so much despite their lack of material wealth, but I believe the discipline and perspective gained through their everyday lives actually gave them the tools to achieve greatness.

From Base Camp to Camp One, Chris and I had carried packs and pulled big sleds: but to get to High Camp, we'd be navigating through an icefall and up a steep headwall, so we'd have to leave our sleds behind. We'd be limited to those things we could physically carry on our backs. So at Camp One, I was again faced with the classic mountaineering quandary—what to leave and what to keep. I forced myself to pause and focus, carefully thinking about every piece of gear I might need from head to toe. Certain items were essential to me for the final push, like two pairs of thick gloves in case one pair was blown away. In Antarctica, if fingers become exposed to the elements for even one minute, they could be lost to frostbite.

What could I do without? My toothbrush came to mind. I had already cut the handle off it to save weight, but now I chose to endure bad breath for a few days and left it behind. Down booties, extra socks, my precious Walkman, and even my peanut M&Ms all went next. I loaded my pack with only the essential gear; hauled it onto my back; and, quickly realizing I could never carry it all, began again the painful process of deciding what else I could live without. Our med kit, originally the size of a shoe box, was whittled down to fit into a plastic ziplock bag. An ice ax could double as a splint for a broken femur, and duct tape could patch a ripped tent as well as a bleeding wound.

One issue was eating at me, however. Before our trip, a television show asked me to carry a video camera to film the summit from a blind person's perspective. I reluctantly agreed. I recalled one of my climbing partners who once cut all the tags off his climbing clothes, piled the tags on a scale, and proclaimed happily, "I just saved four ounces. Now I can bring an extra energy bar." I had laughed, yet at the same time I knew that if I was caught in a terrible storm for a week, four ounces of extra food might just be the difference between life and death. In this light, bringing the video camera seemed like sheer lunacy, but I had no choice; I had made a commitment, so it went into my pack.

Two days later, we left early for the summit from High Camp, as soon as it was warm enough to move out. In my pack were only the necessities, with the exception of the pesky video camera. At twenty pounds, the pack felt light on my shoulders, but eight hours later, the pack transformed itself into what mountaineers refer to as the "Pig." I was in great shape, but the Pig was slowing me down to a crawl. Chris, as usual, yelled for me to hurry up. "Visibility's dropping," he shouted. "A storm's definitely coming in." After all our training, sacrifice, and waiting, I couldn't believe it, but a six-pound video camera was about to cost me the summit. So I yanked the camera from my pack and left it in the snow to be picked up on the way down.

Five hundred feet higher, we were still moving too slowly. The wind was now picking up, making us brace against it. Finally, Chris and I made the decision to drop our packs altogether and go for it. I stuffed an energy bar, a little water, and the extra pair of gloves into my down suit. We had climbed higher and gotten closer to our goal, and my perspective on the things I really needed had sharpened and narrowed—just like the pinnacle itself.

Right below the summit, we faced the greatest test, a narrow rocky ridge. The frigid wind hammered us as I carefully felt my way across, but I felt secure and strong. I had been freed from the Pig.

On the summit, the temperature was close to fifty below zero. My legs were cramping, and Chris told me that my lips were blue from cold. Believe it or not, when I took a leak, it actually froze before hitting the ground. I had a new, personal definition of cold that I still use today.

By the next day, the wind and blowing snow near the top of Vinson were ferocious. If we had added just one more day hauling extra gear, we wouldn't have made it. Instead, we had learned to pack light and pack right, and as a result, we had stood on the top of Antarctica.

Although climbers flying to Vinson may try to cheat the system by stuffing extras into their down suits, there's no cheating in life. Either we pack with deliberation, considering what's important to us, or we are crushed by an array of diversions. It's significant that the word *deliberation* contains the word *liberation.* If we pack light and pack right, we set ourselves free, so that when adversity rises up in the path of what really matters, we are poised to harness its tremendous power.

The lesson that is continually reinforced by my business clients applies to each one of us, and everything we heap onto our lives: when you're constantly drained by sheer weight, it's nearly impossible to move toward being great.

In taking on Summit Five, you will both reassess and repack your *stuff*, *time*, *work*, and *self*, shedding unnecessary burdens that may be sapping your strength or slowing you or your organization down. In each section you will conduct a Pack Check to focus your load. Summit Five will culminate with you completing your own Adversity Advantage Packing List, reequipping yourself to optimize the three A's—*alchemy*, *agility*, and of course *adversity*.

Summit Five also taps into my expanded research in an area called Happiness Economics—the study of the relationship between finances and fulfillment. You will learn the defining difference between net worth and Life Worth—the enduring source of happiness. This summit is about maintaining your agility, energy, and focus to perform your own alchemy. At an individual level, it helps you take a cold, hard look at the way you pack your life, expend your resources, and fuel yourself, so that you can fulfill the promise of this book. Like the other Summits, Summit Five addresses you as an individual and also as a member of a team, family, organization, and community. It begins by exploring our relationship with our *stuff*.

STUFF

*You can never get enough of what you don't need
to make you happy.*
—ERIC HOFFER

Everyday greatness means rising above mediocrity, even when the gravitational pull is enormous. It means moving forward and up, when everyone else is camping. Sometimes it can even mean escaping comfort and welcoming adversity. Recreational campers can load a giant RV to the roof with every whim they can imagine. Sure, all that stuff will compromise their gas mileage, slow them down on curves, and take up some space, but they're just trying to get to the next campground to plug in and hang out. They willingly sacrifice agility for comfort. You might say that they are on an adversity-free quest—to make the journey as easy as possible.

Check your own packing—what you currently carry through life. How much of what you own, and what you do, is really climb critical? How much of it is really just consumption of resources? Ultimately, do the things you pack into your life—the items you accumulate, the decisions you make, the work you do, the ways you invest your time and money, the way you manage your health—weigh you down or lift you up?

Do you spend so much energy earning dollars for more square footage and more stuff that you have sapped your ability to convert adversity into fuel for some higher quest? If you've ever missed one of your kids' events, or a gathering with good friends, because you decided to take on an extra project to help pay off some self-induced bills, you know what I mean. Are you so weighed down with all your stuff that you find it less and less possible to pursue rich opportunities? If so, don't feel bad. Most people report that their stuff does more to weigh them down than raise them up. That's why "more" isn't always more.

Perhaps you can relate. Has there ever come a time in your life when more has become less—especially when it comes to your stuff? Proper packing takes clarity and discipline, especially in the face of adversity. Stuff is the largest category in Summit Five, since it seems to have the greatest power to pull us astray. Our material items and our money are inextricably intertwined. Stuff costs money. Stuff can add complexity. Stuff demands mindshare. And whether at work or at home, money spent on one thing means money not spent on something else. Most people are weighed down considerably by the wrong stuff.

Why More Has Become Less

You don't have to be slogging extra weight up a mountain in Antarctica to come to grips with why more can be less. While waiting in the ticket line at the San Luis Obispo airport, I struck up a conversation with Leo, one of the uniformed baggage-screening officials of the Transportation Screening Association (TSA). I said to him, "When it comes to people and their stuff, I bet you guys pretty much see it all."

"Yeah, well, it's kind of funny you should mention that," he said. "People pay extra to bring overloaded bags full of the most amazing stuff. The other day a guy had to pay eighty dollars because his cappuccino machine put his bag over the limit. Next thing you know, you'll find a collapsible hot tub! Sometimes the airlines actually have to bump passengers because the bags weigh so much." Leo shook his head in disgust.

According to Gregg Easterbrook, author of *The Progress Paradox*, however you measure it, Americans (we are by no means alone in this) have been wealthier and better off and have gained greater material wealth in the past fifty years than at any other time in our history. His entire book and his supporting research are dedicated to the subject of how more stuff leads to no more happiness, and in some cases less happiness.

Today's middle class enjoys greater luxuries and conveniences than the royalty of the not-so-distant past. A mere century ago, time-savers and lifestyle enhancers such as washing machines, desktop computers, automobiles, telephones, refrigerators, dishwashers, ovens, leaf blowers, microwaves, in-home entertainment systems, and even—for many people—running water were all unimaginable. Over recent decades, the average home in the United States has grown from 1,100 to nearly 2,400 square feet and has added more rooms for fewer people. More people own homes, packed with more stuff at higher prices, and funded by higher incomes, than ever before. Nonetheless, more than half of us report that life is getting worse. Specifically, people's perception that, despite the obvious gains, things are on a downslide, robs them of their happiness. When it comes to material gains and happiness, more of the first does not necessarily lead to more of the second. In fact, the inverse can become true.

Packed wrong, more can be less. More stuff leads to more complexity, which leads to less time, less peace of mind, and less capacity to take on more important challenges. That's why, sometimes, the more we add, the weaker we become. Then, when adversity hits, the reflex to "take it on" becomes a plea to "take it away!"

Erik invited me to be a part of his support team for the Primal Quest, the premier adventure race in the world. It goes through some very rugged terrain and involves paddling, biking, running, climbing, and crawling for 450 miles over ten days with no real rest or comfort—so it was the ultimate test of endurance and packing. Erik had his team supplies, so they were no issue. But I needed to cover my own and be prepared for any contingency, including long waits. Not knowing what we might face out there, I was extremely concerned that I pack right. And sometimes the more you pack, the less you experience.

One day, while my ninety-two-year-old grandfather was visiting from out of town, he ambled into the living room where, on a giant tarp, I had carefully laid out all my supplies for the ten-day trek.

"Holy cow! This must be quite an expedition you're going on. Look at all this snazzy stuff," he marveled, surveying the layout.

"Yeah, this is a serious trek, and you've got to plan and pack just right to make sure you don't carry a hundred-pound pack, yet you don't get into serious trouble fifty miles from the trailhead because you have forgotten something. It's all about defining the essentials," I said in my best backcountry-expert voice.

"Essentials, yeah, well, of course. I can see that." My grandfather picked up a small, nearly weightless contraption. "Well, what's this?"

"Oh, well, er, that's a collapsible coffee press."

"And this monstrosity?"

"Oh, that's the most ingenious thing! It's an inflatable, convertible seat sling to sit by the campfire and sleeping pad so you can't get bruised by the sticks and rocks." I demonstrated it.

My grandfather smiled. "Gotta have one of those. And I suppose these little red tanks store some kind of fuel?"

"Yeah, these are pretty amazing! See how light they are?" I tossed one into the air for dramatic effect. "They store all the fuel for this impressive little device—the high-altitude cookstove—so you can always have hot food and water, in minutes!"

"Very impressive. Amazing technology. So tell me, Mr. Backpack Guide, how much does all this weigh?" my grandfather asked, waving his arm to indicate the entire room-wide spread.

I scratched my head, surveyed the room, and did a quick calculation. "We'll probably carry about fifty-five pounds each," I proudly proclaimed, convinced that Grandpa would be nothing less than impressed by the ingenious advances in backcountry technology.

But my grandfather slowly shook his head and let out a long whistle. "Well, I must say. Things sure have come a long way from the days when we used to throw a simple ten or twenty-pound knapsack full of clothes and whatever scraps of food we could find over our shoulders and go disappear into the woods for days on end. It's a wonder we survived without all these neat gadgets," he said, glancing at me with a characteristic warm glint in his eye. "But somehow, we got through. Had a hell of a lot of fun too, I gotta tell ya." He chuckled warmly. "Man, we sure could cover the miles with such light packs. But it sure as heck would have been easier if we'd had all this! I guess we just did what we had to do. Between the weather, trail conditions, lack of maps, and foraging for food, it seemed like new challenges were constantly thrown at our feet, so we had to figure it out as we went along. Sometimes it was pretty tough. But I imagine having all these neat gadgets along must make it more fun."

I was humbled and silenced, as my ears slowly flushed red with the realization that my wise grandfather had just taught me a loving lesson about what really mattered. I envied him for how agile and inventive he must have been. I realized that buying, managing, and carrying all my ingenious comforts might be robbing me of both miles and adventure—preventing me from enjoying the pure wilderness experience he had taken on much more simply, far more nimbly, and, yes, much less expensively. I had more, but would experience less. He had less but was able to do more. And I realized that by being more equipped, I was actually more poorly positioned than he to respond quickly and effectively to whatever might happen, or whatever weather we might encounter. By packing light and right, he had learned to relish adversity. Good lesson, and one I will hold dear for my remaining years.

Grandpa taught me that too much stuff or the wrong stuff, or both, can pull you down the Adversity Continuum. The more stuff we have, the more we have to maintain and manage, and the less nimble we become. So, whatever we stuff into our kids' lives or our own lives, homes, bodies, grocery carts, and daily calendars, we all face the basic question, "How much is enough?" Or, better yet, "Which stuff is the right stuff?" Today's era of over-choice also requires you to consider not just if you have too much stuff, but also if you have the right stuff—those things that directly help, rather than hinder, your everyday greatness and overall worth. And we're not normally taught to think of our money or our stuff in these terms.

Which Stuff Is the Right Stuff?

I'm always asking myself and others, "What's climb-critical?" In other words, what is truly essential to accomplishing the most important things we set out to do? And what is merely desirable? Want versus need. This is the rub. And it takes tremendous honesty, if not courage, to separate the two. My humble observation is that, as a society, once we move beyond genuine need to expected desires, we suffer the mired and potentially ugly culture of entitlement. Most of the people with the money to buy this book spend much of their resources on things they want, but do not need. Food, water, shelter, safety, and arguably love are requirements. Everything else falls somewhere on the continuum of desires from "fairly essential" to "completely frivolous." Which stuff is the right stuff? The right stuff is the stuff that most *enables* and least hinders your efforts to deliver your own version of everyday greatness—to do the things you are meant to do in life. Muster the life-freeing discipline to apply that filter, and only the right stuff remains.

How Much Is Enough?

This second, related question builds on the first. Since most of us live well beyond "need" and well within "want," most of what we have is, by definition, unnecessary. Tough, but true. But pleasures are not evil. They need not detract from your higher calling. They can enhance. Climbers need to rest and rejuvenate themselves. They need to have fun in order to focus on the next piece of rock. But once pleasures or wants obscure or—worse yet—*become* the calling, you have a problem. Desires should enable, not detract from, your highest efforts. That is the acid test for anything you seek to purchase or consider tossing.

I recently attended a deeply moving funeral service for Milton Thornton, an African-American with a New Orleans lineage who had, at eighty-one, succumbed to the ravages of age. Milton came from the most humble roots, and he was just one of those selfless, God-fearing, hardworking, resilient-spirited, dedicated fathers, husbands, community leaders, and citizens who inspire everyone to be more. He helped his neighbors, started his church, fathered three children, prayed for everything, and hardly missed a day of work. His everyday greatness created a strong, values-based, tight-knit contributing family and community, during years of often overt racism. When I saw the assortment of people who had flown in from everywhere to attend the service and heard their heartfelt stories of how Milton Thornton had changed and improved their lives, I realized how rich he had been in the things that count, and how many men of much greater means would envy his deeper wealth.

When we visited the modest home where he and his wife, Barbara, had raised their boys and had lived for nearly fifty years, it made me realize again how little one needs in order to do what one needs to do. When I asked Aaron, his younger son, if his parents had ever felt shortchanged by life—considering their sacrifices, their old car, their spare vacations, and their tiny abode—he spread his arms, taking in the roomful of extended family, and said, "My father always knew what really mattered, and this—this is his fortune. This was always, well, *enough.*"

How much is enough? Exactly as much as it takes to do the thing you're meant to do. Beyond that, employing the disciplined eye to separate, even spring-clean wants from needs, along with the disciplined credit card to take on only those pleasures that truly enhance and never impede your path will leave you fueled, agile, and ready to take on life with all its adversities.

Net Worth versus Life Worth

The cost of a thing is the amount of . . . life which is required
to be exchanged for it, immediately or in the long run.
— HENRY DAVID THOREAU

If you enjoyed a sudden, unexpected financial windfall, what would you do with it? What effect would the cash and how you use it have on your three A's—agility, alchemy, and adversity? Would you use it to pack heavier and "wronger"? Or would you use it to pack lighter and better? And if so, how?

You've probably noticed that you can't really get very far into a meaningful conversation about stuff without eventually talking about money. And you've probably noticed that people who demonstrate any sort of greatness tend to do something different with their money. They use it to elevate, not accumulate. They use it to help fund greater challenges, rather than to distance themselves from having to face challenges in the first place. Money has strategic importance, as a way to fund what matters most, not to demonstrate who has the most.

One of the most useful exercises to help you rethink the role of money in your life is the Net Worth–Life Worth Grid (below). First I'll explain my terms. Then you will complete the grid to gain new insight into your current situation, direction, and life aspirations. Finally, you will identify potential ways you may wish to adjust your life.

NET WORTH

Net worth is something you hope to have in the plus column. It is simply whatever's left when you subtract everything you owe from everything you have. So net worth can be either positive, if you have more than you owe; or negative, if you owe more than you have— the sad reality for a growing number of credit-card-frenzied folks worldwide. For many people, increasing their net worth as much as possible is their ultimate financial goal.

LIFE WORTH

In contrast to net worth, Life Worth is the value you get from and give to life. It is, therefore, a gauge of your everyday greatness. In other words, it's whatever you have left when you subtract all the negatives (those things that harm or diminish your quality of life) from all the positives (those things that are most enriching). It has two parts: the stuff you give to life (love, energy, charity, thought-

fulness, kindness, and more) and the stuff you get as a result (fulfillment, peace, and contentment). Or, more simply, when you pause
and reflect, how would you answer the question, "What's your Life
Worth?" Ouch! Tough question.

If you are unhappy with your answer in any way—for instance,
if your first thought is, "Not as much as it should be"—then this
may be the perfect time to put *The Adversity Advantage* principles
and tools to use. Adversity, properly used, feeds Life Worth. Handled poorly, adversity hobbles Life Worth. You have to be an alchemist to optimize Life Worth.

Life Worth defines everyday greatness. You can stand on a
mountain of net worth and be utterly miserable, but you cannot
stand on a mountain of Life Worth and be anything less than fulfilled. The more Life Worth you enjoy, the more you deliver. And
part of everyday greatness is getting outside your own skin and enriching those around you. When it comes to packing light and
packing right, the challenge is to direct your net worth or money to
optimize your Life Worth.

NET WORTH–LIFE WORTH GRID

The Net Worth–Life Worth Grid will help you understand where
you are now, where you hope to end up, and in what direction
you're heading. It will also help you recognize the role adversity
plays in reaching your goal. The vertical axis represents net worth
(NW), or simply how much money you've got when you take away
all your debts. High is a lot of net worth; low is a little. The horizontal axis represents your Life Worth (LW), the value you give to
and get from life. Right is high Life Worth; left is low.

▶ Step One—Your Ideal. Put a large, bold **X** at the spot on the grid
that represents what you are striving for in life. In other words, what
spot on this grid best represents the balance of net worth and Life
Worth you would like to achieve?

▶ Step Two—Current Reality. Put a bold dot (•) at the spot on the grid that indicates where you are now. In other words, if the people who know you best were brutally honest and they were to put on this grid a dot based not on your words or intentions but on your actual deeds and behavior—where you invest your time and energy—where would they say your balance of NW and LW–related effect really is invested?

▶ Step Three—Direction. Now, attach to your dot an arrow that indicates the direction you are currently heading in. This should be based on your current life circumstances. Are you moving toward more net worth at the cost of less Life Worth? Are you moving toward less or more of both? (See the following example.)

NET WORTH–LIFE WORTH GRID

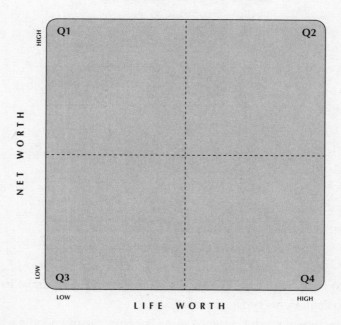

Consider your grid. What's your ideal combination of net worth and Life Worth? Did you opt for more Life Worth or more net worth? Or did you go for the extreme in both? Approximately nine out of ten people choose more Life Worth over net worth. Some choose the max for both. While a lot of people set off to accumulate net worth at the expense of Life Worth, it is extremely rare for someone to ultimately choose higher net worth than Life Worth as the ideal. Why not choose all Life Worth and no net worth? Because most of us are not willing to live like Mother Teresa, who probably had phenomenal Life Worth, but died owning only her robe, sandals, Bible, and rosary beads. It takes some net

SAMPLE NET WORTH – LIFE WORTH GRID

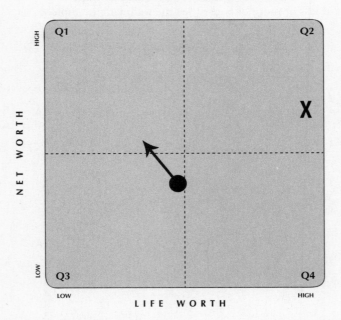

worth to fund your Life Worth. Good news: you don't have to be broke to achieve everyday greatness.

In my line of work I run into some very interesting people when I travel. One stormy afternoon, as I was waiting through some rolling weather delays at Logan Airport in Boston, I overheard a gentleman of some unidentifiable northern African ethnic mix talking on his cell phone. Judging by his worn sleeves and ripped carry-on bag, he certainly did not appear to be wealthy. But he was very animated and emphatic about money. "Three hundred twenty-four dollars! Do you hear me? That's all it takes. Three hundred twenty-four dollars! Every time we raise that much, we buy a new pump and save another village! . . . Yes? . . . Me? . . . Tired? How can you even think of sleep knowing what three hundred twenty-four dollars can do?" He waved his arms dramatically to punctuate his words. Call after call, he emphasized the same thing. "Three hundred twenty-four dollars! That's all it takes!" Finally, when he hung up and went to refill his water bottle, I leaped out of my chair and joined him in line to quell my now boiling curiosity. I asked him what, exactly, $324 actually buys, "Since I could not help overhearing . . ."

His eyes lit up, and he turned to face me. "It buys the most priceless tool, my friend. For three hundred twenty-four dollars you can buy the miracle invention of our time, I tell you! You buy a foot pump for irrigation and pure, pure drinking water! You've seen this thing, yes? They are fantastic! You pump like this (he mimicked something akin to a stair-climber exercise machine) and you get more water than you can even use! It grows food; it builds self-sufficiency; and it saves many, many lives." I looked around, half-expecting the entire crowd of people within earshot to be reaching into their purses and wallets to buy some Life Worth. Using the next dollar of net worth to directly fund Life Worth—using the fruits of your hard-fought adversities to make a richer life—that's what it's all about.

How happy are you with your current reality, or today's balance of net worth and Life Worth? How close is it to where you wanted to be by this age and stage in life? Do you let the pursuit of comfort get in the way of your higher cause—everyday greatness? Like millions of people, are you sacrificing more and more Life Worth to increase your net worth, hoping that you will someday buy some Life Worth in your later, possibly capacity-depleted years, years marked by less adversity and more comfort? Or are you using adversity, at the cost of comfort, to increase Life Worth—perhaps suffering a little; making focused, purposeful sacrifices today for a long-term greater good?

THE ROLE OF ADVERSITY IN LIFE WORTH

Within the first couple years of our marriage, Ronda and I faced some unexpected adversity. One day as she was standing in the kitchen, a jar of strawberry preserves she was holding slipped right out of her hands. The incident was both odd and chilling. We shared a moment of silent, amazed fear. Not one to complain, she finally revealed that she had been experiencing a strange tingling in her head, and sometimes her hands didn't work well. She had been holding off telling me, for fear that it might be a brain tumor, something from which a friend had recently died. She had just hoped it would go away. We immediately scheduled a checkup with the doctor. I remember the incredible sense of intimacy with her and the vulnerability I felt for her as I watched the live MRI scans of her brain. The diagnosis, confirmed by two doctors, was irrefutable. She had multiple sclerosis, MS. Our doctor explained, matter-of-factly, that MS is progressive. It can be aggressive or episodic, devastating or livable, fast or slow. There was no way to know which type she had. We just knew that life, as we had known it, was forever changed. How it was changed seemed largely up to us. My paternal grandfather, whom I never met, died of MS at an early age. I knew its potential to devastate a person. We were determined to do all we could to reduce the chances that she would ever suffer such a fate.

Months before this watershed event, a prominent venture capitalist had taken a tremendous interest in my AQ-based work and business, convincing me and my team that, "because of the uniqueness and robustness of your intellectual capital," we could develop one of the largest training and consulting firms in the world. We found the idea of such a far-reaching impact exciting. Like many other people, this venture capitalist saw the huge potential profit as the real measure of success. He was fond of saying, "Remember, it's not a crime to be filthy rich."

But making this happen wouldn't be easy. Wisely, my emerging partner made it clear that to grow such an enterprise would require nonstop, relentless dedication for at least the first few years. And it would induce "unprecedented stress." Some of us thought he was being melodramatic, but I sensed, from other such ventures I had witnessed, that he was more right than wrong, maybe even conservative in his estimate. I was pumped up by the challenge, the potential risks, and the envisioned upside. So we began to go down the promising path of building PEAK Learning into a global powerhouse, in earnest. We looked at office space, assembled Wall Street investors, and more. The wheels were in motion. Then came the news about Ronda's MS.

So we were at a critical juncture in our lives: net worth versus Life Worth. On one hand, we had two wonderful young boys, Chase and Sean. Because Ronda had just been diagnosed with MS and there was no guarantee that she'd be able to walk the next morning, or ever again, being there with and for her and the boys was the most important aspect of my life. It still is. On the other hand, I had a once-in-a-lifetime opportunity to be the CEO of a major company, perhaps even go public, and retire early with a big vault bulging with money with which we could do as we pleased. I even began to rationalize that, if I could come out the other side of the tunnel of relentless sacrifice within five years, we could potentially have the resources to help deal with anything that might go wrong. Even though building the large company would require enormous compromises and continued travel, it could prove to be the noblest thing to do. Right?

Choices like these are highly personal, and I know that my choice is not right for everyone. But the thought of missing whatever good days were left with our family all together—days free of the more serious hardships of MS—was unacceptable.

To me, no amount of money was worth selling the Life Worth values of family, togetherness, and the freedom or agility to be there with and for Ronda, just in case. Today, the same dynamic tension continues, though in a different fashion. I limit my travel to 25 percent of my working days, and this means I have to say "no" as frequently as "yes" to clients' requests. I have had to shift my focus from quantity of dollars to quality of impact. Sometimes that's difficult. Ronda still has MS. But to this day, decades later, we've been enormously blessed: by exercising, eating right, strengthening her mind, and living sensibly, she has been able to keep it largely at bay. In fact, if you ever were to attend one of her workshops on "You're Only Young Twice" or one of the fitness classes she leads at the health club, you'd never have a clue about the battle she fights every single day.

The fact is that although I'd do anything to take the MS from her and make it mine, I'm immensely grateful for Ronda's illness for at least one clear reason—the ways in which it has helped us to re-order our lives around what matters most. One gift of adversity is its unique power to press the "reset" button on what we pack into life. For Ronda, the boys, and me, it made us rethink how we invest our time and resources. Ronda now has the most intense appreciation of life. And it's infectious. For you, the gift may be something else. But whatever it is, your adversity, properly harnessed, can be your personal elevator to enjoying a level of Life Worth you could never have achieved without your hardship.

Adversity is the catalyst for Life Worth. It is the richest ore from which we can build our selves. Smelted correctly, it offers the highest concentration of lessons, growth, and improvement available from any single source.

REPACKING FOR LIFE WORTH

One of the most cathartic and energizing exercises can be spring-cleaning your current stuff in terms of Life Worth, in order to lighten your load so that you can more effectively take on life and its potentially rich adversities. Where do you begin?

Only you can decide what is or is not sacred when you consider the three A's—agility, alchemy, and adversity. Be simple and tough. If something enhances your capacity for the three A's, keep it. If it clearly hinders your capacity by weighing you down, delete it. You may even want to eliminate stuff that does nothing but make you soft. I've seen people eject all their televisions in order to do more crafts, games, and reading. Others have tossed the golf cart to force more exercise, or reallocated space in their yard to grow their own organic produce. One couple replaced their giant commercial refrigerator with a smaller one, which meant they had to walk the mile to the store more frequently.

The stuff you spring-clean can range from major investments—like high-maintenance rental units that suck a lot of Life Worth while delivering modest net worth—to all the meaningless books on your shelf that bury the ones that really matter. You may intentionally get rid of a costly extra car in order to enjoy an enriching bike ride or walk to work. Or you may shed years of accumulated clothes to make room for climb-critical garments for doing the things that matter. Like some people, if you really get on a roll, you may decide to downsize your home in order to upsize your Life Worth—and spend your time and money on more meaningful things, which might include travel, education, doing good works, or something else more enriching.

PACK CHECK

Before every ascent, Erik does a methodical pack check to make sure he has what he needs. The Pack Check is our challenge to you. It is your opportunity to come to grips with some tough questions, shed self-imposed drags on your greatness, and pack both light and right. As you work through your Pack Check category by category, we encourage you to take real action on your conclusions. As you do, life gets lighter and more focused. You regain some vital agility and energy to perform your own alchemy with adversity.

PACK CHECK–*STUFF*

What five pieces of stuff, big or small, can you shed in order to most dramatically lighten your load, improve your agility, and strengthen your energy? Pause and imagine shedding those things *now*. Well . . . ? List them.

    Note: It may help you to break your stuff into categories by size (big, medium, and small) or by type (recreational, personal, work, family, etc.).

    On a scale of one to ten, to what extent does all your stuff affect your agility, affect your energy, and help or hinder your greatness? Reflect on all you have. Then circle the number that represents your most truthful response.

Overall, my stuff . . .

completely hurts my agility			neither hinders nor hurts my agility				completely helps my agility	
1	2	3	4	5	6	7	8	9	10

completely saps my energy			neither hinders nor hurts my energy				completely fuels my energy	
1	2	3	4	5	6	7	8	9	10

makes me worse and less			makes me neither better nor worse, less nor more				makes me better and more	
1	2	3	4	5	6	7	8	9	10

suffocates my Life Worth			has no effect upon my Life Worth				maximizes my Life Worth	
1	2	3	4	5	6	7	8	9	10

The one significant change I will make in how I use my money to more directly fund my Life Worth is: _____

_____

_____

The one challenge or adversity I will confront to lighten my burden and increase my Life Worth is: _____

_____

_____

So far, the most important lesson I've learned about *stuff* is: _____

_____

_____

TIME

How we spend our days is, of course, how we spend our lives.
—ANNIE DILLARD

The first category, *stuff*, had to do with how you fill your space and spend your money to help or hinder the three A's. This category, *time*, is about a far more precious resource. It is about how you use your day and spend your life. People who harness adversity have a positive urgency coursing through their veins. Fueled by their latest challenge, they are anxious for the high-octane buzz the next worthy challenge delivers when they take it on, take it in, and convert it into life-enriching lessons and experiences. Being fully alive is addictive. Just as indifference is the enemy of passion, worthless time is the enemy of achieving everyday greatness, and it is the demon of any enterprise. Yet the gravitational pull toward time wasters is perhaps greater than ever.

One of the challenges overweight people face is that they consistently underreport what they consume. On analysis, they are often shocked to learn how many empty calories they actually ingest. The same can be said for those of us who are on the verge of softening our "adversity muscles" through a similar type of delusion. What do you consume during the "off" hours of your day or week? How much of what you watch on TV, surf for on the Web, read, or do is truly nutritious or enriching? What portion of it is simply scintillating, alluring, undeniable mind candy? When you are in the doctor's office, do you pick up *National Geographic* or *Popular Science* to learn something new about the world, or do you grab the slick gossip or fashion rag just to flip through and "kill some time"? Do you spend travel time learning, conversing, playing, singing, pondering, or creating? Or do you knock off the latest pulp fiction, watch mindless DVDs, or thumb-twitch through a video game to up your score? The more time and effort you put into making life numbing, the weaker you become in facing up to adversity, and the tougher it is to embrace adversity's force and harness its vital fuel.

Erik doesn't train for mountains by walking on a treadmill in a climate-controlled gym while watching television. He trains by running, biking, and climbing along trails and rocks, often in tough conditions, so that he can maintain his edge. As Erik's Eastern European counterparts on Mount Vinson demonstrated, you can't pursue only comfort and expect greatness. Sometimes you have to take on the unpleasant. William James said, "Do every day or two something for no other reason than that you would rather not do it." We all have to train for the life we want to live.

Steve Jobs, the legendary CEO of Apple Computer, warned graduates at a recent commencement address, "Your time is limited, so don't let it be wasted living someone else's life." Each day, according to his own account, Jobs wakes up, looks at himself in the bathroom mirror, and asks himself how he would feel about doing what he is about to do with his day, if he knew it was his last. If his answer falls short, he changes his day. He drives his own Life Worth. Everyday greatness is something you must strive for, every day.

So, how do you load up your time with Life Worth? Do you become an "obligation martyr"—filling your life with so many responsibilities that they drain your life force and your Life Worth? Begin with your personal calendar. As you look at the list of things you've scheduled throughout the next month, you may want to take out a piece of paper and answer each of the questions in the following challenge.

THE TIME CHALLENGE

LEVEL ONE CHALLENGE–THE BASICS

- ► Which items on your calendar are most climb-critical? Why?
- ► Which items on your calendar are least enriching? Why?
- ► What are two or three things you could shed from your week that score particularly low on Life Worth, in exchange for something that scores much higher? List them.

LEVEL TWO CHALLENGE–ADVANCED

1. Take out a blank sheet of paper. Set it next to your calendar, and down the left-hand side, list all the different roles you play in life (mother, daughter, sister, boss, coworker, student, community member, volunteer, teacher . . .). Space them out so that you have room to write.
2. Next to each role, write down the thing you already have scheduled for the coming week that will enhance Life Worth most. There may be some blanks.
3. Now, for each role, write down one challenge or adversity you would like to take on to become even more effective in that role.
4. Next to each role, write down one simple thing you will commit to do over the coming week that will enhance Life Worth.

Just as most dieters don't pile junk food into their meal plans, most of us don't intentionally schedule mediocrity into our days. As one student leader aptly put it, "I just love this challenge, because it makes me shift my week from life dearth to Life Worth!" Take on worthy pursuits, build in worthy challenges, and you will increase your overall Life Worth and the three A's.

PACK CHECK—*TIME*

What specific obligations can or should you shed to most dramatically lighten your load, improve your agility, and increase your energy? List two to five items on a separate sheet of paper.

On a scale of one to ten, to what extent do your current obligations affect your agility, affect your energy, and help or hinder your everyday greatness? Reflect on how you spend your time. Then circle the number that represents your most truthful response.

My obligations and time demands . . .

completely hurt my agility			neither hinder nor hurt my agility					completely help my agility	
1	2	3	4	5	6	7	8	9	10

completely sap my energy			neither hinder nor hurt my energy					completely fuel my energy	
1	2	3	4	5	6	7	8	9	10

completely hinder my Life Worth			neither hinder nor hurt my Life Worth					completely help my Life Worth	
1	2	3	4	5	6	7	8	9	10

make me worse and less			make me neither better nor worse, less nor more					make me better and more	
1	2	3	4	5	6	7	8	9	10

The one change I will make in how I use my time to more directly increase my Life Worth is: _____

_____

_____

The one challenge or adversity I will add to my life to increase my Life Worth is: _____

_____

_____

So far, the most important lesson I've learned about my use of *time* is: _____

_____

_____

WORK

I believe you are your work.
Don't trade the stuff of your life, time,
for nothing more than dollars.
That's a rotten bargain.
—RITA MAE BROWN

Work is an excellent opportunity to hone *Adversity Advantage* skills. Most jobs entail adversity, but they are also a major potential source of Life Worth—an opportunity to demonstrate everyday greatness. Your approach to work may mirror and will probably influence the way you live your life outside work.

I know that some jobs can really stink. But if you attack work, any work, with resolve and creativity, you energize yourself and create positive momentum by leaning into the wind. By contrast, if you approach work as dead time, or even as just a source of income, you waste a major opportunity to build your three A's.

Because of its enormous potential for both Life Worth and adversity, work deserves its own compartment, as you load your life. Done wrong, work can be a big drain on Life Worth and energy. The countless adversities you confront at work can consume you to the point where they smother your ability to turn the lead of your life into gold. Done right, work can be among the most enriching facets of your life. But most of us mindlessly accumulate the tasks, obligations, and responsibilities that make up our workday, with little or no thought to Life Worth.

The Adversity Advantage is not about making it through the adversities of your workday. It is about using the adversities of your workday to some genuine advantage. It's also not about how well a job suits your ideal scenario of Life Worth. It is about how effectively you infuse whatever work you do with Life Worth so that you finish your day energized, or used up in a good way. And this is important, since work generally takes place during the sweet spot of life.

Prime Time—The Human Energy Grid

If we define *contributing* as giving more than you take, then we can ask: (1) What are the prime energy years of a contributing person's life? (2) What are the prime energy hours of a contributing person's day? (3) What are the prime energy days of a contributing person's week?

My team at PEAK Learning and I had the opportunity to ask those questions of more than 100,000 employed people across many industries, jobs, and cultures. Their answers? (1) Between the ages of twenty-five and fifty-five. (2) Between seven AM and three PM. (3) Monday through Thursday. These numbers represent over 90 percent of people's answers.

Are you surprised that weekends didn't get a bigger play? I was! There are two main reasons people give for this oddity. First, weekends have become recovery time for most people. They are the time we take our foot off the accelerator, pull out of the fast lane, and ease over to the rest stop. For example, for people practicing some organized religions, the Sabbath—a time for rest, reflection, and spiritual connection—is half the weekend. Second, some people are energized in anticipation of and during their work. Work is a vital outlet for which they are primed to pour forth their natural gifts. Why is work such a big deal? Altogether, the data tell us that the vast majority of us spend the prime energy hours of life at work.

Books have been written on this subject. But there are two main ways to pack your work life lighter and better. One is to infuse your current pursuit with Life Worth; the other is to pick a pursuit that is inherently rich in Life Worth.

> The data tell us that the vast majority of us spend the prime energy hours of life at work.

Elevating the Day Job

The first way to properly load the work compartment of your life is to infuse your current job with more Life Worth. Most jobs can't be classified as overt quests to save the world or transform human life as we know it. Most work is more mundane. In fact, in many ways, the more mundane or lacking in worth a job may be, the greater the opportunity to infuse it with Life Worth. So, while some jobs naturally lend themselves to becoming more purposeful than others, we find that any job can have meaning if you approach it with a little creativity and the right mind-set, and if you are willing to see yourself, not external circumstances, as the primary source of Life Worth. Paul and I each have been inspired when we see people do their work while making Life Worth a priority.

It saddens me greatly when I meet people who feel stuck in unfulfilling jobs, because these jobs are all they know, or because they have to pay the bills. They tell me heart-wrenching tales of how they trade their values and spirits for a paycheck. Yet they *know* there's a better way. Maybe I sound idealistic, but I believe work should improve, not deplete, your Life Worth. Changing jobs may seem like the obvious way to dramatically elevate the Life Worth you generate through your work. But in many cases it may be nobler to reinvent how you do what you currently do to create greater Life Worth.

My neighbor Joe comes to mind. He's one of the hardest-working, straightest-talking guys I know. He spent twenty-five years in the logging industry in central Pennsylvania—a tough way to make a buck—often getting paid to do the wrong thing. Over the years, the easier, more accessible timber had already been cut, while the price of lumber sagged. Higher costs and lower prices really put Joe's family business in a squeeze.

Finding little lucrative work in commercial logging, Joe found people who had inherited tracts of forested property. He was hired to clear-cut their land so that they could sell the timber for whatever price they could get. Prematurely cutting down young trees destroyed the ability of the forest to rejuvenate, but his customers were too motivated by money to care about the long-term effects. As Joe says, "We had to pay the bills. You know? Money decides." He loved the forests, but his job was forcing him to destroy the thing he valued most. Joe's gut would tie in knots, because he knew there was a better way.

Five years ago, Joe decided to move the business to Gilpin County, Colorado, where he continues to log. But now, instead of compromising, he educates and guides people to do it right. Because of clear-cutting, many of Colorado's forests have lost their diversity of life. The same kinds of trees have grown up in the same time period. They tend to crowd each other out, so that none of the trees can get the necessary space and sunlight. On top of that, owing to serious droughts in Colorado's forests, acres of trees have been fatally stricken by mountain pine beetles, which bore holes deep into the trunks of ponderosa and lodgepole pines. Joe told me that the most sustaining factor in a forest is a fire, because it burns away all the small, weak, or diseased trees plagued with pine beetle rot, and allows the healthier trees to grow big and proud. So, he sees himself as the human replacement of the forest fire, removing certain trees so that others can flourish.

Joe also adds to the diversity of the forest by planting a variety of species that will all help each other survive, rather than stunting each other. He has also developed a specialized way to plant the fledgling trees, increasing the odds that they will make it through their first cold winters. With scraps from the trees he cuts down, he builds birdhouses and places them strategically throughout the forest to lure mountain bluebirds and western tanagers, which dine on pine beetles.

Joe has evolved eons beyond the traditional role of a logger. He sees himself as a vital part of the forest, not as a predator. Through his experience facing adversity, he now helps nature reclaim the delicate balance upset by humans, and his example inspires others to treat the forest properly. He creates health, sustainability, and a good life for his family. "I'm just trying to make a difference in life." I've seen firsthand how Joe uses his love and knowledge of the forest to positively affect what's important to him. He's doing a similar job, but in a totally different way, and his Life Worth has dramatically improved. Sometimes you just have to do what you do a little differently.

Instead of working in the stately forests of Colorado, how would you like to stand outdoors in gale-force winds and fog to sell fish? On the central coast of California, a local fishing pier has two seafood shops that present a marked contrast. It's a working pier jutting about one mile into a large, protected bay in the Pacific Ocean. Seals piled three deep bark and loll around on a nearby raft, and seagulls swoop down in hope of the random dropped morsel. Throughout the day small fishing boats unload their modest catches to be cleaned and sold.

On the north side of the pier is a seafood shop with a re-spectable assortment of the day's catch. It has a price list on a white-board outside a window through which you shout your order. More often than not, you have to repeat yourself to make sure the person on the other side, who seems viscerally irritated at being inter-rupted by a customer, acknowledges you with a low grunt before disappearing into the back to search for and package your order. The seafood is fresh; the service is a little rough. It's pretty much what you'd expect from such a joint. Good seafood, reasonable prices, miserable servers. Can't blame them. Who wants to wrap smelly fish all day in that cold, wet fog?

On the opposite side of the pier, about 100 yards away, you will find Winston Lee's open-air seafood shop. The first thing you no-tice is how impeccable his tanks, countertops, and deck are—quite a feat for something under the relentless onslaught of mildew and raw salt air. Regardless of the weather, the crowds, or the time of day, Winston greets each customer with a big, warm smile, and often a song. "I just love what I do," Winston explains. "Good seafood makes everyone happy and healthy. It is the best thing to eat and helps you live a long life. I have the best job in the world. All day, even in the rain, I make people happy with my seafood, because I sell the best seafood anywhere!" On the surface, he performs the same job and service as his competitor. But instead of just bemoan-ing his fate, slapping fish into butcher paper, and sending people on their way, Winston honestly cares about enriching people's lives— through seafood. He works hard to give each customer something extra by offering advice on what is freshest, and on recipes, prepara-tions, combinations, and bargains. His pride, resilience, and sense of mission are contagious, and apparently very good for business. People line up at Winston's humble shack, even though the other seafood shop often has greater variety.

Here's one point. If Winston can turn standing out in the open on a cold, wind-battered pier all day long selling seafood into a quest, then you can pack your own job with more Life Worth. And when you do, everyone wins.

Here's another point. Both jobs involve plenty of adversity. Fog, cold, rude customers, smelly fish, inconsistent quality, undependable fishermen, and thin profit margins can all add up to a pretty tough day. One shop owner is shrunk by adversity, but the other is ennobled by it. One is consumed by adversity. The other consumes it to fuel his day. One is a "realist." The other is an alchemist.

From Paycheck to Reality Check

The second, and more dramatic, way to pack light and right in your work is through job selection. Some people use adversity to directly fuel their Life Worth, even if it means giving up a good solid job and taking on the kind of work many of us could not bear. For Dan Greer, it was the death of three family members that helped awaken him to Life Worth.

After ten years as a software quality-assurance engineer, Dan knew he wanted to do something different, but had no idea what. Then his thirty-two-year-old sister died of breast cancer, leaving behind a husband and two small children. Next Dan's mother died, also of breast cancer; and three months later his father succumbed to alcoholic liver disease. Dan was the primary caregiver for both his parents during their final days, with the help of a local hospice organization. "There were two messages here," he realized. "You're not guaranteed any amount of time. And if you're saying, 'The pay is good. I can retire by fifty,' you have to ask yourself, 'Am I happy while I'm getting there?' " Dan's experience helping his parents taught him the power of doing something deeply important. So he and his wife agreed that it was time for Dan to walk away from the IT industry and take on Life Worth by working full-time with the hospice group. Now, each week he takes home less net worth and more Life Worth than he did in his old job. "I felt that Hospice Partners was where I belonged," Dan said. "I had found my tribe and my mission." Dan's alchemy is turning the dark side of adversity into light.

Other people are able to transform themselves from being rich in assets to becoming rich in the things that count. Here is one of the most extreme but enlightening examples I've ever encountered.

Richard Evanson was a cable network mogul, living the fast life in San Francisco. He cashed out for millions, but found himself miserable, learning firsthand that money doesn't buy meaning. His relationships failed, he developed a drinking problem, and he was on a downward slide. This is not an uncommon theme among people who mistake net worth for Life Worth. Lose the job, prestige, and paycheck? Crash and burn. Then Evanson heard that a remote, barren island was for sale in Fiji. On a whim, he bought the island for $500,000, and spent three years living a hermit's life and getting himself together. Finally, restored and refocused, he reached the point where he was ready to share not only the island but also his vision of the way life can be.

Today, Turtle Island is not only one of the world's most exceptional resorts but also a model society handcrafted from the ground up in every detail to maximize Life Worth for its 2,500 citizens. Evanson, who is called "Big Papa," has planted more than 1 million trees and has made the island self-sufficient: it grows its own food and generates its own energy. He even provides outlets rich in Life Worth for his guests. On a regular basis, Evanson buys and auctions off to guests of Turtle Island all the sea turtles from the fishermen, who otherwise would need to kill and sell them for their valuable shells. The rescued sea turtle's shell is marked with indelible paint—harmless to the turtle, but rendering it worthless to the fisherman. The funds are then dispersed to island residents to help pay for projects critical to them. Evanson's society is based on egalitarianism, contribution, love, kindness, and environmental harmony. He has no throne, and everyone has a seat at the table.

To help better everyone's lot, he funded a learning center, a vocational school, a medical center, and other facilities for his fellow Fijians, free of charge. Why? When he dies, he wants his son and his beloved islanders to say, "He really cared about us." When he was offered $100 million for the island, Evanson said, "I didn't have to think for a moment before saying 'no.' I have learned no amount of money can buy this kind of happiness." Today Turtle Island stands alone as a nearly utopian society—a model of what's possible when people are selfless and are willing to pioneer some possibilities in the face of adversity. Examples this extreme help awaken us to the horizons of alchemy—turning life's adversities into Life Worth.

People like Dan Greer and Richard Evanson intentionally took on more adversity to fuel their Life Worth. Easier was less. Tougher was more. Whether within the constraints of your current work or in the creation of something entirely new, the same principle is likely to apply to you.

PACK CHECK–*WORK*

What adjustments could you make at work to enhance your Life Worth, lighten your load, improve your agility, and strengthen your energy? List two to five.

On a scale of one to ten, to what extent does your current work affect your agility, affect your energy, and help or hinder your everyday greatness? Reflect on your work. Then circle the number that represents your most truthful response.

My work . . .

completely hurts my agility	neither hinders nor hurts my agility	completely helps my agility

1   2   3   4   5   6   7   8   9   10

completely saps my energy			neither hinders nor hurts my energy					completely fuels my energy	
1	2	3	4	5	6	7	8	9	10

completely hinders my Life Worth			neither hinders nor hurts my Life Worth					completely helps my Life Worth	
1	2	3	4	5	6	7	8	9	10

makes me worse and less			makes me neither better nor worse, less nor more					makes me better and more	
1	2	3	4	5	6	7	8	9	10

The one change I will make in my work to improve my Life Worth is: _____

_____

_____

The one challenge or adversity I will add to my work to increase my Life Worth is: _____

_____

_____

So far, the most important lesson I've learned about my *work* is: _____

_____

_____

SELF

Look to your health; and if you have it, praise God,
and value it next to a good conscience; for health is the second blessing
that we mortals are capable of,
—a blessing that money cannot buy.
— IZAAK WALTON

How fast can your car go if the engine is running on half of its cylinders? Likewise, how far can you ascend if you are exhausted, out of shape, spiritually empty, and emotionally spent? What happens to your three A's? Even if you pack your life light and right—with the stuff, obligations, and work that enhance Life Worth, it is still you who has to take on the terrain. Agility, alchemy, and adversity demand your best. You have to treat yourself like a world-class athlete so that you can give your best to everyone else.

Stephen Covey tells us to "sharpen the saw," or invest time in ourselves before our effectiveness slides. If you are not careful, you can become a lopsided martyr to Life Worth by helping others so much that you hurt yourself. According to the implicit law of Life Worth, you can't pour out any more or any better than you take in. Harnessing adversity takes physical, emotional, mental, and spiritual strength. Building and optimizing all four capacities is essential. That's why people driven by Life Worth do not hesitate to schedule time in their day to refuel and rejuvenate. They intuitively understand why they have to constantly elevate their own game in order to elevate those around them. Do a scan of the people you most respect. Chances are that a large proportion of them invest in themselves as the engine of Life Worth for others.

People deprived of Life Worth may work out for short-term or empty reasons such as mere vanity or show. Rather than boost their three A's, they are working out for the superficial compliments they receive from others on their looks, how they fit into a shirt or bathing suit, or how much weight they can lift. But looking great is not the same as being great. Alchemists feed their fuel cells—focusing on the kinds of learning, exercise, meditation, relationships, nutrition, and prayer that rejuvenate them—not just for themselves, but first and foremost for others. We're talking about a father who wakes up at four-thirty AM to swim laps in spite of his fatigue, because he is driven to give 110 percent to his family; or the friend who knows that by suffering well through her adversity she is helping others to do the same with theirs. It's Winston Lee riding his bike to his job selling fish on the pier so that he arrives energized and clearheaded for the adversity of the day, or Dan Greer doing yoga so that he is centered and strong enough to help others through their pain.

It's important that you, as our readers, know how Erik and I attempt to live our message. Erik has climbed the Seven Summits— the highest peaks on each of the seven continents. He has already changed people's perceptions of what's possible. You might argue that his job is done, that his life goal has been achieved. And if he retired, like a professional athlete whose contract is up, who would fault him? Climbing is a tough business. Yet for Erik, climbing is but one way to teach others around the world to be and do more.

Instead of retiring, Erik begins many days at home with a two-hour bike ride up Lookout Mountain with a neighbor who meets him at five-thirty AM at his front door; or by making an intense morning climb with a friend, often a teammate from the Everest expedition, up one of Colorado's "fourteeners" or a nearby rock face. This keeps his body and mind ready for the next big challenge. Importantly, it hones him so that he can tackle the rest of his workday, writing or preparing for his next talk or meeting with a group of schoolchildren. And even though he is one of the top speakers on the corporate circuit, Erik asks more than he tells—the hallmark of a learner. He is constantly expanding his mind through exploration, much as he expands his soul through the humbling and uplifting nature of his craft. Why is Erik so relentless in his evolution? Because giving less than his all to Emma and Ellen, his daughter and wife, as well as to his friends and clients, is utterly unimaginable. And by living his example through deeds rather than words, Erik inspires us all to become better, to become more.

In my own modest way I too wake up each day striving to live what I teach. Some days I fail. But if I am going to coach CEOs on how to use these principles to optimize their businesses and their lives, I must do all I can to model these lessons, as a business owner, researcher, husband, father, son, community member, and more. So at home, I begin almost every day paddle-surfing in the ocean. I join my son or a good friend; we throw our kayak-surfboard hybrids (my sons still surf "old school") into the ocean at the crack of dawn; and we bash through the waves, riding as many as possible during a non-stop hour of aerobic crank, breathtaking natural beauty, and adrenaline-induced fun. With our paddles, we get ten times as many rides as standard surfers. We see the sun rising, the fog moving, and the otters and seals laughing at our antics. It's complete spiritual, emotional, and physical rejuvenation.

On other mornings I run the trails with my dog. I try to really experience the sounds, smells, and beauty of the day. On the road, I make sure I'm the first to hit the workout room before each program, no matter how little sleep I've had. It always pays off. On mornings when I'm weary from long or late travel, I am positively haunted by all the people I have the privilege of affecting through my work, in any form, so I drag my bones out of bed and work the energy flywheel by exercising, ideally outside, to get some spiritual benefit for myself as well.

And if I am going to be any kind of researcher, I have to feed my mind. I can get a little nerdy, but I bring a stack of articles and magazines on every airplane flight, and I absorb as much as possible, cutting out articles and trying to refresh my thinking. Hardly a moment is wasted. Likewise, every moment at an airport when I'm not working, I am in a newsstand thumbing through and picking the next books or magazines to feed my mind with nourishing material. In my hotel room, I keep the TV off, and I read or do research online. I could do much better, but I find that these habits help me stay somewhat current and reasonably sharp.

Life is short. Optimize your Life Worth.

PACK CHECK–*SELF*

What adjustments could you make in the way you treat yourself to enhance your Life Worth, lighten your load, improve your agility, and increase your energy? List two to five.

On a scale of one to ten, to what extent does the way you treat yourself affect your agility, affect your energy, and help or hinder your everyday greatness? Reflect on this. Then circle the number that represents your most truthful response.

The way I treat myself . . .

completely hurts my agility			neither hinders nor hurts my agility					completely helps my agility	
1	2	3	4	5	6	7	8	9	10

completely saps my energy			neither hinders nor hurts my energy					completely fuels my energy	
1	2	3	4	5	6	7	8	9	10

completely hinders my Life Worth			neither hinders nor hurts my Life Worth					completely helps my Life Worth	
1	2	3	4	5	6	7	8	9	10

makes me worse and less			makes me neither better nor worse, less nor more					makes me better and more	
1	2	3	4	5	6	7	8	9	10

The one change I will make in my *self* to improve my Life Worth is: _____

_____

_____

The one challenge or adversity I will add to my week to refuel and increase my Life Worth

is: _____

_____

_____

So far, the most important lesson I've learned about my how I treat my *self* is: _____

_____

_____

THE ADVERSITY ADVANTAGE PACKING LIST

How ironic it would be to let your adversities get in the way of your doing anything to take greater advantage of them! I discovered long ago that it's easy to put down a book, be inspired to action, and then actually do nothing—not because you're a weak or bad person, but because life and its many adversities get in the way.

So I like to make things simple and practical. That's why I have shrunk life down to these four compartments, each with a one-word name. And that's why I created the Adversity Advantage Packing List.

The questions in the Packing List are challenging. They require some real thought. They are designed for you to ask yourself first, and others second. You can use them as a friend, parent, or leader to improve lives and businesses.

Starting with you, you have three choices. (1) You can skim right past this challenge, and do nothing. (2) You can approach it superficially or academically, complete the Packing List, and do nothing. (3) You can take it on! Our advice is to pause, reflect, and dig deep to unearth some real life-enhancing answers that you will act on to improve your three A's and fuel your everyday greatness.

THE ADVERSITY ADVANTAGE PACKING LIST

The point of this exercise is to focus on something you can do now and as an ongoing process to help you pack light and pack right so you can optimize your three A's—agility, alchemy, and adversity.

Packing light and right is not just about shedding unnecessary weight, although each Pack Check helped you lighten your load. Packing is also about strategically adding those things that are most climb-critical.

STUFF

As you think about everything you own, what item or items could you purchase or add that would improve your three A's?

Example: We have one client whose face lights up when he describes how he and his wife keep their new, convertible backpack-style overnight bag packed at all times, so if anything unexpected hits, they know where to go, and can leave at a moment's notice. This makes them more agile, so while everyone else scrambles, they are already under way. They also use it for spontaneous getaways. Their pack symbolizes their agility for taking on life.

TIME

What is a new obligation, or something you will add to your schedule to improve your three A's?

Example: As of six months ago, a dear friend runs stairs three times per week (indoors and outdoors). Now her children (who are twelve and fourteen years old) run with her. Not only does running improve her fitness and energy, she says, but whether catching a train, beating a traffic light, or leaving a burning building, there are moments in life when you have to run to make it. She wants to make sure they make it. To her that's part of everyday greatness.

WORK
What will you add to your work to make it richer in Life Worth?

Example: Natalie is a self-funded, full-time student, working at two part-time jobs, just to make ends meet. Her jobs pay the bills, but she discovered that the light of her otherwise insane week was being a Big Sister to an eight-year-old girl. So now she brings her little sister to work with her at her job at the University Center information desk four hours per week, where the girl is a big hit with the students and faculty. Her little sister loves being "picked up for work."

SELF
What will you add to your life to optimize your energy, your outlook, and the three A's?

Example: Peter is a design consultant and father of three who works out of his home. His day starts at five forty-five AM and often goes past ten thirty each night. His multiple roles as husband, professional, parent, community member, and son to elderly parents often leave him wiped out at the end of the day. As a result he sometimes finds himself short-tempered and humorless. Peter now sets his alarm for five fifteen, adding thirty minutes to jog with his dog a few miles around the park and local neighborhood before the world wakes up. He starts each day fired up and ready for the onslaught.

"Wouldn't it be nice?" is one of the most common responses to any prescription that can make us better. "Sounds great. I really should do that, but wouldn't it be nice if I had the time (energy, capacity . . .)?" "Wouldn't it be nice if my boss (spouse, kids, teachers, team . . .) gave me permission and space to do these kinds of things?"

I encourage you to ask a different question: Won't it be great?

Won't it be great when you begin to apply these principles and practices to your own life? Won't it be great to help your organization or team rethink what they bring along whenever they take on anything tough or worthwhile? Won't it be great to feel yourself become more focused and effective, as you do these things to pack light and pack right, to improve your three A's and develop the kind of everyday greatness that enriches you, those around you, and your organization?

Life is simply too short and too precious to load it down with anything or anyone who depletes our potential to become and do our best. As a father, husband, community member, and business owner, I recognize that it is actually my moral obligation to keep myself as honed as possible so I can have the greatest impact on the areas that truly matter to me—and this includes helping other people increase their own Life Worth. The success of every ascent I attempt is largely determined by how effectively my team and I pack and prepare in these same four life compartments: stuff, time, work, and self. Slowly, and learning from many mistakes, I have developed the capacity to make the tough choices needed. You can too.

As a climber, I can't imagine a place where the consequences of those choices are more apparent than on a vertical wall of rock and ice; and as I've gained more experience, this is where I'm increasingly putting my efforts. These big technical faces are exciting and challenging. If there is to be a chance for success, everything has to go perfectly: ultimate efficiency between team members, stable weather, and every ounce of gear measured precisely and serving a critical purpose. On Vinson, we carried our houses on our backs, but it's a step up to carry your house while climbing a vertical face.

The second reason why these faces appeal to me more now has little to do with climbing. With a family, it feels wrong to be away for the months that are needed to climb major high-altitude peaks. By climbing steep, technically demanding faces in places like Canada and Europe, I can be home in just a couple of weeks. It's a nice balance between the sport I love a lot and the people I love most.

Until about thirty years ago, climbers lacked the knowledge and techniques to make quick, safe ascents of these faces. So they resigned themselves to a style called "siege climbing," in which they inched their way up the face, anchoring permanent ropes to the wall, foot by foot, pitch by pitch, until they reached the top. By the end, they'd have ropes running from top to bottom. This allowed them to summit while never losing their toehold to the ground. The problem was that these attempts would take months of effort; massive resources; and a huge, unwieldy team.

But a few pioneers, equipped with some new tools and a new mind-set, and tired of the constraints of siege tactics, saw a different way forward. They called it "Alpine climbing." In this style, climbers wait for a stretch of good weather, and, with everything they need on their backs, commit themselves to an all-out push to the summit. In just a few days, a small team of climbers can accomplish what previously took a month and a small army. One by one, the world's great faces have been knocked off in Alpine-style, defying conventional wisdom and expanding expectations about what's achievable. Because of the increased level of commitment and the difficult choices it forces climbers to make, I consider Alpine-style climbing to be more true, more pure, and ultimately more rewarding when the summit is finally reached.

Currently, I have my sights set on the ultimate Alpine-style adventure, the north face of the Eiger, 6,000 vertical feet. This is one of Europe's most notorious climbs. Putting it in perspective, the Eiger north face has seen fewer ascents than Mount Everest. For me, making it to the top will be like bringing the concept of pack light, pack right to a whole new stratosphere.

Alpine-style climbing is definitely the way to go, but to do it effectively takes commitment, discipline, and courage. So the ultimate question of this chapter is this. Like the other alchemists we've met, are you willing to forgo your safety net and go Alpine-style through life, to give up the stuff that weighs you down so that you can have the greatest impact on your life and the people in it? Paul and I believe the answer should be a resounding "yes."

When we make difficult choices, deciding on a direction and eliminating the extraneous, there will always be sacrifice and plenty of suffering along the way. If you believe strongly enough in your climb, however, it is actually possible to embrace the hardships and be strengthened by them. That's exactly what Summit Six, Suffer Well, is all about.

SUMMIT FIVE—PACK LIGHT, PACK RIGHT

GUIDING PRINCIPLE

What you pack into your life and organization can help or hinder your three A's—alchemy, agility, and effectiveness with adversity. In order to take advantage of the adversities that come your way, you have to Pack Light, Pack Right.

Stuff

- We have more choices and stuff today than at any time in history.
- More can be less—the more we accumulate, the more it can weigh us down, killing our agility.
- Life Worth is the value you get from and give to life. The key to long-term happiness is to use your net worth (funds) to optimize your Life Worth.
- Spring-cleaning your stuff to keep only what is "climb-critical" can lighten your load and strengthen your focus.

Time

Many people become martyrs to obligation, packing so many "requirements" into their day and month that they cannot focus on the things that really matter. It's also easy to be tempted by the things that provide immediate excitement or rush, rather than the things that provide long-term benefits.

Work

For most people, the prime energy hours of life are spent at work. Dedicating them to something that enhances Life Worth is essential. You can enhance Life Worth at work by reinventing not just what you do, but how you do it.

Self

People who remain agile and effective with adversity find creative ways to keep their energy flywheel moving by resisting easy temptations to feed their bodies, minds, and souls empty "calories," and by focusing on enriching, nutritious fuel. Small investments yield dramatic results.

SUFFER WELL

MOUNT KOSCIUSKO
Summit: 7,310 feet–tallest peak in Australia

> I cannot imagine a fate more awful–a fate worse than death–
> than a life lived in perfect harmony and balance.
>
> –CARL JUNG

The question in life is not whether you will ever have to suffer. Rather, it is this: When you do suffer, how will you suffer? Will you suffer poorly, or will you Suffer Well? As with the tougher forms of adversity, you probably don't crave or actively seek opportunities to suffer. In fact, the very thought of suffering may feel unbearable and make you want to slam this book shut.

However, it turns out that suffering can be the highest-octane fuel for greatness. Suffering has been the focus of all major philosophers and religions. Confucius, Kant, Nietzsche, and Sartre, among countless others, weave pain and suffering as essential strands in the human condition. The Bible, the Torah, the Koran, and the Book of Mormon are all filled with stories and lessons of suffering as a means to a higher plane of awareness and spirituality. Buddhists use fasting, or denying the body its natural needs, as a pathway to greater purity, peace, and enlightenment.

Suffering is also one of the main and most consistent themes of the great books. When I was a teacher, we discussed classics like Homer's *Iliad* and *Odyssey* as well as Virgil's *Aeneid.* They are filled with stories of heroic people who must endure unspeakable pain, loss, and disillusionment in order to lead, rise above disaster, and emerge victorious. What is the Book of Job in the Old Testament about, if not a test of suffering? What would we know about the human spirit and its capacity to endure if Miguel de Cervantes and Shakespeare had not written so eloquently of Don Quixote and Hamlet? Which books would still be "great" if they were stripped of the cathartic theme of human suffering as a means to clarity, character, strength, faith, and advancement?

As an alchemist, you can convert suffering into meaning and beauty, elevating everyone within range of its force. Perhaps there is no everyday example of alchemy that can transcend childbirth. Before my wife, Ellie, gave birth to our daughter, I had a secret opinion that men were the tougher sex; but after witnessing Ellie endure hours of labor with dignity and calm, I no longer have a shred of doubt which sex is tougher. Her most protracted and agonizing pain resulted in a breathtaking, heart-lifting miracle.

If you've ever been close to anyone who has really suffered, it may seem insensitive to suggest that there are good and bad ways to suffer. After all, people facing hardship may be doing the best they can. But this book is not about them as much as it is about you. In business and in life, there is ample opportunity to suffer. Summit Six will take on the difficult topic of suffering and, from my experiences and Paul's, give you our best ideas about what it takes for you to Suffer Well.

You may be wondering why I chose the easiest of the Seven Summits as the opening for this particular subject. The real work of Everest and McKinley, as well as four other summits, was behind us. In my opinion, Kosciusko's summit was only a ceremonial finish line. When I told a local Aussi of our plans, he responded, "Ah! Lovely Kosciusko! Not so much a climb as a stroll really. I did it with my dog last summer." As soon as I finished, there were hours of interviews planned over a satellite feed to news programs around the world. We even had a bottle of champagne for a celebratory toast at the summit, but it seems that whenever you finally let up and assume something will be easy, life presents you with a reminder that it's all about transforming adversity.

From the moment we arrived at Kosciusko, during the Australian spring, a series of huge low-pressure systems, half the size of the continent, repeatedly dumped snow over the mountain. The winds near the top roared at eighty miles per hour. After waiting five days for the weather to clear, and with no improvement in sight, we made the decision to go for it. What match would little Kosciusko be against hardened mountaineers, who had gutted it out on the tallest mountains in the world?

Only half an hour out of the parking lot, as the howling wind roared down the slopes and drove hard bullets of ice directly into our faces, I already began questioning the wisdom of continuing. One of my teammates was actually lifted up by the wind and sent sliding 100 yards down the snow slope. When he waved up at us, and we knew he wasn't hurt, we all let out a relieved laugh.

It seemed as if the winds had focused their attention on our team, because next I was struck by a tremendous gust. The wind flung me back into Eric, who was right behind me, and we both went down in a pile. We were a tangled heap of arms and legs as we slid twenty feet down the hard-packed slope before Eric managed to dig in his ice ax and stop us. Back on our feet and working our way upward again, we were learning a new definition of suffering and had the bruises and windburn to show for it.

As we got above tree line, we were faced with an indistinct wind-scoured landscape, made even more disorienting by the blizzard. Jeff took the lead and had to navigate with a compass; and for three hours, we wandered around through the whiteout looking for the actual summit.

Finally, after trudging up a last snow face, with the wind fighting us at every step, Jeff described to me the truck-size boulder layered in ice that signified my seventh summit. It took four of us holding tightly to our banner to pull it out of my pack and raise it for a few summit shots, as the wind tried to rip it away. Then, still sticking stubbornly to our summit celebration, we popped open the champagne. The cork sailed away, zinging, I assume, past all seven continents on its way downward. As I took a drink, the wind tipped the neck of the bottle forward, caught the liquid, and plastered half the contents across my face and my Gore-tex suit. The irony wasn't lost on us; this summit, typically host to T-shirt clad tourists, young children, and dogs, was doing its best to blow us off the mountain. In fact, of my Seven Summits, little Kosciusko's brutal winds topped them all. Nothing else was even close.

In hindsight, I know that had we confronted this kind of adversity on our first summit, it might have beaten me down and sapped my will to the point that I would never even have attempted the other summits. But by the time we reached Kosciusko, I knew that suffering was not only absolutely unavoidable but also, I'd argue, necessary. It's not that I'm a masochist who looks forward to being tested; but the immense suffering I had experienced in the mountains and beyond was like eating a well-balanced meal. The cake might induce euphoria, but the broccoli and carrots, although hard to swallow, fortify and sustain us. Suffering gives our lives depth; without it, our summits would feel meaningless. On Kosciusko, shivering behind a boulder, all I could do was laugh. For that matter, we must have all looked like lunatics, covered with frozen champagne and braced together against the hurricane-force gale as we howled with laughter. Suffering, with all its awful significance, had been beaten into my lexicon of adversity.

On the way up Kosciusko, as on the other Seven Summits, the wind had been an impediment, driving us back; but as I clipped into skis and headed down, I realized that instead of working against us, the wind might actually work for us. The gale now blew at our backs, and we used its energy as we use adversity itself, to propel us forward. It was a wild ride.

Character cannot be developed in ease and quiet.
Only through experience of trial and suffering can the soul be strengthened,
vision cleared, ambition inspired, and success achieved.
— HELEN KELLER

In business, suffering well means putting up with political backbiting, naysayers, long hours, rejection, uncertainty, constraints on resources, downturns, and drudgery in the name of a higher cause or a worthy breakthrough. It means doing whatever is necessary to make things right, when the gravitational pull is toward watching them go wrong. It means getting pierced in the back by a sheath full of arrows, taking on sacred cows, putting up with unbearable assignments, embracing impossible deadlines, enduring mindless meetings, and suffocating amid incompetence, but sticking to a vision no one else yet embraces. It means paying a price others may be unwilling to pay to achieve a goal others may be unable to reach. It means facing up to the hardships inherent in anything significant, and taking on a task together, not with the hollow words, "Good luck, team," but rather with the meatier blessing, "Suffer well!" Live these words, and greatness will emerge.

Suffering well means suckling on the rich nutrients of life's bitter defeats, and emerging more powerful, formidable, and focused as a result. Or, if you are on the downslide, suffering well means using the hardships of your reduced capacity as an impetus to shift your focus from yourself to others. It means feasting on fear and failure, leaving them behind as desiccated remains of battles hardfought and well won. Suffering well means applying "positive pessimism" to weather even the most dismal days, and to lead others through dark times.

Abraham Lincoln is considered one of the great American presidents, who took on and endured one of the most difficult chapters in American history. Experts throughout history have remarked admiringly on the situations Lincoln had to endure, and the adversities and setbacks he overcame to achieve his goals. Yet, arguably, it was the war within Lincoln—his internal suffering—that fed his greatness.

Lincoln was torn between a driving ambition that made him a born achiever and a debilitating depression that made him question his desire to live. His relationship with pain and tragedy began in his childhood and continued throughout his life. His father was harsh, rejecting, and physically abusive, treating Abraham like a possession he could throw around. He refused Abraham an education. Biographers describe Lincoln as "tall, gangly, ugly," and "ignorant."

By the age of ten, Lincoln had experienced and witnessed the deaths of his mother, adoptive grandparents, and infant brother. When Lincoln lost his great love, Ann Rutledge, to typhoid fever, he was so depressed that his friends kept a suicide watch for days, and he remained in deep despair for months.

Like a silent demon, Lincoln's despair would invade his dreams, and torment his soul, throughout his presidency. But by all accounts, Lincoln's suffering fed his deep empathy and compassion for the suffering of others. His own troubles were so deep that he could not bear the unjustly imposed troubles of others. Arguably, this attitude fueled his quest to right some deeper wrongs in the world and inspire a better history for all. His last speech advocated voting rights for blacks, because Lincoln had an uncanny ability to understand and therefore address their suffering.

To suffer well is to use hardship to transcend ego, so that you get out of your own way in doing what needs to be done with your life. It means coming to grips with lost opportunities to have suffered better, and thinking proactively about impending opportunities to suffer more strongly next time. To suffer well is to marinate in pain rather than anesthetize yourself against it. To suffer well is to forge your character and harden your resolve in a white-hot flame, rather than shield yourself from its searing heat.

To suffer well is to be the alchemist who converts pain and hardship into momentum and life force. Suffering well means committing yourself to enrich those closest to you with the pure ore of your deepest strengths, when it matters most. To suffer well is to distill and perhaps share the meaning from each difficulty. In short, to suffer well is one of the most noble and important things we can do in life.

It is not enough to simply grasp the concept of suffering well—
to say, "OK. I get it. When life gets brutal I've got to shine with optimism and strength." Words disappear readily in harsh winds. And
paint-job optimism cracks under the pressure of pain. We need
weather-tested tools that we can grab and use when hardship hits.
At this point you need:

1. A good working definition of suffering.
2. A description of the Common Cracks and Chasms that people
    stumble into when they suffer, so you can avoid them.
3. A good grasp of the types of suffering.
4. Your first Suffer Check—a way to turn into the storm and come
    to grips with the nature and magnitude of your own, or others',
    suffering.
5. Ways to become a positive pessimist so that you may more
    effectively mix humor and reality.
6. Clarity on the difference between suffering poorly and suffering
    well.
7. The Suffer Well—a tool that master sufferers can use to become
    alchemists and turn adversity into profound advantage.

SUFFERING DEFINED

Before you consider my biased words on a subject of such gravity and sensitivity, you may want to consider that during the
past twenty years and more, when I have been out in the world
researching, teaching, and conversing about the human relationship with adversity, I have heard the most extraordinary and ordi-
nary tales of human suffering. Some are tragic. Many, like Erik's,
are deeply inspiring. Over time, I discovered some common themes
and lessons.

To suffer is to *endure something painful*. And, as with adversity, the more something matters to you, the more painful it may be. Suffering is also relative. A single mother of two struggling at a minimum-wage job who loses a twenty-dollar bill may genuinely suffer, while a millionaire who drops a few hundred dollars in a poker game may merely smile at the loss. A child with a splinter in one hand may cry out in anguish, but a soldier with a leg full of shrapnel may weep with relief over surviving such a close call. Suffering is sometimes determined by duration. Suffering usually implies chronic or protracted discomfort. If something terrible passes quickly, we don't usually apply the word *suffer*. And suffering usually implies pain of some depth or severity. If something is a mild discomfort, like a slightly chilly room, we don't usually think of the word *suffer*, unless we're being melodramatic. However, being forced to endure a weeklong mountain blizzard without supplies is more likely to involve real suffering.

The power of suffering is its ability to *strip* away superficialities, ego, and distractions. Actually, STRIP is an acronym, because, in short, the factors that make up suffering are:

▸ Severity—the magnitude of the pain.
▸ Time—how long you must endure the pain.
▸ Relativity—how severe your pain is when you are compared with those around you and your situation is compared with your own past or other hardships.
▸ Importance—how much the thing for which you are suffering matters.
▸ Price—how much you may or will lose as a result of the adversity.

The unique way suffering can STRIP you down to your essential self can be both freeing and powerful. Suffering can both require and generate energy. Together these five factors determine whether or not you suffer, and the degree to which you suffer.

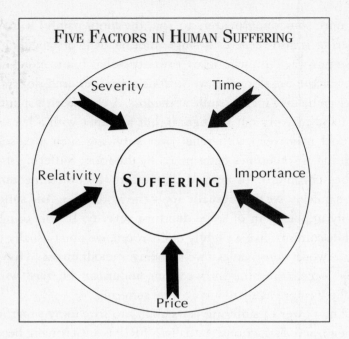

FIVE FACTORS IN HUMAN SUFFERING

Severity   Time

Relativity   SUFFERING   Importance

Price

TEN COMMON CRACKS AND CHASMS

After visiting the United States, Mother Teresa said that "the poorest place in the world is not Calcutta, it is here, since although you have everything, you have nothing." Although you might argue against her conclusion, Mother Teresa's point has merit. Throughout my travels I have discovered that some of the poorest people, for whom suffering is a constant state, can be the most generous and joyful. And I have seen people who live entirely insulated from adversity but who suffer in ways that hobble the happiness of anyone within reach. Suffering can make us richer. Failure to suffer well can leave us impoverished.

We couldn't do justice to the subject of suffering without pointing out the very common, entirely human cracks and chasms we all at some point stumble into. One might just as easily label these "coping mechanisms." Call them what you will, but if they are done too well or too often, they hinder your ability to suffer well. Besides, the purpose of this book is not to coddle you. It is to *strengthen* you. So review these mechanisms with that purpose in mind.

1. Whining

When is the last time you heard someone say, "You know, I really like that person; he (or she) is always whining"? Most people despise whining, especially coming from someone else. Whining immediately brings to mind a tired child tugging on the arm of a bedraggled parent at the local amusement park, pleading for a treat or "One more ride. Puhleeeeze? Come on, just one more? We *never* go on the big rides enough. Puhleeeeze?"

Why is whining so irritating? Maybe it's the tone of voice, which is typically feeble, pleading, high, and pathetic. Or maybe it's a perceived lack of merit in the whiner's case. If the child has been treated to a fun-filled day, begging pathetically for one more ride comes off as selfish and unfair. So, when the leaders of our client organizations say, "There's an awful lot of whining going on right now," they are implying that, from their perspective, people's complaints are out of line with what's being asked of them. To the intended receiver, there is a huge difference between expressing legitimate concerns and whining. Whining also implies inaction. When people whine, they are, at best, venting rather than acting.

But isn't suffering the perfect excuse to let fly and finally whine? Sure—again, who can blame you? Think about the big stuff. Your beloved spouse has just dropped a bomb, informing you that he or she is having an affair, switching sexual orientation, clearing out the bank account, and leaving you forever. Then your best friend stops by, asking innocently, "So, what's going on with you?" Chances are you'd let fly. Then there's the smaller stuff, to which whining really applies. The line at the grocery store was unbearable, the gas pump was shut down, you got a parking ticket downtown, and your phone company put you on hold for what seemed like a lifetime. Time to whine. Or, maybe not. Maybe you'd rather do something slightly more constructive, like complain.

2. Complaining

To complain is to express unhappiness about something. Complaining gets a bad rap. But saying we can't ever complain is like saying we shouldn't be honest. Sometimes we need to express our unhappiness about something in order to come to grips with it and get past it. So complaining has a potential purpose, even an upside.

The problem with complaining is that, overdone, it makes us weak. It doesn't tend to hone our determination. Worse, complaining can be highly contagious. Complaining begets complaining. And, like whiners, complainers draw complainers. Let loose on all the things you're unhappy about at school, at work, or at home, and you've invited everyone else to do the same. Chances are people won't leave a team complaint session energized and exuberant. Instead, they will leave depressed and deflated. In other words, rather than using our suffering to make us more, complaining makes us less. Complaints are like relational cockroaches. They're everywhere, but no one enters a room hoping to encounter one. We could go on and on about complaining, but if we did we'd be, well, complaining.

3. Blaming

For decades there has been a school of psychological research indicating that in order to stay intact when something bad happens, you should never blame yourself. Blame others. By externalizing bad events, you preserve your self-concept. There's one slight problem here, or maybe several problems. When we blame others, we give up control. If someone else is the cause, it's within someone else's power, not ours, to fix the situation.

When we blame, we also miss out on a vital piece of our own development. In my first book, I addressed the role of shame and guilt in forging one's character and modifying one's behavior. I also explained the virtue in blaming oneself appropriately—one learns from one's mistakes and then moves on. In short, if we don't own our actions, decisions, consequences, and fate, we can't do anything about them, and we rob ourselves of the wisdom and humility required to suffer well. It's really Erik's fault that we even added blaming to the list.

4. Identifying

Identifying is what happens when we become one with our suffering, in a bad way. As in an abusive relationship, we can get too close to our suffering, making it hard to leave. This is what happens when a cancer patient unconsciously comes to need his or her cancer, since it has become the source of long overdue attention and love. It's what happens when we internally label ourselves according to our suffering: "the guy who went bankrupt," "the A student who flunked," "the friend who can't commit to a relationship and always dines alone," "the woman with one arm," "the man with the scarred face," "that guy with the terrible migraines," "that woman who lost her kid in a terrible accident."

Identifying can come from within ourselves or from others, or both. As we've just noted, it often sounds like labels. "Widower," "cancer survivor," "recovering alcoholic," "manic-depressive," and "disabled person" are all identifiers, among countless others. These labels can be beneficial: they provide a sort of shorthand for understanding another person's condition; and they also provide a sense of belonging with others who share a similar label, as in support groups. The problem arises when the labels move from descriptions to *definitions*. I can't pretend to know what some people suffer. But I do know that a former business colleague dampened countless potentially wonderful relationships by beginning each opinion with, "As a victim of physical abuse . . ." or "As an abuse victim . . ." It was her identity. I saw a similar distancing effect with a manager who labeled himself a "depressive." Isn't it interesting to notice how much more final that sounds than saying, "I have had episodes of depression"? You can hear the E, or endurance dimension, of his AQ working against him because he has adopted that identity. He privately confessed to me that he loved the company holiday party but never attended it because he once read that people are "uncomfortable around depressives." My heart went out to him as I imagined all the other opportunities he denied himself as a result of his self-imposed identity.

Defining ourselves and others by labels is extremely limiting. To define Erik as "the blind guy who climbed Everest" is to completely ignore the successful man, husband, father, son, speaker, charitable leader, and businessman who also happens to be blind.

By identifying too closely with our suffering and its related label, we may fail to evolve through that suffering, and we rob others of the chance to do the same. All this talk about suffering is enough to make one numb!

5. Anesthetizing

One of the most socially acceptable chasms we slide into when we face suffering is anesthetizing. Immediately, if not constantly, we anesthetize ourselves against the hurt. Sometimes it's as straightforward as swapping pills for pain. At other times, we numb ourselves in more insidious and complex ways.

An unbearable home life or an excrutiating divorce is so often—consciously or unconsciously—numbed by a workaholic lifestyle. I see a disconcerting number of executives who rely more and more on the adrenal rush of their day jobs as a way to offset harsh realities at home.

Likewise, I see people of all ages anesthetizing themselves against the real and mounting hardships of school or work through a variety of readily available numbing devices. The market for creative anesthesia seems to know no bounds. These devices range from the technical to the chemical and biological. Technology offers immediate sedation through television, the Internet, video games, and more. Likewise, the chemical options continue to expand. While they are used for escaping (see number six, below), recreational drugs, alcohol, and medications are also commonly sought as anesthesia. People use these and other creative methods to reduce or remove the actual sensation of pain, whatever form it may take. If we can't feel it, we don't have to deal with it. The problem is that if we don't deal with it, we can't use it to make ourselves and others better. If we anesthetize ourselves, we can't suffer well. This is one reality we cannot escape.

6. Escaping

"You can run, but you can't hide" is the warning label that should accompany all suffering. Suffering is like a heat-seeking missile. The point is that no matter how far you run, or how creatively you hide from your pain, its lessons and impact will somehow find you, often when you least expect them.

Postponing and its sibling, procrastinating, are forms of escaping. A woman we met whose sister had drowned in a tragic accident explained it in eerily accepting terms, just weeks after her loss. Then one day, two years later, in the middle of the children's section of a local department store, she heard her sister's favorite childhood song, which suddenly triggered racking sobs. The guy sitting next to me on the airplane fifteen minutes before I wrote this told me how his boss told his entire team to prepare for another reorganization. But he said, "We were all so reorg-weary that we kinda gave up. We believed that by doing our jobs well and waiting things out, we'd escape the ax. But we didn't, and people are devastated."

We escape by trying to outrun adversity. I see businesses trying to hide their fatal flaws in more and more aggressive growth, but the truth always catches up. One business had significant flaws in its new "flagship technology," but rather than fix the problem, it burned through dozens of overcompensated sales mercenaries who were paid to close orders, and let the nightmares rain down on tech support. I watched in fascination as its stock soared and then plummeted like a pent-up avalanche. It saddened me deeply when I heard of a senior executive who mimicked some of her peers' poor choices by engaging in a series of extramarital affairs, momentarily escaping her crumbling home life and her isolation.

The truth is, to repeat, that you can run but you cannot hide. Escaping often induces suffering. And the vast majority of suffering is unnecessary. That twists my guts. But these stories are common. And sure, it is normal and understandable to postpone or escape hardship. But it is more powerful and courageous to enter the storm, embrace the hardship, and harness its cleansing force. Sometimes we have to let adversity sandblast our souls.

People are boundlessly creative in inventing new ways to escape their suffering. But rather than letting suffering find you, you gain far more power by finding it and harnessing it to your advantage. Maybe we're just rationalizing.

7. Rationalizing

"A person's strengths, overextended, can become weaknesses." This adage applies to us all. The human capacity to explain why we do what we do is nearly boundless. The good news is that this is how we make sense of the world. The bad news is that if we get too good at it, we can explain or rationalize almost anything, especially suffering poorly.

One of Erik's colleagues recently said, "I imagine you must just possess some superhuman gene for suffering. I know for sure that I don't, so I could never deal with the kind of pain you do, or accomplish the kinds of things you accomplish. You're obviously some sort of genetic aberration" (a nice term for "freak").

Erik responded by gently pointing out, "Actually, I'm just like you. I hurt, doubt, suffer, and cry. Whatever capacity for suffering you think I have is really the long-term result of the decisions I've made and the challenges I've chosen to take on. There's nothing I'm doing in my way that you could not do the equivalent of in your way. That's the whole point of my message, to shatter people's perceptions of what's possible."

Rationalizing is healthy when it helps us make sense of our lives and come to grips with the compromises we may have made to get here or there. It's unhealthy when we reason ourselves out of what's possible, including our ability to use our suffering to become better people and teach others how to take it on. Admit it. You can't deny it.

8. Denying

In contrast to anesthesizing, or numbing pain, *denying* is refusing to acknowledge its existence. If we refuse to acknowledge that adversity exists, we don't have to deal with it. So, the temptation to deny is potentially immense. It's easier to deny that your credit card is overloaded, or that you spend way more than you earn, than it is to shore up the discipline to set things right. It is more fun to delude yourself that your job (life, marriage, family, health) is going great than it is to shine a bright light on the situation and do the work necessary to repair the cracks.

Culture plays a powerful role in our relationship with suffering.

Some cultures (such as Italian, Jewish, and Middle Eastern) are more comfortable with what others would consider histrionics and the baring of one's soul. To people of these cultures this is normal, honest, and healthy. Others (such as Scandinavians and Asians) would consider such displays and conversations about one's pain and suffering to be inappropriate at best, believing instead that one should suffer with quiet dignity.

The mistake we make is applying our cultural lens to other people's behavior. If we see people who never speak of their suffering, we may assume that they are denying it exists. On the other hand, if we see people who speak openly and emotionally about their suffering, we may assume that they are "milking it" to get attention. In both cases, we may easily be mistaken.

Denial is not a judgment. It is a relationship. It happens when we fail to completely accept the full magnitude of our suffering, the resulting consequences, or the severity of the source. And while denial protects us, it also denies us the tremendous power and opportunity of our suffering. Denial falls under the category of "avoiding adversity" on the Adversity Continuum.

There's no use pretending that denial isn't real.

9. Pretending

While denial is a refusal to accept what is real, pretending is acting as though what we know exists does not exist. Pretending is acting. It implies a falsehood—we are projecting a perception that contrasts with what we know to be true. Like the other chasms we slide into when we suffer, pretending can serve a positive purpose. Much research has supported the notion that smiling, even when we least feel like it, can create positive changes within our bodies. We're taught, "Fake it till you make it" and "Don't let 'em see ya sweat." What's the moral? We're taught that even when you're miserable, you should pretend you're not. *The Art of War* by Sun

Tzu teaches us that all war is based on deception. Those who deceive best win. And the inducement to deceive can be enormous. When you know that pretending that a given project is "going just great" will calm the boss, when in fact the project is in trouble, one could advocate pretending as an effective strategy. It buys you time, and it keeps the boss out of your face. But pretending, like all forms of deception, while human and common, eventually spawns mistrust. What happens when the boss finds out the truth? How likely is he or she to believe your next status report? When you pretend to your family that everything is financially solid when it is not, how long will it take until you are found out, and what lessons will this situation teach? Everyday greatness implies making tough choices. Deception elevates no one. Being an alchemist elevates us.

Pretending goes awry when it becomes a barrier between others and our suffering. If we get too good at pretending, we deny others the lessons and experience our suffering can offer them. It holds our loved ones at a distance when their closeness and connection are most important. And since pretending can go both ways, when others pretend our suffering is not real or does not exist, they deny us the opportunity to suffer well. Pretending is natural, but it can backfire. There's just no use whitewashing the truth.

10. Whitewashing

Almost everyone at some time or another engages in a more subtle form of pretending—whitewashing. We embellish when we make something more than it is. When you say that a good regional school is "one of the top ten schools in the state," you are embellishing on the fact, which is that the school is highly regarded. Today, job applicants' embellishing of their résumés has become a widespread concern.

We whitewash when we try to make something look better than

it is, by prettying it up a bit. Whitewashing can be endearing. Every time a woman uses a little extra makeup on a day when she is a little under the weather, she is whitewashing. When I quickly shove the obvious dog hair under the rug before my bride comes home, I'm whitewashing. Likewise, whenever we minimize or reframe a bad event, we may be whitewashing a bit. One might argue that public relations, marketing, and politics are careers based on expertise in whitewashing. When these services are done right, we accept and even demand them. There are times we want or need to see the better side of a situation. And let's face it, whitewashing beats the heck out of catastrophizing.

As with the other cracks and chasms, whitewashing loses its endearing quality when it merely hides and keeps us from experiencing what's real. A good friend whose mother is suffering from breast cancer explains her frustration: "Every time I call, my mother tells me she's doing fine, getting along OK, and not worrying too much. She never tells me how scared she feels, or what the doctors really say about her situation. I sense she is using positive thinking to whitewash the truth. Here she is, going through the biggest challenge of her life, and I've never felt so distant. It's like she's put a veil over the whole thing. And it's driving me nuts!"

When you review the ten Cracks and Chasms, keep these principles in mind:

- It is human nature to use these.
- To a point, most can be used positively and for good reasons.
- Overused, all become destructive.
- These are often used with the best of intentions.
- We *all* use them.
- If abused, they prevent us from suffering well.

TYPES OF SUFFERING

Like joy, adversity comes in all shapes, sizes, and durations. Some adversities, like a car accident or a stock market crash, are highly defined, with potentially enduring effects. Others, like the loss of a job or a loved one, can be instant and severe. Adversities such as ill health, drifting friendships, a dying marriage, and boring work may be gradual, amorphous, and vague. Suffering can also be voluntary or involuntary—a distinction that is not always easily judged.

Every time people run a marathon, take on a monumental task, or induce a major change, they may be *choosing* to suffer, for either the perceived payoff or the joy of the grind. You can see the exhausted exaltation on the face of a sleepless scientist working relentlessly to solve a mystery, or the unmatched gratification in the visages of your team members who suffered real hardships to deliver a superior result. And you sense in each of Erik's stories that at some level he enjoys the suffering—to the point that, if it were removed forever, he would feel an irreplaceable loss. Perhaps the gift of self-induced suffering can be the sensation of being fully alive.

At some point or other, perhaps during the eighth round of edits, writing a book can become a grind. Yet I'm awake at one AM for the third night in a row, writing this paragraph, asking myself why my wife's wonderful sympathy feels so odd. Sure, fatigue can set in at odd times, and there are real sacrifices involved in any worthy challenge, but why does her compassion feel so misplaced? Then it dawns on me. It's because I *love* doing this. There's something energizing about the hardships that come from stretching your capacity, from emerging better and more as a result. Testing one's limits can bring unique pleasure unmatched by lesser challenges. I also believe that self-imposed suffering can prove a useful training ground for involuntary suffering.

You will recall that most of us are hardwired to respond more effectively to the big stuff than to the small stuff, owing to the powerful fight-flight mechanism. You will also recall that adversity arises when something negatively affects, or is predicted to negatively affect, something or someone you care about. I believe that consciously suffering for the sake of bettering or helping something or someone you care about is one of the elevating tendencies anyone can readily adopt.

Like our capacities, both voluntary and involuntary suffering can be categorized into four main areas. Because of how deeply interconnected we are, suffering in one area is more than likely to induce suffering in another.

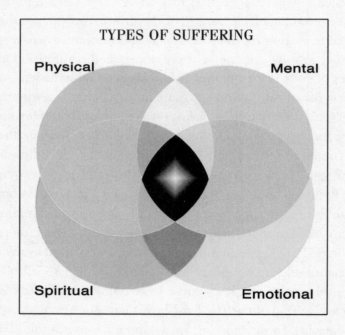

TYPES OF SUFFERING

Physical

Mental

Spiritual

Emotional

Physical suffering is the most obvious type. Our bodies tell us when something hurts. If it hurts severely enough and long enough, you are likely to suffer. Physical suffering is often the kind we talk about most openly, and it often evokes the greatest sympathy.

Physical suffering covers an enormous range of experiences, from mild but chronic discomfort like a headache to being stuck on an airport tarmac for several hours to the most unspeakable agonies, which need not be enumerated. Certainly, the hundreds of millions of people worldwide who suffer from chronic disease or crippling hunger know more about physical suffering than we could ever pretend to articulate from the comfort of our current lives and health.

> *Pain is God's megaphone.*
> —C. S. LEWIS

Emotional suffering is the kind that can make your heart ache, your limbs heavy, and your gut twist in knots. Unresolved worry, fear, frustration, anger, helplessness, resentment, anxiety, envy, anguish, hatred, disgust, and even love are the classic array from which both the poet and the playwright draw for many of their most vivid creations. Our discovery is that despite their masterful "game face" reflecting cheer and control, most people go through moments, if not extended periods, of significant emotional suffering over the course of a normal week or month. And again, like adversity, the severity of the pain is determined by STRIP—perceived *severity, time, relativity, importance,* and *price.* The greater these are, the more pronounced the pain.

Unlike physical suffering, emotional suffering is fairly contagious. One person's worries can easily become another's. This transference can go deep, affecting the chemistry and physiology of the other, as if the emotional suffering originated with him or her. This is one reason learning to suffer well is so vital—it reduces the burden we transfer to others. Pretending to suffer well fools no one, at least over time. But the real deal is invariably elevating.

Physical and emotional suffering are somewhat distinct from the remaining forms of suffering. Our society has created a multi-

billion-dollar industry solely dedicated to the alleviation and miti-
gation of physical and emotional pain through pharmaceuticals and
medicine. Today it is expected that people suffering physically, and
often people suffering emotionally, will seek some sort of treatment
or solution. Nonetheless, and despite our best scientific advances,
our society is heavily sprinkled with people who suffer chronically
both with and without medication, and who suffer more than just
physically as a result. This is why the other kinds of suffering are
likely to kick in over time.

Mental suffering is induced when we can't seem to figure out
and resolve a matter of great importance, like how to best care
for an aging parent when there may be limited choices; how to
graduate before your student loans run out, when you can't ever
seem to get the right classes; or how to deliver a vital project on
time, according to specifications, when critical pieces remain missing or unresolved.

Mental suffering often comes from conundrums and quan-
daries—the inability to find one best, right, or even possible solution, when the need for a solution may be intense. It can also be
induced by confusion or lack of information regarding something
you consider vital. This is why many of our clients suffer when their
companies restructure. They know big change is certain, but they
don't know how to take care of themselves and their loved ones
when their employment, responsibilities, income, identity, location—everything that constitutes their ability to provide—is up in
the air and is being decided by someone else.

As with physical and emotional suffering, mental suffering is
often traceable to a specific problem or situation.

In contrast, *spiritual suffering* often stems from something private and hidden. It occurs when we feel adrift, faithless, purpose-
less, hopeless, and unconnected with the universe. Spiritual
suffering can be chronic and vague, as when we have a gnawing
sense that something is amiss; or it can be sharp and severe, as when

we witness or, worse yet, are victimized by evil—for instance, when we or someone we love is violently and senselessly attacked. Spiritual suffering happens when your soul is in a state of tumult, often as a result of wrestling with big questions that may, in turn, have been sparked by the loss of a loved one, a brush with death, or any personally jarring event. Spiritual suffering can arise when one suffers a crisis of faith, or when one feels insignificant and that life is devoid of meaning.

Spiritual suffering is what happens when we know we have fallen short or done wrong in some matter of great importance. It is the chronic hurt that comes from knowing that we let our lower self override our higher self, and that an opportunity has now passed. It is also often triggered by the other three kinds of suffering. Perhaps this is why so many people consider spiritual suffering to be the most significant and most potentially elevating form.

Suffering, cheerfully endured, ceases to be suffering
and is transmuted into an ineffable joy.
—MAHATMA GANDHI

Of course, separating the forms of suffering in this way can be dangerous, much like learning the main systems of the human body in a high school biology class. It would be easy to treat the types of suffering as if they operated in isolation. But the reality is that most people who suffer in one of these four ways suffer to some extent in at least one other way. For example, if you were fired from your job, with cause, despite your "best efforts," you might be quite upset emotionally. And trying to find a job in a limited market when you have a poor reference might make you suffer mentally, and the resulting stress could lead to sleepless nights and overall fatigue. Also, of course, those moments of drifting, or feeling as if "God has abandoned me" might induce spiritual suffering. So most suffering involves and even shifts between two or more forms.

SUFFER CHECK

Have you ever been in a room where you experience an enormous sense of relief when the refrigerator motor or heating unit turns off, even though originally you didn't notice that it was on? Suffering, like chronic pain, can operate in a similar way. It can have a wearing effect on your energy, mind, and spirit, without your ever knowing it is even there. And then when and if it ceases, you experience a tremendous lift. In Summit One, we introduced the principle of turning into the storm. In the same spirit, the idea now is to use the principles in Summit Six to discover and come to grips with the source of suffering before it wears you down.

Now that you understand the various types of suffering, I want you to perform your own Suffer Check. It's simple. You list the greatest source of suffering in your life (at work, or at school, or . . .), and you rate it according to STRIP. Your score will give you some indication of what's really going on. That's a great place to start.

The fact is that you may not be experiencing any suffering in your life right now. If this is genuinely the case, you may wish to apply the Suffer Check to someone you care about.

SUFFER CHECK

The purpose of this exercise is to get you to take stock of where and how you suffer, so you can begin to harness suffering for the high-octane advantages it can bring.

WORK AND LIFE

Currently, what is your single greatest cause of suffering at work? (If applicable.) Currently, what is your single greatest cause of suffering in life?

STRIP down to the truth by rating each type of suffering on a scale of one to ten. Apply each of the following criteria:

WORK   LIFE

Severity—the magnitude of the pain
(1 = unnoticeable, 10 = agonizing)

Time—how long you must endure the pain
(1 = momentary, 10 = forever)

Relativity—how severe your pain is when you are compared with those around you and
your situation is compared with past or current adversities
(1 = unnoticeable, 10 = agonizing)

Importance—how much the thing for which you are suffering matters
(1 = trivial, 10 = absolutely vital)

Price—how much you may or will lose as a result of the adversity
(1 = nothing, 10 = everything)

Scoring your results:
5–15—You are experiencing little, if any, discomfort. At worst, your discomfort may prove wearing
over time but is unlikely to spur you to bold action.

16–30—You are experiencing noticeable discomfort, which warrants your attention and ingenuity.
How can you reduce, eliminate, or (ideally) harness its energy to achieve a positive outcome?

31–45—You are experiencing real pain, which if harnessed could improve your reality.

46–50—You are experiencing extreme suffering, which if harnessed could dramatically elevate you
and the people around you.

Regardless of what form or degree of suffering you experience, the fact remains. You can suffer poorly, or you can suffer well. All four forms share that basic truth.

The only way to be happy is to love to suffer.

— WOODY ALLEN

POSITIVE PESSIMISM

My friend and climbing partner Chris Morris is famous for a little trick he uses to deal with suffering. He calls it "positive pessimism."

We'll be sitting out in a raging storm. I've gone a month without a shower. The wind is driving snow directly into my face. I'm wondering what insanity led me to this nightmare in the first place. That's when Chris will look up with a big cheesy smile on his face and say, "Sure is cold out here . . . but at least it's windy." One time, we had been moving through the cold for ten hours. We were all wasted. Chris turned to our team and said, "Boys, we sure have been climbing a long way . . . but at least we're lost." In the Khumbu Icefall, as Chris was halfway across his first ladder over a giant crevasse, he came out with the classic, "This ladder may be rickety . . . but at least it's swinging in the breeze."

Positive pessimism is a wonderful, light way to take the edge off the suffering you're enduring at the time. If you can throw out a positive pessimism when you're really hurting, it helps you maintain a little control over your predicament by giving you a healthy perspective. Reacting to the gravity of a situation with humor and humility speaks loudly about your character and helps those around you to stay optimistic. Whenever I'm suffering and Chris comes out with a positive pessimism, I think that maybe things aren't so bad after all.

On Aconcagua, I had just struggled to the 22,841-foot summit. I was barely hanging in there. Chris gave me a big hug and croaked, "Big E, you may be blind . . . but at least you're slow!" As hammered as I was, I laughed and shot back with, "Chris, you're not the nicest guy in the world . . . but at least you're stupid."

I've seen people use positive pessimism in all aspects of life. Once a guy was hiking with me in Colorado and was struggling to keep up the pace. From behind me I heard him say, "I may be fat . . . but at least I'm old."

How about a well-placed positive pessimism in the office? "I'm going into a three-hour meeting . . . but at least I didn't have time to eat lunch." Or: "We didn't get the big account . . . but at least our stock price went down." At home, try this one: "Honey, we may be on a really tight budget . . . but at least our heating bill doubled." Or: "We may be moving into a smaller house . . . but at least your mother is coming to live with us."

With a week to go until this book was due to the publisher, I went into my computer file and found that the entire chapter I had been writing for a week had been deleted. My first reaction was to do something violent, but then I thought of my good friend Chris Morris and said aloud to the empty room, "I may have lost the chapter . . . but at least I'll be up for the next three nights rewriting it."

BAD SUFFERING

What does it mean to suffer poorly? And how dare we judge how nobly or weakly anyone suffers, when suffering is so intensely personal? Bad suffering is not so much about our perception of others—pointing our finger at people and labeling them as "weak" or "unworthy." Rather, how poorly or well one suffers can ultimately be determined only by the one suffering, and perhaps by the higher force of the universe. Simply put, bad suffering occurs when the experience makes us less rather than more.

When we become meaner, smaller, or more selfish as a result of our pain, that is bad suffering, even if it is understandable. If we further hurt ourselves or hurt others because we hurt, we are suffering poorly. When we reduce our Life Worth and the Life Worth of those around us because of our pain, we suffer less nobly than we perhaps could. When the net effect of our suffering is that we have damaged the belief and faith of others, we have, indeed, suffered badly.

It sounds harsh, but the truth is that suffering can be the ultimate excuse to stop trying. When you suffer genuine mental, physical, emotional, or spiritual pain, who could ever blame you for checking out, being miserable, and making everyone else miserable in the process? Who could judge you for subtracting from the world through your suffering? After all, you're suffering!

Suffering can also become a cultural norm within organizations. I'll never forget one client with whom I worked many years ago. I was helping the company work through a major change, and I immediately noticed that it was weighing heavily on everyone. Each time I'd meet with the executive team in their boardroom, which was decorated in the style of "modern mausoleum," they would come in with heads bowed, faces anguished, and shoulders hunched as if bearing the burden of the world. Each time we'd meet, I would work even harder to help them see the potentially positive, even exhilarating upside of their change. Finally, a senior vice president of marketing sighed, turned to me, and said, "In case you haven't noticed, Paul, this is not *fun*. In fact, nothing about our company is *fun*. Truth is, surviving in business these days is damned tough. So, I suggest you put your optimism aside, just help us work through the grim realities of this change, and stop trying to convince us of how wonderful it can be." I sensed that this wasn't the first time he had given his grim speech. You'd think the company made caskets or bombs. Amazingly, it produced consumer electronics. Needless to say, the hallways were filled with the walking dead. The company's change effort was excruciating, and its stock price sagged as its competitors beat it on the buzz, energy, excitement, and innovation that drove real numbers.

Suffering poorly is your right. Suffering well is your opportunity.

GOOD SUFFERING

Good suffering is elevating. It is the opposite of bad suffering. The result of suffering well is making oneself and others better people because of what we've been through or are currently going through.

Good suffering can press the personal reset button. It can clear everything superfluous off our radar screen. Good suffering often involves a sort of catharsis, in which the pain we endure brings with it exceptional clarity on what really matters, along with a positive impatience when we are focusing on anything less. It sweeps us clean of pettiness, making us more magnanimous and selfless. Good suffering often spawns hope by helping others believe that whatever they must someday endure, it doesn't have to end horribly. By watching you suffer well, they begin to believe that they could too.

Suffering becomes beautiful when anyone bears calamities with cheerfulness, not through insensibility but through greatness of mind.
—ARISTOTLE

To suffer well, you will want to:

- ▸ Use suffering to help and enrich others.
- ▸ Use it to become a better person—demonstrating your highest character and virtue in the face of pain.
- ▸ Turn inward, and privately harness it to expand your capacity for hardship.
- ▸ Use and transcend it by attacking life with renewed determination.
- ▸ Be human—acknowledging when it's hard or it hurts—and don't pretend it does not exist, robbing yourself of the potential lessons.
- ▸ Ask for help when you need it.

- ▶ Turn your suffering into a cause.
- ▶ Be open about it—letting others learn from what you are going through.

THE SUFFER WELL

Because suffering is so personal, it's difficult and perhaps inappropriate to provide one universal manual for how to do it. But I have found a tool—the Suffer Well—that can apply in almost any circumstance. Here's how it works.

A drinking well is filled with fresh water. You dip your bucket as deeply as necessary to draw forth the water you need. Likewise, the Suffer Well is filled with vital questions that, when answered, will draw forth the knowledge you need to suffer well. You can dip into and draw forth any or all questions, in any sequence, depending on the nature and severity of your suffering. Answer them from the heart, and devise your approach to suffer well.

How?

How am I going to elevate myself and others, starting now? We are moved to tears when a person transcends pain in an effort to make something better for others. Express to others, in words and deeds, your own appreciation, beauty, love, gratitude, faith, or wisdom, especially when the suffering is most intense.

Who?

Who is most affected by how I suffer? The answer might not be obvious. Beyond those closest to you, there may be people in the next ring of family, friends, and associates who are profoundly affected by how you suffer. Erik never even knew Terry Fox, the guy who ran across Canada on a prosthesis, whom Erik watched on TV with the last bit of his sight. But Erik's life was forever changed by the uplifting way he suffered. Picture the people you most want to elevate.

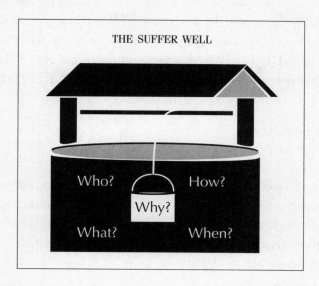

What?

What is your CORE with regard to your suffering? In Summit Three you learned about your CORE, and how it is like a lens through which you see and navigate in life. It applies doubly to suffering. Gauge your CORE and address these questions:

▸ Control—What are the facets of this suffering that I can potentially influence?

▸ Ownership—What can I do to step up to make even the smallest positive improvement in how I, and others, experience my suffering?

▸ Reach—What can I do to minimize the downside of my suffering and maximize the potential upside?

▸ Endurance—What can I do to get past this as quickly as possible? What do I want life to look like on the other side for me and others?

Why?

Why do I want to suffer well? Chances are that when it comes to suffering well, you won't do it without a compelling why. Your why may have to do with other people, the legacy you choose to leave, or your personal dignity. Think about and try to put into a sentence your rallying cry—your reason for taking it on. "Rather than suffer poorly, I choose to suffer well because . . ."

When?

By when will you have said or done something that demonstrates your commitment to suffer well? Time takes on a new dimension when you are suffering. And scheduling a goal is often a powerful way to help you endure the short term. Committing yourself to a date or time can be highly motivating, helping your body and spirit rally for the cause.

Research reveals a somewhat inverse relationship between happiness and the degree to which one focuses on oneself. Getting outside your own skin, and focusing on others, especially in times of suffering, can reduce your pain and create an upside to what can be an otherwise down experience. Likewise, you may know people who've been able to endure terrible difficulties by focusing on a compelling goal, or reason. It can literally keep one alive. So, addressing the how, what, who, why, and when of suffering can help you work through even the toughest moments. When you have to endure hardship, dip into your Suffer Well, pull out and address whatever question appears, and you will be on your way to elevating others through your hardship.

Erik and I are deeply humbled when we stumble on people who live up to this elevating mind-set.

During the spring of 2004, I spoke at the kickoff event for the Kate Svitek Memorial Foundation near Philadelphia, Pennsylvania. Frank and Ellen Svitek established this foundation to honor their daughter Kate and spread her wish to help people better understand the natural world and the lessons it can teach. The foundation provides financial support to students like Kate, who want to explore and discover the outdoors.

Shortly after graduating from college and moving to Bend, Oregon, Kate was killed in a snowboarding accident while off duty from her job at Mount Bachelor Ski Resort. Her death was a deep loss to those who knew her. To her parents, it tore apart a family that they described as "perfect."

In their invitation to me, Kate's parents said that I shared the same outdoor spirit and passion for discovery as their daughter. Having me join them on that special day would help them honor Kate's memory. Traveling to Pennsylvania, I was a little hesitant, because I also shared a part of their story. Only two years after I went blind, my mother was killed in a car accident. The news nearly destroyed me. Compared with the pain of losing my mom, going blind felt almost trivial. The depression I experienced was transformed into a physical suffering. The pain was so intense that I wondered if it could actually cause my heart to stop beating and my blood to stop coursing through my veins. While the pain has subsided a little, the loss remains with me. I carry it in my heart every moment of every day.

So I had a notion of how a family reacts to the news that a daughter is gone. I thought to myself: how could two parents be expected to carry on with life when a part of their souls had been ripped from them? And what could I offer to this family that could even come close to filling the void that now lived in their hearts?

Death, I believe, is the ultimate adversity. It's not the same thing as failing on a mountain or losing an investment in the stock market; it is adversity to an unfathomable degree. We cannot avoid it, adequately prepare for it, or ever be expected to bounce back from it. The death of a child is something that no parent should ever have to bear. It tests the very nature of the human spirit and the human capacity to endure. So how can enduring the severe pain of death ever be considered good suffering?

Kate's mother, Ellen, told me that in the weeks after Kate had died, she purposely drove her car without a seat belt, thinking that if she were killed in an accident, her chances of being with Kate again would be greater. And to this day, Kate's father, Frank, is moved to tears when he shares stories about Kate's adventurous spirit and love of the outdoors. During our conversations, he had to pause repeatedly and fight back tears just to complete a sentence. And when he couldn't, Ellen would complete sentences for him. It made me realize that even today, their suffering is simply so great that, just to endure, Frank and Ellen must live as a single spirit.

I learned that Kate was a passionate climber and, in high school, had attempted Mount Rainier in Washington. In describing her first try, she wrote, "Although I didn't make it to the summit that sunrise, being near the top of the world gave me a new perspective on life. I realized the importance of challenging one's own limits and ingenuity even if you are not able to achieve a goal. That sunrise placed into me a sense of wonder that had nothing to do with whether or not I made it to the summit. It is not always necessary to achieve an ultimate goal, because the reward of self-satisfaction is enough from within."

Kate's experiences on Mount Rainier had a lasting impact on her parents. In fact, on her second attempt she took her father along as a climbing partner. Even though they fell short of the summit, they made an important discovery—that through physical suffering, the body can do so much more than the brain thinks it can.

Perhaps this discovery led Kate to a third attempt, in which she finally reached the summit. And six months after Kate's death, exactly a year after Kate had stood on the top of Mount Rainier, her father reached the summit, too. Standing on top in her honor, Frank saw a rainbow. He told me that he believed it was sent by Kate to help him live on.

Frank and Ellen Svitek will suffer intensely the rest of their lives, but—as with the rainbow Frank saw appear above the summit of Rainier—from that

suffering arises a beautiful and noble calling. In only three years, the foundation has given out almost three dozen scholarships to underprivileged students to attend programs like Outward Bound and the National Outdoor
Leadership School. Kate's spirit will live on through the many students who
otherwise would not have had the opportunity to follow in her footsteps.

Every night before bed, Kate's mother reads the testimonials from grant
recipients and cries. Her suffering is noble, important, and lasting. Nathaly
Filion, a grant recipient, wrote, "I have learned so much about myself, the natural world, and my passion for the outdoors. I thank you from the bottom of
my heart."

While the pain and suffering from Kate's death cannot be erased from
Frank's and Ellen's hearts, there is a message we can learn from their work:
by discovering a purpose to our pain, we learn what it means to suffer well.

In business, the finest executives I know share a capacity to suffer well. They shoulder enormous stress, unfathomable uncertainty, weighty responsibility, substantial risk, chronic pressure, and
nearly impossible, often competing demands with the same up-
beat determination with which a child chases a puppy. When a
leader doesn't suffer well, the entire organization suffers.

Rick Wilson is a national leader for a global business. He does
the job of three leaders with very little defined direction and must
deliver exceptional results in all three areas. Because Rick is so
capable, his bosses have never gotten around to fulfilling their
promise to hire additional executives to shoulder some of his many
responsibilities. The reason Rick does not pressure his bosses to
hire more people is that on most days, he truly thrives on the challenge, to the point where it fuels him, and he would not want it
any other way.

Rick also has multiple sclerosis—MS—which is exacerbated by
stress. He has harnessed his adversity to fuel his zeal for living life to

the fullest while he can. He skis expert runs, exercises, and engages in numerous hobbies and sports. On his good days, no one can keep up with him. But Rick has occasional rough days too. And when he does, you can see a special sparkle in his eye, as if to say, "Now I can *really* show them what I'm made of!" Despite his pain and hardships, Rick is a constant inspiration to the thousands of people who report to him. Why? He suffers well.

People like Rick make it look easy. Sometimes it's not. The challenge in suffering well comes when we confront the common, entirely human, cracks and chasms discussed earlier.

THE SUFFER SHIFTER

Now that you have learned how we define suffering, the common cracks and chasms, the four types of suffering, the five factors of suffering, your current level of suffering, and the powerful difference in business and in life between suffering poorly and suffering well, you're ready to make a shift within yourself, or for someone you know. The Suffer Shifter is a simple and hopefully meaningful exercise that you should first apply to yourself. Again, if you are the rare person who has no discomforts in life, you can use it to benefit others.

My advice is that you take some moments of real thought to derive your best answers to the questions I pose, so you can gain the most advantage from the adversity your suffering or that of others can bring.

THE SUFFER SHIFTER

The purpose of this exercise is to help you shift your suffering and hardship from bad to good. Once you complete it, you may wish to discuss your conclusions with the people around you who are most involved with the situation or situations in which you suffer. Their understanding, support, and involvement may prove extremely helpful.

Pain point: The one area in which I currently suffer most is:

_____

_____

_____

On the basis of all I have learned about suffering poorly, one specific thing (see Chasms) I commit myself to stop doing or do less of is:

_____

_____

_____

On the basis of all that I have learned about what it takes to suffer well, one specific thing I commit to start doing or do more of is:

_____

_____

_____

As a result of these commitments, I and the people around me should enjoy the following benefits (list):

_____

_____

_____

_____

_____

_____

Whenever a big accomplishment nears its end, you face a moment of truth. Do you make this moment the apex of your life, or do you continue your ascent? The moment it's over, the aspiration that was your focus and fueled your passion becomes a memory, something you did "yesterday," "last month," "several years ago," and, eventually, "once." It's very tempting to stop, or "camp," as Paul describes settling into your suffering-free comfort zone, especially if you suffered a lot just getting there.

When the goal is accomplished, when you've breathlessly arrived at your destination, and that dramatic shift from present to past occurs, you face the question "What's next?" I faced that question when I stood on top of Kosciusko, after completing my seven-year quest. I didn't want to spend the rest of my life being the guy "who once climbed the Seven Summits." The Seven Summits were my "what." I was driven by my "why." If I was going to spend my life helping people rethink what's possible, I needed to find new challenges to extend my mission. And that meant voluntarily taking on more suffering.

Climbing a mountain is tough, but nothing has ever made me suffer more than the Primal Quest, the toughest adventure race in North America, if not the world. It involved 460 miles; 60,000 feet of elevation gain; nine days; and no time-outs. Initially, my partner from Everest, Jeff, and I thought the idea of climbing, caving, mountain biking, running, rafting, and kayaking against the world's elite adventure racing teams sounded like a great challenge. However, shortly after we began the race, our thoughts changed. Fatigue began to ravage our bodies; the climbs became increasingly formidable; and as more and more teams dropped out of the race, Jeff and I began to call it the "Suffer Quest."

Suffering was actually the key component of our race strategy. Earlier that year, our team of four had tried a five-day race across Greenland, but because it was only half the distance of "Suffer Quest," the pace was twice as fast. With all the teams at sprint pace, our team fell days behind. I tore my calf muscle trying to keep up on the rugged terrain, and we ultimately dropped out. However, to have a chance to complete the extreme distance of "Suffer Quest," we predicted that teams would have to gear down and settle into a steady pace. I knew I couldn't beat teams on the basis of speed or even skill, but we might just be able to out-suffer them.

The first leg of the race was a thirty-mile, nine-hour kayak across Lake Tahoe. I was in front setting the pace, and it worked well for the first five hours. In the final four hours, a strong headwind kicked in and caused the cold waves to crash over my head. When we pulled the kayak out of the water, I was hypothermic. But thankfully the next leg, a 100-mile tandem bike ride over the Sierra Nevada, warmed me up again.

As I started the race, I was still plagued by the calf injury from Greenland. Two days into the race, the calf screamed with every step. I thought that if it got any worse, there was no way I would be able to keep moving. Ten hours later, however, my calf was the least of my worries, because my knees felt as though they had been hit with a sledgehammer. Ten hours after that, I couldn't feel the pain in my knees anymore; it had moved to the giant blisters on my toes.

By day four, teams began to drop around us. Some had begun the race too quickly and burned themselves out; others had capsized in the white water, and the members had banged themselves up; some participants had gotten heat stroke, and others had gone into shock as their bodies became depleted of electrolytes. One guy had fallen asleep on his bike and crashed.

Since we were catching only an hour of sleep a night, my team was suffering from sleep deprivation—or, as adventure racers like to say, we had been "bitten by the sleep monsters." At one point, as we were bouncing down a mountain trail at midnight with Jeff guiding us from the front of the tandem, he admitted he couldn't see the trail anymore; his eyes were so fatigued they simply weren't working. As we rode for the next hour, I continually slapped him on the back, sang songs, and told dumb jokes. "Whatever you do, absolutely do not fall asleep," I yelled in his ear. Finally, he rebounded, but a few minutes later, I fell asleep myself. The bike swerved and I sprang awake.

It seemed that every time we conquered a huge series of hills on the tandem and convinced ourselves we were about to top out, we'd round a corner and be confronted by an even bigger mountain. We couldn't figure out how they had rigged this race with hills that eternally went up and never went down. Rather than being demoralized, though, we responded each time by turning to each other and cracking up. I figured it was better than crying. The last night, through a forty-mile boulder field, I was actually hallucinating on my feet. Since I was once a teacher, I'd hear my fifth-graders cheering me on from an imaginary playground. Then I'd shake my head and realize exactly where I was.

Eight days and twenty-three hours after beginning, our team crossed the finish line, one of only forty-two teams to complete the race out of the eighty elite teams from around the world that had started. No blind person had ever attempted an expedition-length adventure race; and the rumor, as I later learned, was that some teams thought we wouldn't make it past the first day.

At the finish line at four AM, I heard a giggly little voice yell, "Daddy." At first I thought I was hallucinating again, but as the voice ran and wrapped its arms around my legs, I realized that Emma and Ellie were there to meet us. That voice made all the suffering I had endured for the last nine days worthwhile.

I'm convinced that our ability to outlast and, in many cases, ultimately outperform dozens of far more experienced teams was not just due to our fitness, systems, or cohesiveness as a team; it was also due to our capacity to suffer well. Suffering seems to be the one experience we all share and the one thing most of us would gladly give up. But over the course of these Summits, you and I have learned that suffering can be the lead that alchemists turn into gold.

As you reach the conclusion of your Summit Challenge, or any goal you may set for yourself, you will face the same quandary I did when I stood on my seventh summit. What's next? As you turn the page to begin the final Summit of this book, Summit Seven, you will pull together everything you've learned so far and apply it to elevate your life, and the lives of those around you, to deliver greatness every day.

SUMMIT SIX—SUFFER WELL

GUIDING PRINCIPLE

To suffer is to endure something painful. Suffering is part of life. The question is whether you will suffer poorly or suffer well. Suffering well means suffering in a way that elevates you and those around you. It is the one opportunity for everyday greatness we are all granted.

Suffering Well

- Use suffering to help and enrich others.
- Use it to become a better person—demonstrating your highest character and virtue in the face of pain.
- Use and transcend it by attacking life with renewed determination.
- Be human—acknowledging when it's hard or it hurts—and don't pretend it does not exist, robbing people of the potential lessons.
- Ask for help when you need it.
- Turn your suffering into a cause.
- Be open about it—letting others learn from what you are going through.

Suffering Poorly

- Suffering poorly means becoming less, and bringing others down as a result.
- When we become meaner, smaller, or more selfish as a result of our pain, that is bad suffering, even if it is understandable.
- If we further hurt ourselves or hurt others because we hurt, we are suffering poorly.

Ten Common Cracks or Chasms to Avoid

Whining, complaining, blaming, identifying, anesthetizing, escaping, rationalizing, denying, pretending, and whitewashing.

Types of Suffering

Spiritual, physical, emotional, and mental.

Five Facets of Suffering (STRIP)

1. **S**everity—How bad is it?
2. **T**ime—How long does it endure?
3. **R**elativity—How does it compare with other suffering?
4. **I**mportance—How much does it matter?
5. **P**rice—What is the potential cost?

DELIVER GREATNESS, EVERY DAY

KILIMANJARO

Base Camp: 3,000 feet

Summit: 19,340 feet—tallest peak in Africa

We give others the courage to do great things
by our own example of doing great things.

–STEVE ACKERMAN, THE FIRST PARAPLEGIC
TO PEDDLE AROUND THE WORLD ON A HAND CYCLE

As we set forth on this final Summit—Summit Seven—together, I wonder if you fully appreciate how much terrain you have successfully covered so far. While each person's journey through *The Adversity Advantage* is highly personal, I hope and predict that you have already strengthened your relationship with adversity, so that you can begin to use it as a true advantage in your life. Paul and I wrote this book to help you use life's hardest moments for the most uplifting pursuits. It is about your new role as an adversity alchemist, converting life's tough stuff into the gold of everyday greatness.

We also wrote the book to show you the powerful difference between wrestling adversity into submission, or conquering it for your own satisfaction, and using adversity to elevate yourself and the lives of those around you. The book is about the vital role adversity plays in shaping the kind of leader you aspire to be, and that may mean developing your organization, driving your team forward, or helping your family thrive, in the harshest weather.

I've climbed Kilimanjaro two times now, and the contrast between my two very different ascents helped me discover that there's much more to life than standing proudly on top of a mountain and declaring to the world, "Look at me! I did it!" Being an alchemist, I learned, meant more than overcoming immense physical obstacles like extreme cold and brutal winds. It meant helping others transform their own challenges into triumphs.

I organized the first trip to Kilimanjaro as my second continental summit, but also—and equally importantly—to give my father, Ed, and my wife, Ellie, a taste of bigger mountains. I wanted them to experience the same joy that I did, and I thought Kilimanjaro would be the perfect setting. However, I didn't do my homework or plan properly, as I learned to do on later expeditions. Instead, I hired a less than reliable guide who had us camp very low on the mountain on the night before our summit attempt. His decision made for a hellishly long and brutal summit day, 5,000 feet and twenty hours in all, and it took a toll on our team.

One guy in our group was so wasted that he turned back, and on the way down he began giving away all his climbing gear, repeating to anyone he passed, "I'm never climbing again." At one point, a woman in our group curled up in a ball and refused to move. The guides had to haul her down. The worst part of the climb came an hour below the top when my dad and Ellie both decided to turn back. Later, Ellie called our long day the "endless nightmare."

Although I suffered from altitude sickness and during the last hour was stopping every thirty feet to throw up, I gutted it out and reached the summit. I had surmounted adversity and achieved my goal. Good for me. Why, then, did I feel that I had failed? The two people I loved most in the world were somewhere below me. Were they OK, or were they suffering? I hadn't summoned my strengths to help them or encourage them on, as others had done for me. Standing on top, instead of celebrating, I cried.

Eight years later, I began corresponding with an extraordinary athlete, Douglas Sidialo. He lived in Nairobi, Kenya, with his wife and two daughters. In 1998, Douglas was driving past the American embassy when he saw a flash of light. That was the last thing he ever saw. He woke up in a hospital three days later, an innocent casualty of the simultaneous bombings of the United States embassies in Kenya and Tanzania.

Rarely are blind people employed in Africa. When Douglas became blind, he and his family had to survive on his wife's small salary as a teacher. When Douglas told me that his dream was to climb Kilimanjaro someday, I couldn't sleep for the next three nights. My brain churned with an idea that might help Douglas and his family and possibly many others, too.

The plan sprang from the knowledge of two opposing experiences: the emptiness of my first summit on Kilimanjaro and the joy I experienced on Mount Everest when so many of my team stood on top with me. I attributed our crowded summit on Everest to everyone's desire to be a part of something great. That uncompromising belief and commitment drove us all to the summit. With a higher "why," people often rise above themselves and go all the way. I suspected that the same magic could be replicated on Kilimanjaro.

So, I decided to form an integrated team of sighted and blind participants, not elite athletes but everyday people like stay-at-home moms and corporate folks. Ninety percent of the sighted participants were middle-aged and had little mountaineering experience. Their job would be to guide the blind people to the top. Besides Douglas, the blind folks included people from four continents. Just to make things interesting, we also brought along Carl, a visually impaired and hearing-impaired participant from Denver; and Bill, who was sixty-nine years old and was not only blind but also missing part of his right arm and some fingers from his left hand as a result of a blasting accident in Alaska.

For the first step, I brought the team to Colorado for a training hike to hone our systems and build team strengths. Since most of the sighted people were novices at guiding blind people, everyone struggled to figure out how to best work with everyone else. Instead of taking the standard six hours to complete the hike, the trek took twelve hours, and only two blind people actually made it to the top. But by sticking it out together, they had shown they had the will to do something great. They now needed to gain the skill, and I hoped this less than momentous beginning was just the adversity they needed to spur them forward.

At the base of Kilimanjaro, I told them that this climb was not just about getting individuals to the summit. The end goal was to summit as a team, really taking care of one another. The sighted and blind partners came prepared with new systems they had developed for guiding. Some duos held opposite ends of two trekking poles. With others, the blind person lightly held a strap on a backpack. With still others, the sighted person rang a loud bell for the blind person to follow.

Our first test came only two days into the trek, as one of the blind climbers was struggling through the seemingly endless boulder fields before camp. Three teammates stayed behind to help him through. The African guides offered to actually carry him into camp, but the team tenaciously refused. They came in at eight PM, after a twelve-hour day, and the folks who had arrived earlier already had tents set up, sleeping bags laid out, and a hot meal waiting. Higher up on the Barranca Wall, a steep 1,000-foot rock scramble, I witnessed sighted teammates working patiently and carefully to talk Douglas through every step. As I knew very well, one wrong move meant a 200-foot slide.

On summit night, everyone snaked up the headwall in a long line. We moved as a single unit. Not one person sprinted ahead to the summit. By six AM, as the team finally surmounted the headwall and stood at Gillman's Point, still an hour below the true summit, people were exhausted. One team member was almost passing out over his ski pole. Another was seeing double, and a third had sprained his ankle and limped painfully with every step. I recognized the problems and said to the team, "Guys, let's call it good. I think we should stop here," but I was immediately and unanimously overruled. An hour later, we stood on the roof of Africa as a team, and it was exhilarating to see how these non-mountaineers had taken it on and risen up to pioneer possibilities.

Life at 19,000 feet can be brutal. Normally, a large proportion of people tire and don't make it to the top. But, to my delight, my theory about giving the team a higher purpose proved true. We got twenty-three out of twenty-eight to the top, far more than we ever could have otherwise. It's as Paul says, "People will show up for a task, but engage fully in a cause."

On our last night on the mountain, one teammate stood up at dinner and said, "We've had such a rewarding experience together, one that none of us will ever forget. So I propose we leave a lasting legacy of our time together." The result was the Kilimanjaro Blind Trust Foundation, which the team formed to provide scholarships for blind children throughout East Africa. The foundation will be administered by Douglas.

I had climbed much bigger and more challenging mountains, and I had used adversity countless times to drive me on to a summit. But few of those successes gave me the same sense of fulfillment and Life Worth as joining five blind people from four continents, and helping the first blind African to stand on the roof of his continent. We didn't just surmount adversity that day. We used it to elevate everyone involved. Paul and I call this "delivering everyday greatness." And through Summit Seven, you will pull together everything you've gained so far and emerge prepared to deliver your brand of it, every day.

I like the phrase "your brand of it," because everyday greatness is not a generic skill set. It is highly individualized, like personality. This means that you get to deliver everyday greatness in your own unique, authentic way.

But it's important to point out that there is a fundamental difference between *epic greatness*, the "great people of history" whose biographies fill the library shelves, and *everyday greatness*, the kind of greatness we are exploring together here. It's like the difference between looking skyward to a distant, daunting, windblown peak versus having a series of handholds within easy reach all the way up the mountain. One is an occasional epic event; the other is a whole lot more accessible, more of an ongoing effort and an everyday opportunity.

Besides, the reality is that most people are not striving to be a "great person in history," like Gandhi, Nelson Mandela, or Sojourner Truth, who rises up and does the right thing in the face of immense adversity, changing the course of human history in the process. But we all still strive to have our lives matter, to close our eyes for the final time knowing that even a small piece of the world is better for our having been here.

Slow Man, the latest book by the Nobel Prize–winning author J. M. Coetzee, tells the story of a man who near the end of his life realizes that while he has done little significant harm, he has done no good either. He will leave no trace behind. He will have slid through the world. He imagines arriving at the pearly gates and being asked this powerful question: "Did you not understand why you were given life, the greatest gift of all?"

I think of the virtues that make up everyday greatness—resilience, magnanimity, compassion, fortitude, goodwill, and integrity—like charity. There are people who deliver them more readily and generously when life is good than they may when times get tough. This is true of many leaders who—unlike Churchill—are far better at gelling their teams when they are on a roll than when they are slammed against the rocks. But with charity, what speaks more clearly about your character—giving when you have an endless vat to draw from, or giving when you have nothing to give? Likewise, what matters more—elevating others when your mood, the setting, and the conditions are just right, or doing so in the heat of battle? If it were easy, we would call it "everyday normality" instead of everyday greatness.

So, how do *you* deliver greatness, every day? Consider the people you most admire. You may wish to jot down your answers so that you can discuss, or repeat, the following exercise with others.

WITNESSING GREATNESS EVERY DAY

The following exercise can be completed either through conversation with others or through writing and reflecting on your own. The richest benefit comes from exploring each question in some depth.

1. Who in your life do you currently most admire? Why? What does that person do, or demonstrate, that makes him or her worthy of your admiration?
2. Who do you currently most admire at work, at school, or in your community? Why? Likewise, what does that person do, or demonstrate, that makes him or her worthy of your admiration?
3. Answer each of the following questions as best you can, as they relate to both people.

SUMMIT ONE. TAKE IT ON
- How does that person Take It On?
- Where does that person fall on the Adversity Continuum?
- If you had to guess, what assumptions do you think that person makes about adversity (Adversity Assumptions)?

SUMMIT TWO. SUMMON YOUR STRENGTHS
- What is the toughest or most important thing you've seen that person pursue?
- What skills did that person possess and develop to make it happen?
- What strengths does that person summon in the face of adversity? Which ones do you most admire?
- How do the teams that person assembles or joins complement his or her strengths to achieve a higher goal?
- How does that person create positive interdependence, being roped together with others?
- What does he or she bring to any team? Rate that person's overall A Factor (strength in the midst of adversity), W Factor (why), and E Factor (ego).

SUMMIT THREE. ENGAGE YOUR CORE

► Do you think that person has a high, moderate, or low Adversity Quotient (AQ)?

► To what extent does that person tend to focus on what can be influenced (C = Control), step up to make things better (O = Ownership), contain bad things (R = Reach), and see or get past adverse events (E = Endurance)?

► On a scale of one to ten, how effectively does that person engage his or her CORE?

SUMMIT FOUR. PIONEER POSSIBILITIES

► What possibilities, big or small, has that person pioneered?

► How does that person respond when someone says something important is impossible?

► What Signature Systems have you seen that person apply?

SUMMIT FIVE. PACK LIGHT, PACK RIGHT

► On a scale of one to ten, where does that person score on Life Worth?

► What examples can you think of when that person has forgone a desire in order to achieve something more important?

► How effectively does that person strategically invest time, energy, and money on the things that matter most? To what extent does that person invest in his or her own well-being?

SUMMIT SIX. SUFFER WELL

► What (if any) suffering, big or small, have you seen that person endure?

► How did that person handle it? What effect did his or her approach to suffering have on others?

Overall, how would you describe that person's relationship with adversity? Would you have chosen that person if he or she had never faced any adversity or had scored much lower on the Adversity Continuum?

Hopefully, this exercise has already led to some rich discussion and insight. The wake-up call for me, more than twenty years ago, was the realization that, while each person is different, there are powerful similarities in how the people whom others most admire relate to adversity. Such people could be famous, or people close to you. It doesn't matter. These people set forth relatively noble ambitions and faced significant adversity along the way; then, through whatever struggles and suffering they encountered, they ultimately elevated themselves and others, turning adversity into a meaningful advantage, performing some form of alchemy resulting in everyday greatness. And that discovery led me on to my lifework and my research on AQ, and beyond.

Let's take it one level deeper. In the introduction, I explained that I found Erik an exemplar of everything this book is about. And I told you that part of my job was to decode his emotional DNA in such a way that you could replicate it inside yourself, in your own way, for your own Summit Challenge and your life. I also pointed out that while it would be easy to distance yourself from Erik's example, considering him to be a freakish, superhuman emotional mutation, he is in fact a regular guy, who did something you or anyone can do—use adversity to your advantage. You can replicate in your life, with your adversities, all the ways Erik, as an alchemist, turned his lead into gold. The point is not to convince you of how amazing Erik is or to have you leave this book chanting his name (although his daughter, Emma, would get a great kick out of that).

The point is to hold Erik out as an instructive example of what's possible when the principles and tools offered throughout this book are applied. Let's see how we did. Repeat the exercise you completed above, applying the same questions to Erik, on the basis of what you know or have learned about him from this book.

DEMONSTRATING GREATNESS EVERY DAY

Like the preceding exercise, this can be completed either through conversation with others or through writing and reflecting on your own. Draw on all that you've learned about Erik to answer each question as best you can.

In your own words, what, if anything, do you most admire about Erik? In what specific ways has he been an adversity alchemist, turning life's lead into gold, or converting adversity into fuel for everyday greatness? On the basis of what you've read and know, answer the following questions.

SUMMIT ONE. TAKE IT ON
- In what ways does Erik Take It On?
- Where do you think Erik falls on the Adversity Continuum?
- If you had to guess, what assumptions do you think Erik makes about adversity? That is, what are his Adversity Assumptions?

SUMMIT TWO. SUMMON YOUR STRENGTHS
- What is Erik's Summit Challenge?
- What skills does he possess and did he develop in an effort to make it happen?
- What strengths does Erik summon in the face of adversity? What strengths did he have to develop? Which ones do you most admire?
- How do the teams he assembles or joins complement his strengths to achieve a higher goal?
- How does he create positive interdependence, being roped together with others?
- What does Erik bring to any team? Rate Erik's overall A Factor (strength with adversity), W Factor (why), and E Factor (ego). Give each a score of one to ten.

SUMMIT THREE. ENGAGE YOUR CORE

- ► Do you think Erik has a high, moderate, or low Adversity Quotient (AQ)?
- ► To what extent does Erik tend to focus on what can be influenced (C), step up to make things better (O), contain bad things (R), and see or get past adverse events (E)? How do you know? What evidence do you have to support your answers?
- ► On a scale of one to ten, overall, how effectively does Erik engage his CORE?

SUMMIT FOUR. PIONEER POSSIBILITIES

- ► What possibilities has Erik pioneered?
- ► How do you think Erik responds when someone tells him that something important is impossible?
- ► What Signature Systems has Erik designed and applied?

SUMMIT FIVE. PACK LIGHT, PACK RIGHT

- ► On a scale of one to ten, where do you think Erik scores on Life Worth? Why?
- ► What examples can you think of when Erik has turned down a tempting whim or desire for the sake of something more important?
- ► How effectively do you think Erik invests his time, energy, and money in the things that matter most? To what extent do you think Erik invests in his own well-being?

SUMMIT SIX. SUFFER WELL

- ► What (if any) suffering, big or small, has Erik had to endure?
- ► How did he handle it? What effect do you think his approach to his suffering has had on others? On you?

Overall, how would you describe Erik's relationship with adversity? If he scored much lower on the Adversity Continuum, how would he, and your answers, be different?

I could ask you to do the same exercise a third time for the person you most admire in the entire span of human history, and my guess is your answers would be very similar to those you've already given. Clearly, there are some key points. The people you admire most:

1. Are those who tend to harness their adversities, be Adversity Alchemists, and score highest on the Adversity Continuum.
2. Tend to demonstrate the principles of *The Adversity Advantage* in their daily lives, earning your respect, trust, and admiration.

So, if these are the common practices, principles, and tools of the people we most admire, here is the most important question. *Of all of the characteristics, choices, and tendencies that you've listed above, which ones* can't *you re-create and put to use within yourself and within your own life?* I assume that your humbling and inspiring answer is, "None."

Everything you've learned in Summits One through Six can be used to deliver your brand of greatness every day. Now, you need your game plan.

YOUR EVERYDAY GREATNESS GAME PLAN

Your Everyday Greatness Game Plan is both portable and personal. You may choose to make it part of your personal development plan at work or home, and track your progress through your weekly planner. Imagine if the people around you were also striving to apply the principles of *The Adversity Advantage* to deliver greatness every day. Can you imagine the impact that could have on your family, your team, or your business?

You may decide to share the journey with others—including loved ones, coworkers, and colleagues—agreeing to create your own "rope team" by holding one another accountable for the commitments you make. Or you may simply have a weekly cup of coffee to share your progress, discoveries, and challenges with your best friend. Whether personal or shared, your Everyday Greatness Game Plan will help you and the people around you win with and benefit from adversity.

There are two potential pathways. One path—the Singular Challenge—involves focusing on these tools and applying them directly to your Summit Challenge—the one thing you've always wanted to do but have not done (see page 40), or in other words, a single worthy aspiration for which you have enormous will and energy. The benefit of this approach is it enables you to focus on one thing.

A second path, the Multiple Challenge, involves applying these principles and tools specifically to the pains or adversities that you listed under each Life Category in your Adversity Inventory in Summit One (see page 39). If you take this approach, you will want to leave ample room to list your ideas for turning each of these adversities to your advantage, within each Life Category. The benefit of this approach is its breadth. It potentially covers most of the facets of your life.

How do you decide which approach is best for you? I would suggest that you consider the source of your greatest pain, and your greatest potential fulfillment. If not having accomplished your Summit Challenge or some other aspiration causes you gnawing pain, or the thought of making it happen lights you up from within, then that might be a sign to focus on this one thing. If, however, certain items on your Adversity Inventory score higher on the pain and excitement meter, then that is your indication to focus on those.

No matter which option you select, you may wish to jot down your ideas and notes regarding the most important Summit Questions that follow. You want to be obsessed with the question, "What can I do, or what Adversity Tools can I use, to convert this adversity to some advantage that benefits me and others?" You'll capture your best ideas and then hone them to develop your first steps and timelines, culminating in your Everyday Greatness Game Plan. And you'll get the most from this activity with that goal or outcome clearly in mind.

Summit One–Take It On!

You will begin by choosing either the Singular or the Multiple Challenge Path. Decide now and apply all that follows to your choice.

On the basis of all that you've learned, jot down your best thoughts about how you could take on and harness the adversity in a way that not only reduces your pain or achieves some goal, but also actually elevates others in the process. As an Adversity Alchemist, how could you turn the adversity into something good?

As you think about your challenge, what lower-level behavior do you need to cease (avoiding, surviving, coping . . .), and what higher-level behavior can you practice (turning into the storm, facing the facts, harnessing . . .)? What's the one thing that, if harnessed, would have the most significant impact on your life and on those around you?

Summit Two–Summon Your Strengths

As you consider your challenge, how can you summon your strengths to deliver greatness? Recall that Will + Skill ⇨ Strengths. In other words, when you apply your will to develop new skills, especially in the face of adversity, you emerge with more overarching strengths. You gain invaluable assets or qualities.

What strengths do you currently possess that will serve you

best in relation to the challenge? What strengths do you lack or need to develop to succeed with each challenge?

What's the most compelling reason for taking it on? If you don't have a compelling reason, you probably won't prevail. What's the why beneath the why that drives you to take this on? What is the deeper reason that this really matters to you?

Specifically, what skills do you already possess to help you succeed? What ones do you need to develop? Which skills do you have the will to use or develop to the level you need to attain?

Beyond your Regular Strengths, what Adversity Strengths do you possess that you can apply to this challenge in a way that elevates others? If you had to focus on one or two such strengths, which would you select as most important?

Who needs to be "on rope" with you to take on this challenge? Who should *not* be on your team? What strengths do you need from your team members in order to achieve your goal? Who brings the right combination of AWE: the A Factor (strength with adversity), the W Factor (a compelling why), and the E Factor (a healthy, substantiated ego)?

Summit Three—Engage Your CORE

As you consider this challenge, how can you engage your CORE in a way that is uplifting to others? So far, what role has your AQ played with respect to this challenge? Specifically, how will it affect you, and others, when you consciously engage your CORE to respond more effectively?

For any challenge, ask yourself the CORE questions. "What can I potentially influence in this situation; and of these items, which are most important to me (C)? Where and how can I step up to make the most immediate positive difference, or how can I improve things in even the smallest way (O)? What can I do to contain the potential downside (R)? How can I optimize the potential upside (R)? What do I want life to look like on the other side of this adversity (E)? How can I get there as quickly as possible (E)? How can I respond in a way that strengthens and inspires the people around me?"

Summit Four–Pioneer Possibilities

As you consider your challenges, what challenge would most people consider impossible but would change the game if it could be made possible? What can't you currently do? If you could do it, how would you do it? Are you focusing on the right challenge? What worthy goal sparks your *motivation*, *strength*, and *excitement*?

You will recall that adversity is the perfect force to tap your deeper reserves of innovation and ingenuity when the tools or means to accomplish what must be done are lacking, Possibility Pioneers invent them, often using whatever sparse resources are available at the time. What Signature Systems can you cobble together and draw on to make the unlikely happen? How can you Practice to Perfect?

Summit Five–Pack Light, Pack Right

One of the greatest impediments to giving your challenges the focus, energy, and resources you need is the natural tendency to become distracted and burdened by life. It's easy to slip into the role of a martyr to obligation and rob yourself of the life force it will take to be an Adversity Alchemist and deliver greatness every day.

So, how can you pack light and pack right by focusing your time, money, and energy on things that generate the greatest Life Worth, or the value you and others get from and give to life? How can you spring-clean your stuff, your calendar, and your relationships in order to redirect your resources toward the things that matter most? What do you need to toss out or reduce? What do you need to move to the front of your life, and what needs to be added? If you had three bins labeled "Toss," "Keep," and "Add," what obligations and commitments would go in which bin?

How well do you use the energy flywheel in your own life by investing the time it takes to receive the energy that comes from better health and overall well-being? If you had to strengthen one area of your health and capacity—spiritual, mental, emotional, or physical—which one would you choose, and why? What is one simple way you can bring it back to life?

Summit Six–Suffer Well

The path to achieving most elevating goals involves some degree of suffering. And while that is unpleasant, at best, it's a good thing. You can suffer poorly, or you can suffer well. Rather than using suffering as a reason to stop and turn back, use it to fuel your ascent, and as the high-powered opportunity it really is to elevate others.

Being brutally honest with yourself, consider in what ways you are likely to suffer. How would those who know you best describe how you have tended to suffer in the past? What changes do you need to make to ensure that, as you pursue this challenge, you suffer well? Specifically, how can you shoulder the full force of the adversity in a way that elevates and perhaps earns the genuine admiration of the people around you?

Crafting Your Game Plan

The next steps are simple, but important. You will want a piece of paper with the words "Adversity Advantage: Everyday Greatness Game Plan" written boldly at the top. Or you can use the following exercise as your template. Then you will use all that you have learned and listed to insert your best thoughts and ideas. The most important thing is to give your game plan your finest effort. The more thoughtful and specific you are, the greater your likelihood of gaining the fullest possible advantage from your adversities.

ADVERSITY ADVANTAGE:
EVERYDAY GREATNESS GAME PLAN

THE ASPIRATION OR SUMMIT CHALLENGE
Of them all, the specific aspiration or challenge I choose to take on first is:

_____

YOUR ADVERSITY
The greatest potential adversity I may face along the way is:

_____

When I face inevitable, unforeseen adversities, I will:

_____

THE ADVANTAGE
When I successfully convert this adversity to an advantage, the ways I will probably benefit include:

_____

The ways others will probably benefit include:

_____

YOUR STRATEGY
Of my entire list of possible ways that I can turn this adversity to an advantage, my specific initial approach will be to:

_____

The first adversity tools that I need or intend to apply are:

_____

Specifically, the way I intend to apply them is to:

_____

The Adversity Strengths I intend to use or develop (or both) include:

_____

I commit myself to get started no later than:

_____

YOUR ROPE TEAM
The person or people I want with me on my "rope team" to accomplish my goal include:

_____

The strengths needed from the team to accomplish my challenge are:

_____

THE SUMMIT
My vision of how life will be different once I have successfully implemented my Game Plan is:

_____

_____

_____

Putting Greatness into Action

You now hold your Everyday Greatness Game Plan in your hand. But, if you unleash its true force, you must also hold it in your heart. And that may be the remaining challenge. Here is Erik's and my concern. Do you, *can* you, fully comprehend what you are about to unleash? Because we believe that, if you did, you would let nothing get in the way of putting your Game Plan into immediate motion.

Part of the challenge is that you have probably read books designed to help you strengthen yourself, your team, your relationships, and your organizations. This may not be the first time you emerge from a book with some sort of action plan, parts of which you may have actually implemented. And that may be just fine. But on the basis of all we have witnessed over the decades of our research and lives, Erik and I firmly believe that this book, this Everyday Greatness Game Plan, is entirely different.

Your relationship with adversity undergirds, influences, and drives everything in your life. As Stephen Covey pointed out in his eloquent foreword, these teachings can fuel a noble and richer life. Your relationship with adversity is utterly foundational to all you aspire to be and do. So, done right, your Game Plan can infuse greatness into every facet of your world. In fact, our positive warning is this: *Greatness is potently contagious.* Once unleashed, it can readily take root and flourish in what would be otherwise lifeless soil.

So, to help elevate your thinking as to what's possible once you unleash your Everyday Greatness Game Plan, we leave you with this final story, in Erik's words, of how a humble life anywhere in the world and all the lives within its current and future reach can be forever transformed when the principles and tools of *The Adversity Advantage* are put to good use.

EVERYDAY GREATNESS—A TIMELESS LEGACY

It wasn't until I met Sabriye Tenberken that I learned of her amazing story. She was from Bonn, Germany. Like me, she had been blinded at age twelve by a degenerative retinal disease. But she didn't let that tragedy kill her vision. Like you, she saw herself making a positive mark in the world. So,

instead of merely coping with her adversity, she stepped out to make a difference. She first applied to join a government-funded program to help underprivileged people in other parts of the world. But the German government
flatly denied her application, making it clear that her disability would pre-
clude such work. They told her it was impossible. Like a true Adversity
Alchemist, Sabriye remained undaunted.

She simply rerouted her focus by taking a keen interest in one particular
troubled spot in the world, Tibet. As a first step, she completed a master's
degree in Tibetology so that she'd have some skill to match her will. When
she discovered that there was no Braille alphabet for the forty-two syllable
characters of Tibetan—a complex language—she created a Signature System, developing a Tibetan Braille alphabet in just two weeks. As she explained, "It was a matter of necessity. I had picked Tibet as the country where
I later wanted to do development work. Because a Braille system didn't exist,
I had no choice but to create one."

Creating this alphabet was just the beginning. Her biggest challenges
were yet to come. Apparently, although Tibet is widely regarded as a
mountain paradise, its people suffer blindness at a rate twice the global average, largely owing to high altitude and sun exposure. (The proportion of
blind Tibetans is one in seventy.) Also, the blind children are considered to
be cursed with demons, and their blindness is considered a punishment
to the family for misdeeds by someone in its lineage in a previous life.
Thank goodness, rather than turning away, Sabriye decided to turn into the
storm.

In 1997, having scraped together her sparse resources, Sabriye entered Tibet with nothing but her cane. And she did a most courageous thing.
She traveled the rigorous mountain countryside on horseback with a Tibetan
health counselor to check on the plight of the blind. But despite her warm
heart and good intentions, she received a cold reception.

"It was depressing," she explained. "We met kids who had been tied to
beds for years so they wouldn't hurt themselves. Some couldn't walk because their parents hadn't given them the space to develop." When she
told me that, it felt like a knife in my heart. Like Sabriye, I couldn't help hurting

for every blind or disabled kid in Tibet who'd been marginalized by ignorance and myth.

So, along with her Dutch partner Paul Kronenberg, a development aid worker she met in the Tibetan capital, Lhasa, she summoned her growing strengths to unravel the red tape and do the work they needed to do. In Paul she found a teammate who supplemented her strengths to achieve something she could not do alone.

She faced countless setbacks, once getting extreme altitude sickness and three times losing her visa (a loss that forced her and Paul to make the arduous three-day trip over the mountains into Kathmandu, Nepal). However, she used each adversity to fuel her determination and vision. Finally, in May 1998, Sabriye opened the first school for visually impaired children in Lhasa. "We faced a lot of prejudice and bureaucracy," she explained to me. "Sometimes it was hell, but I enjoy challenges!"

In eight years, Sabriye's training center has grown from only two students to over fifty. She lays the foundation for growth by teaching her children many of the principles Paul and I present in this book. Whenever her students are laughed at in the streets, she teaches them to take it on by standing up and defending themselves.

Once, a nomad called one of her students a "blind fool." The boy turned around and said, "You cannot talk to me like that. I am blind but I am not a fool! Did you ever go to school? Do you know how to read and write? Can you find the toilet in the middle of the night without a flashlight?" Although Lhasa may be the most "blind-unfriendly" capital in the world, with unprotected potholes two meters deep and mopeds and rickshaws darting everywhere, Sabriye teaches her students to summon their strengths to find ways to navigate through the chaos. She encourages them to pack light and right by pushing them to ignore all the distractions and naysayers and focus instead on what's most important, becoming the best-educated kids in Tibet. And the hardships of their daily lives and their struggle for acceptance have already been the best teacher in how to suffer well.

Six years later, I received a life-changing letter from Sabriye.

Dear Erik,

After you have reached the top of the world our Tibetan
neighbour rushed into our center and told the kids about
your success. Some of them first didn't believe it but then
there was a mutual understanding: if you could climb to the
top of the world, we also can overcome our borders and
show to the world that the blind can equally participate
in society and are able to accomplish great things. The
children realized that it does not matter much if you are a
blind child in Germany, the USA, or Tibet; the experience
one has who becomes blind, the embarrassment at first, the
confidence which builds up slowly but steadily, the reaction
of the sighted surrounding is probably for every blind
person the same. . . .

Sabriye wrote to invite me to visit her school. But I thought I could do
more than go and shake their hands. I went to my Everest team and asked
them to come together once again for, perhaps, a more important reason
than summiting a mountain. They agreed. We wanted to help the children
blow apart their own perceptions of what's possible, as well as those embedded in their culture, by taking them on a real mountaineering adventure.

Sabriye chose the six students she thought would be best suited to our
challenge. They were kids full of will but with almost no skill. My team and I
brought over mounds of climbing gear and a collection of the trekking poles
I use to navigate in the outdoors, and we taught them the fundamentals.
Then, we took them on an adventure hike, with lots of coaching, which ended
up being an arduous ascent, up and over a 17,500-foot pass. The terrain was
a lot more rugged than I had anticipated; and one day the temperature
dropped fifty degrees and we all straggled into camp in a driving snowstorm.
But none of the kids seemed fazed. Their will was steadfast, and their skills
evolved quickly as the challenge intensified.

We could have stopped there. But Everest has such deep spiritual and
symbolic importance in these students' culture that I thought it would be im-

measurably more powerful to bring them there. So we came back several months later with the goal of guiding these six blind kids to the Rombuk glacier, a huge tongue of ice on the north face of Everest, just above the 21,000-foot camp.

On the way, we had to traverse a mini-icefall riddled with serpentine columns of ice, jutting pinnacles, and shifting shards, with a zigzagging pathway through the labyrinth. As challenging as it was, it was incredibly tactile, filling them with wonder as they played in that magical palace of ice.

Many kids got sick, and all of them had to struggle. But after three weeks of pushing up rocky trails, through wind and cold, and across crevasses, all six kids, Sabriye, myself, and my Everest team stood at 21,500 feet. Blind kids who had been told they had evil spirits inside them, who had been sold into slavery, who had often run from rocks being thrown at them, all stood higher than any team of blind people in history.

Oddly, though, at our high point there were no shouts of triumph or raised fists. In fact, when we made it to the top of the glacier, many of the kids seemed somber—almost stunned. As great as our success had been, I privately wondered if I had done the right thing. Had I pushed them too hard or just put them through unnecessary suffering? And for what? But as I was getting ready to leave Tibet, the six kids ran up to me, surrounded me, and wrapped their arms around me.

"Erik," Kienzin asked, "we all want to know when will you come back and climb another mountain with us."

I teased them playfully. "Mountains are too high and cold," I said.

"No," they all replied in unison.

"You can't climb mountains, because you're all blind," I said.

"No," Sonom Bonso said proudly. "We are blind, but we can do anything."

Then they piled on top of me, poked me in the ribs, and punched me in the arms. My concerns vaporized.

"We want you to take us to the top of Everest," Kiyla said. "We want to climb higher." I was moved to tears because I knew that their notions of what was possible were forever elevated.

Since then their aspirations have grown. Kiyla has decided that she wants to take over the school someday. She is now in London studying. Two of the other kids set their sights on studying abroad in the United States. Another decided to open her own massage therapy business. And yet another decided to become a teacher. In fact, they all became teachers.

I cannot describe how humbling and inspiring it is to meet these young children who, a few years ago, left their villages as outcasts but then returned walking proudly with their canes, and writing Braille in three different languages. Rather than being shunned, they now teach their fellow villagers. They are now heroes.

One blind German girl decides that she wants to grow up and make a difference. And, like anyone trying to do something worthwhile, she faces immense adversity along the way. But, being an adversity alchemist, she converts adversity into the gold of everyday greatness, equipping young children with the very same principles you've learned in this book, so that they can perpetuate their own brand of greatness for generations to come. That's her legacy, her story for *The Adversity Advantage*.

Twelve years ago, while climbing in Arizona, my buddy turned to me and, out of the blue, said, "Let's try something bigger." That began a quest that carried me around the world confronting some of life's greatest challenges. And along the way, I learned that a spark of greatness exists in all people. But only by touching that spark to adversity's flame does it blaze into a force that powers our lives and brings changes to the world. That's my story of *The Adversity Advantage*.

Since the day you were born and began to navigate life on your own, you have faced your own endless array of challenges. Like wind shaping rock, adversity has had its effect on you. Some hardships may have been erosive, taking a tragic toll. No doubt, there have been times when pieces inside you have even crumbled. However, perhaps those hardships have also worn free your hidden gems, making you stronger and better.

From this point forward, you can and will forever change your relationship with the profound forces of adversity. No longer will you remain passive or helpless against its fury. You, like Sabriye and the countless others we've introduced in this book, will harness your adversity and use it to create advantages you may not have dreamed possible. You will prove, over and over, that bad things can spawn good things. When life beats you down, you will use its force to rise up, to elevate yourself and those around you. You will convert life's difficulties into pure, endless fuel for delivering your brand of greatness . . . every day. This is the human story, your story. Now you become its inspired author.

SUMMIT SEVEN—DELIVER GREATNESS, EVERY DAY

GUIDING PRINCIPLE

There are two kinds of greatness, *epic greatness* and *everyday greatness.* Epic greatness describes the exceptionally rare people in rare moments that dramatically and positively shift the course of human history. Everyday greatness is when you demonstrate the resilience, magnanimity, compassion, fortitude, goodwill, and integrity that elevate yourself and others, especially in the face of adversity.

Witnessing Greatness Every Day

- Whom do you most admire at work? In life?
- What do they do or demonstrate that makes them great?
- How does that person take it on?
- How does that person summon his or her strengths?
- How does that person engage his or her CORE?
- What possibilities has that person pioneered?
- What tough choices does that person make to pack light and pack right?
- If you have seen that person suffer, does he or she suffer poorly or suffer well?

Everyday Greatness Game Plan

- What is your Summit Challenge?
- What is your Summit Adversity, or the greatest obstacle you face in fulfilling your Summit Challenge?
- What advantage can you foresee gaining from this adversity that you could not otherwise enjoy?
- What *Adversity Advantage* tools will you use to harness this adversity?
- What is your Summit Vision? How will life be different once you have successfully performed your alchemy, turning adversity into an advantage; hardship into greatness?
- Who will benefit?

Your Adversity Advantage Story

Erik, Sabriye, and others throughout this book have their *Adversity Advantage* stories that have shaped their lives. Once you put these tools to use, what will be your *Adversity Advantage* story?

NOTES

SUMMIT 3

1. This and related studies can be found on the Global Resilience Project Web page at www.peaklearning.com.

SUMMIT 4

1. Joni Evans and Nicole Keeter, "Your First Million," *O, The Oprah Magazine*, September 2005.
2. This and related studies can be found on the Global Resilience Project Web page at www.peaklearning.com.
3. Story adapted with permission from the original text provided by Mike Savicki. Background sources: Colorado Public Radio, interview with Jay Clapper, www.cpr.org. "America's Schools Use Wind Energy to Further Their Goals," U.S. Department of Energy, www.eere.energy .gov. "Electricity from the Wind: A New Lesson for Schools," www .windpoweringamerica.gov.

ACKNOWLEDGMENTS

First and foremost, Erik and I would like to express our deepest gratitude to our editorial team—Ed Weihenmayer, Tina Shultz, Jeff Thompson, and Mike Savicki—for their immense contributions to this effort. Special thanks to our amazing wives, Ellie and Ronda, who signed up for this lifelong "climb" and sacrificed their rest and sanity on many endless late-night read-throughs. We thank our valued clients and teams, without whom many of these principles would remain untested, our gifted publishers Nancy Hancock and Trish Grader, and their team at Fireside, as well as our expert agent Denise Marcil, at the Marcil Agency in New York. We also wish to express particular gratitude to one of the great men of our time, Dr. Stephen Covey, through whose principles and generosity this book and its authors are immeasurably improved. Without the extended faith, dedication, and sacrifice of all of these exceptional people, along with their proven ability to put these practices into action, *The Adversity Advantage* might never have reached the printed page.

INDEX

ABOUT THE AUTHORS

PAUL G. STOLTZ, PH.D., is the CEO of PEAK Learning, a global research and consulting firm; and the director of the Global Resilience Project. The originator of the globally acclaimed Adversity Quotient (AQ) method and author of the international bestseller *Adversity Quotient* and *Adversity Quotient at Work*, he lives in San Luis Obispo, California. For more information regarding Dr. Paul Stoltz, Adversity Quotient (AQ), or the PEAK Learning suite of assessments, products, keynotes, programs, coaching, and consulting solutions go to www.peaklearning.com, or contact PEAK directly at info@peaklearning.com or (805) 595-7775.

ERIK WEIHENMAYER is the world's leading blind athlete and the only blind person in history to reach the "Seven Summits." He is the author of *Touch the Top of the World* and the subject of the award-winning documentary *Farther Than the Eye Can See*. Erik has been featured on the cover of *Time* and lives with his family in Golden, Colorado.